March of America Facsimile Series

Number 76

The South-West. By a Yankee

VOLUME II

Joseph Holt Ingraham

The South-West.
By a Yankee

VOLUME II

by Joseph Holt Ingraham

ANN ARBOR
UNIVERSITY MICROFILMS, INC.
A Subsidiary of Xerox Corporation

The South-West. By a Yankee

VOLUME II

THE

S O U T H - W E S T.

BY A YANKEE.

Where on my way I went;
——————A pilgrim from the North—
Now more and more attracted, as I drew
Nearer and nearer.

ROGERS' ITALY.

IN TWO VOLUMES.

VOL. II.

NEW-YORK:

HARPER & BROTHERS, CLIFF-ST.

1835.

CONTENTS.

XXVIII.

XXIX.

XXX.

XXXI.

XXXII.

CONTENTS.

XXXIII.

XXXIV.

XXXV.

XXXVI.

XXXVII.

CONTENTS.

XXXVIII.

XXXIX.

XL.

XLI.

XLII.

CONTENTS.

XLIII.

THE SOUTH WEST.

XXIV.

THE rich and luxuriant character of the scenery, which charms and attracts the eye of the traveller as he ascends the Mississippi from New-Orleans to Baton Rouge, is now changed. A broad, turbid flood, rolling through a land of vast forests, alone meets the eye, giving sublime yet wild and gloomy features to the scene. On looking from the cabin window, I see only a long, unbroken line of cotton trees, with their pale green foliage, as dull and void of interest as a fog-bank. The opposite shore presents the same appearance; and so it is, with the occasional relief of a plantation and a "landing place," comprising a few buildings, the whole distance to Natchez. A wretched cabin, now and then, varies the wild appearance of the banks—the home of some solitary wood-cutter. Therefore, as I cannot give you descriptions of things abroad, I must give you an account of persons on board.

There are in the cabin about forty passengers, of both sexes. Two of the most genteel-looking among them, so far as dress goes, I am told, are professed "black-legs;" or, as they more courteously style themselves, "sporting gentlemen."— There is an organized body of these *ci-devant* gentry upon the river, who have local agents in every town, and travelling agents on board the principal steamboats. In the guise of gentlemen, they "take in" the unwary passenger and unskilful player, from whom they often obtain large sums of money. I might relate many anecdotes illustrative of their mode of operating upon their victims; but I defer them to some future occasion. As the same sportsmen do not go twice in the same boat, the captains do not become so familiar with their persons as to refuse them passage, were they so inclined. It is very seldom, however, when they are known, that they are denied a passage, as gambling is not only permitted but encouraged on most of the boats, by carrying a supply of cards in the bar, for the use of the passengers. Even the sanctity of the Sabbath is no check to this amusement : all day yesterday the tables were surrounded with players, at two of which they were dealing "faro;" at the third playing "brag." And this was on the Sabbath! Indeed the day was utterly disregarded by nearly every individual on board. Travelling is a sad demoralizer. My fellow-passengers seemed to have adopted the sailors' maxim, " no Sunday off soundings." Their religion was laid by for shore use. One good, clever-looking old lady, was busily engaged all the morning hemming a handkerchief; when some one remarked near her, " This time last Sunday we made the Balize."—" Sunday! to-day Sunday!" she exclaimed, in the utmost consternation, " Is to-day Sunday, sir ?"

" It is indeed, madam."

" Oh, me! what a wicked sinner I am! O dear, that I should sew on Sunday !"—and away she tottered to her state-room, amidst the pitiless laughter of the passengers, with both hands elevated in horror, and ejaculating, " Oh me! what a wicked sinner! How *could* I forget!" In a short time she returned with a Bible; and I verily believe that she did not take her eyes from it the remainder of the day, unless it might be to wipe her spectacles.— Good old soul! she was leaven to the whole lump of our ungodly company.

There are several French gentlemen; one important looking personage, who bears the title of general, and seems amply to feel the dignity it confers; three or four Mississippi cotton planters, in large, low-crowned, broad-brimmed, white fur hats, wearing their clothes in a careless, half sailor-like, half gentleman-like air, dashed with a small touch of the farmer, which style of dressing is peculiar to the Mississippi country gentleman. They are talking about negroes, rail-roads, and towing shipping. There is also a travelling Yankee lawyer, in a plain, stiff, black coat, closely buttoned up to his chin,

strait trowsers, narrow hat, and gloves—the very
antipodes, in appearance, to the *non chalant*, easy,
care-for-nothing air of his southern neighbours.   A
Methodist minister, in a bottle-green frock coat,
fancy vest, black stock, white pantaloons and white
hat, is sitting apart by the stove, deeply engaged
upon the pages of a little volume, like a hymn-book.
Any other dress than uniform black for a minister,
would, at the north, be deemed highly improper,
custom having thus so decided ; but here they wear
just what Providence sends them or their own taste
dictates.   There are two or three fat men, in gray
and blue—a brace of bluff, manly-looking Germans
—a lynx-eyed, sharp-nosed New-York speculator—
four old French Jews, with those noble foreheads,
arched brows, and strange-expressioned eyes, that
look as though always weeping—the well-known
and never to be mistaken characteristics of this remarkable people.   The remainder of our passengers
present no peculiarities worth remarking.   So I
throw them in, tall and short, little and big, and all
sorts and sizes, to complete the motley " *ensemble*"
of my fellow-travellers.

Among the ladies, besides the aged sinner of the
pocket-handkerchief, are a beautiful, dark-eyed,
dark-haired Virginian, and an intelligent, young
married lady from Vermont, accompanied by her
only child, a handsome, spirited boy, between four
and five years of age.   The little fellow and I soon
became great friends ; in testimony whereof, he is
now teasing me to allow him to scrawl his enormous pot-hooks over my sheet, by way of assisting

me in my letter. An apology for his rudeness, by his mother, opened the way for a conversation; during which I discovered that she possessed a highly cultivated mind, great curiosity, as a stranger in a strange land, and her full share of Yankee inquisitiveness. She was always upon the "guard," resolved that nothing worthy of observation should escape her inquiring eye. She was a pure New-England interrogative. So far as it was in my power, it afforded me pleasure to reply to her questions, which, as a stranger to southern scenery, manners and customs, it was very natural she should put to any one. With a southerner I might have journied from Montreal to Mexico, without being questioned so often as I have been in this short passage from New-Orleans. But unless we *can* answer their innumerable questions, (which, by the way, are most usually of a strongly intelligent cast), travelling Yankee ladies are certainly, unless young and pretty, a little annoying. I mean, always, the inquisitive ones; for there are some who are far from being so. When a northerner is not inquisitive, the fact may generally be ascribed to intellectual dullness, or an uncultivated mind : in a southerner, to constitutional indolence and love of quiet, which are enemies to one jot more corporeal or mental exertion than is absolutely requisite to enable them to glide through existence. I do not rank my fellow-traveller in the class of the troublesome inquisitives—though full of curiosity, compared with the "daughters of the sun,"—but she is no more so than any intelligent person should be in a strange, and by no means uninteresting country.

" The general" is quite the lion on board. It would amuse you to observe the gaping mouths, fixed eyes, and attentive looks around, when the general speaks. He is the oracle—the *ne plus ultra* of excellencé—the phenix of generals!

By this time you must be wearied with my prosing about persons of whom you know nothing, and are probably waiting for more interesting subjects for description. Thus far, with the exception of one bluff, with a few buildings perched upon its summit, there has been no variety in the monotony of the gloomy forests which overhang the river.

" Ellis's cliffs, which present the wildest and most romantic scenery upon the Mississippi below St. Louis, are now in sight. They rise proudly from the river, and compared with the tame features of the country, are invested with the dignity of mountains. They exhibit a white perpendicular face to the river, and are about one hundred and fifty feet in height. Gold and silver ore have been lately found in the strata of the cliffs; but not in sufficient purity and quantity to induce the proprietors to excavate in search of them. Here are discovered the first stones —small pebbles of recent formation—that are seen on ascending the river. The surrounding country, which is nearly on a level with the summit of the cliffs, recedes pleasantly undulating from the river, rich with highly cultivated cotton plantations, and ornamented with the elegant residences of the planters. It is said that few countries in the world possess a more beautifully diversified surface—or one more pleasantly distributed in hills and valleys. In the vicinity also, of this romantic spot, Chateaubriand has laid some of the scenes of his wild and splendid fiction " Atala."

We are now within twenty miles of Natchez. The river is here very circuitous, making the distance much greater than by land. The shores continue to exhibit the peculiarly gloomy and inhospitable features which, with the occasional exception of a high bluff, plantation or village, they present nearly to the mouth of the Ohio. The loud and startling report of a cannon in the bows of the boat, making her stagger and tremble through every beam, is the signal that our port is in sight—a pile of gray and white cliffs with here and there a church steeple, a roof elevated above its summit, and a light-house hanging on the verge! At the foot of the bluffs are long straggling lines of wooden buildings, principally stores and store-houses; the Levée is fringed with flat boats and steamers, and above all, tower majestically the masts of two or three ships. The whole prospect from the deck presents an interesting scene of commercial life and bustle. But this is not Natchez! The city proper is built upon the summit level, the tops of whose buildings and trees can be seen from the boat, rising higher than the cliff. The ascent from the lower town, or as it is commonly designated, " under the hill," is by an excavated road, of moderate elevation. The whole appearance of the place from

the deck is highly romantic. On our left, opposite
Natchez, is Vidalia, in Louisiana, a pleasant village
of a few houses, built on one street parallel with
the river. Here, in a pleasant grove above the
town, is the "field of honour," where gentlemen
from Mississippi occasionally exchange leaden cards
—all in the way of friendship.

On our right, a few hundred yards below Natchez,
crowning a noble eminence, stand the ruins of Fort
Rosalie, celebrated in the early history of this country.
Its garrison early in the last century was massacred,
by the Natchez tribe, to a single man, who escaped
by leaping from the precipice. Here is the principal scene of Chateaubriand's celebrated romance.
The position of the fort, in a military point of view,
commanding, as it does, a great extent of river and
country, is well chosen. Beyond the fort, a peep
at rich woods, green hills, and tasteful country-seats,
is agreeably refreshing to the eye, so long accustomed to gaze upon melancholy forests, and dead
flats covered with cane-brakes. Indeed, the mourn-
ful character of the forests along the Mississippi, is
calculated to fill the mind with gloom. The long
black moss, well known at the north as the "Carolina moss," hangs in immense fringes from every
limb, frequently enveloping the whole tree in its
sombre garb. The forests thus clothed present a
dismal yet majestic appearance. As the traveller
gazes upon them his mind partakes of their funereal
character, and the imagination is ready to assent to
the strong and highly poetical remark of a gentleman on board, with whom I was promenading the

" guard," who observed that it would seem that the
DEITY was dead, and that nature had clothed herself in mourning.

XXV.

SINCE the date of my last letter, a period sufficiently long to enable me to make my observations
with correctness has elapsed ; and from memoranda
collected during the interval, I shall prepare this
and subsequent letters from this place.

We landed last evening at the Levée, amid the
excitement, noise, and confusion which always attend the arrival or departure of a steamer in any
place. But here the tumult was varied and increased by the incessant jabbering, hauling, pulling,
kicking and thumping, of some score 'or two of
ebony-cheeked men and urchins, who were tumbling over each other's heads to get the first trunk.

" Trunk, massa—trunk ! I take you baggage."

" You get out, for a nigger !" exclaimed a tall,
strapping fellow, as black as night, to his brother
ebony. " I'm the gemman, massa, what care de

trunk." "Dis nigger, him know noffing, massa—
I'm what's always waits on um gentlemans from de
boats!" roared another; and stooping to take one
of the handles, the other was instantly grappled by
a rival, and both giving a simultaneous jerk, the
subject of the contest flew violently from their hands,
and was instantly caught up by the first "gemman," and borne off in triumph. This little by-play
was acted, with variations, in every part of the cabin, where there was either a gentleman or a trunk
to form the subject.

On landing, there was yet another trial of the
tympanum.

"Carriage, massa—mighty bad hill to walk up!"
was vociferated on all sides; and

"No, no, no!" was no argument with them for
a cessation of attack; denial only made them more
obstinate; and, like true soldiers, they seemed to
derive courage from defeat.

Forcing my way through the dingy crowd--for
four out of five of them were black, and, "by the
same token," as ragged as Falstaff's regiment, of
shirtless memory—I followed my athletic pioneer;
who, with my heavy baggage poised accurately upon his head, moved as rapidly and carelessly along
the thronged Levée as though he carried no weight
but his own thick cranium. On looking round me
for a moment, on landing, I was far from agreeably
impressed with the general appearance of the buildings. This part of the town is not properly Natchez
—and strangers passing up and down the river, who
have had the opportunity of seeing only this place,

have, without dreaming of the beautiful city over their heads, gone on their way, with impressions very inaccurate and unfavourable. These impressions, derived only, but justly, from this repulsive spot, have had a tendency to depreciate the city, and fasten upon it a bad name, which it is very far from meriting. Like the celebrated " Five Points," in New-York, " Natchez under the Hill," as it has been aptly named, has extended its fame throughout the United States, in wretched rhyme and viler story. For many years it has been the nucleus of vice upon the Mississippi. But, for two or three years past, the establishment of respectable mercantile houses, and an excellent hotel, combined with an efficient police, and a spirit of moral reform among the citizens, has, in a great measure, redeemed the place—changed its repulsive character and cancelled its disgraceful name. Though now on the high way of reform, there is still enough of the cloven-hoof visible, to enable the stranger to recognise that its former reputation was well earned.

The principal street, which terminates at the ascent of the hill, runs parallel with the river, and is lined on either side with a row of old wooden houses; which are alternately gambling-houses, brothels, and bar-rooms: a fair assemblage! As we passed through the street—which we gained with difficulty from the boat, picking our way to it as we could, through a filthy alley—the low, broken, half-sunken side-walks, were blocked up with fashionably-dressed young men, smoking or lounging, tawdrily arrayed, highly rouged females, sailors, Kentucky boatmen, negroes, negresses, mulattoes, pigs, dogs, and dirty children. The sounds of profanity and Bacchanalian revels, well harmonizing with the scene, assailed our ears as we passed hastily along, through an atmosphere of tobacco smoke and other equally fragrant odours. After a short walk we emerged into a purer air, and in front of a very neat and well-conducted hotel. From near this place, extending along the Levée to the north, commences the mercantile part of the "landing," lined with stores and extensive warehouses, in which is transacted a very heavy business. The whole of this lower town is built upon a reclaimed flat, from one to two hundred yards broad, and half a mile in length; bounded upon one side by the river, and on the other by the cliff or bluff, upon which Natchez stands, and which rises abruptly from the *Batture*, to the height of one hundred and sixty feet. This bluff extends along the river, more or less varied and broken, for several miles; though at no point so abrupt and bold as here, where it bears the peculiar characteristics of the wild scenery of " Dover cliffs." The face of the cliff at Natchez is not a uniform precipice, but, apparently by the provident foresight of nature, broken by an oblique shelf or platform, gradually inclining from the summit to the base. With but a little excavation, a fine road has been constructed along this way, with an inclination sufficiently gentle to enable the heaviest teams to ascend with comparative ease. One side of the road is of course bounded by a perpendicular cliff; the other by empty air and a dizzy precipice:

so that the unwary foot-traveller, involved amid the ascent and descent of drays, carriages, horsemen, and porters, enjoys a tolerably fair alternative of being squeezed uncomfortably close against the bluff, or pitched, with a summerset, into some of the yawning chimneys on the flats beneath. For the whole length of this ascent, which is nearly a quarter of a mile, there is no kind of guard for the protection of the passengers. Yet, I have been told, no lives have ever been lost here. One poor fellow, a short time since, having taken a drop too much, and reeling too near the verge, lost his equilibrium, and over he went. But it is hard to kill a drunkard, except with the "pure spirit" itself; and the actor in this "drop scene" being "a gem of sweet Erin," stuck to the sod, and slid comfortably, though rapidly, to the bottom. The next moment he was seen gathering himself up out of a sandheap, with "By St. Pathrick! but that was a jewel of a lape!—and it's my bright new baiver castor that's smashed by it to smitherins."

On arriving at the summit of the hill, I delayed a moment, for the double purpose of taking breath and surveying the scene spread out around me. Beneath lay the roofs of warehouses, stores, and dwellings, scattered over a flat, sandy surface, which was bordered, on the water side, by hundreds of up-country flat-boats, laden with the produce of the rich farming states bordering the Ohio and "Upper Mississippi." Lower down, steamers were taking in and discharging freight; while the mingled sounds of the busy multitude rose like the hum of

a hive upon the ear.   Immediately opposite me lay
two ships, which, with their towering masts, gay
flags, and dark hulls, agreeably relieved the otherwise long and unbroken line of boats. To the north
the river spreads its noble bosom till lost in the distance ; while the continuous line of cliffs, extending
along its shore like a giant wall, seem to speak
in the language of power, " thus far shalt thou flow
and no farther, and here shall thy proud waves be
stayed." To the south, the view is confined by the
near projection of the obtruding cliffs. Yet the river stretches boldly out many miles on its course
toward the sea, till lost to sight within the bosom of
the distant forests which bound the southern horizon. To the west, the eye travels over the majestic
breadth of the river, here a mile wide, and rests for
a moment upon level and richly cultivated fields
beyond, a quiet village and noble forests, which
spread away to the west like a vast sea of waving
foliage, till they blend with the bending sky, forming a level and unbroken horizon. Turning from
this scene of grandeur and beauty to the east,
Natchez, mantled with rich green foliage like a gar-
ment, with its handsome structures and fine avenues, here a dome and there a tower, lies immediately before me. It is the very contrast to its straggling namesake below. The city proper consists
of six streets, at right angles with the river, intersected by seven others of the same length, parallel
with the stream. The front, or first parallel street,
is laid out about one hundred yards back from the
verge of the bluff, leaving a noble green esplanade

along the front of the city, which not only adds to
its beauty, but is highly useful as a promenade and
parade ground.   Shade trees are planted along the
border, near the verge of the precipice, beneath
which are placed benches, for the comfort of the
lounger.   From this place the eye commands one
of the most extensive prospects to be found on the
Mississippi.   To a spectator, standing in the centre
of this broad, natural terrace, the symmetrical arrangement of the artificial scenery around him is
highly picturesque and pleasing.

  On his right, to the south, a noble colonnaded structure, whose heavy appearance is gracefully relieved
by shrubbery, parterres, and a light latticed sum-
mer-house, crowning a gentle eminence in the rear,
and half suspended over the precipice, strikes his
eye with a fine effect.   From this admirable fore-
ground, gently sloping hills, with here and there a
white dwelling, half concealed in foliage, spread
away into the country.   Between this edifice and
the forest back ground rise the romantic ruins of
Fort Rosalie, now enamelled with a rich coating of
verdure.   On his left, at the northern extremity of
the esplanade, upon the beautiful eminence, gradually yet roundly swelling away from the promenade, stands another private residence, nearly resembling and directly opposite to the other, its
lofty colonnades glancing in the sun—a magnificent
garden spreading out around it, luxuriant with foliage—diversified with avenues and terraces, and
adorned with grottoes and summer-houses.   Imagine these handsome residences, flanking the city,

and forming the extreme northern and southern terminations of the broad terrace before the town,
with the mighty flood of the Mississippi rolling
some hundred feet beneath you—the dark forests
of Louisiana stretching away to infinity in the west,
with Natchez—its streets alive with promenaders,
gay equipages and horsemen—immediately before
you, and you will form some idea of this beautiful
city and its environs from this point. But as the
spot upon which the town is built, originally a cluster of green hills, has been, by levelling and filling,
converted into a smooth surface, with a very slight
inclination to the verge of the cliff, a small portion
only of the city is visible. The buildings on the
front street face the river, and, with the exception
of one or two private houses, with galleries and
shrubbery, reminding one of the neat and beautiful
residences on the "coast," * possess no peculiar
interest. The town is entered from the parade by
rude bridges at the termination of each street, span-
ning a dry, dilapidated brick aqueduct of large dimensions, which has been constructed along the
whole front of the city, but is now, from some unknown cause, suffered to fall to ruin. It was probably intended as a reservoir and conductor of the
water which, after heavy rains, rushes violently
down the several streets of the city.

As I was crossing from the bluff to the entrance
of one of the principal streets—a beautiful avenue

---

* The banks of the Mississippi are termed "*the coast*," as far up
the river as Baton Rouge. It is usual to say one lives on the *coast*,
if he lives on the river shore.

bordered with the luxuriant China tree, whose dark rich foliage, nearly meeting above, formed a continued arcade as far as the eye could penetrate—my attention was arrested by an extraordinary group, reclining in various attitudes under the grateful shade of the ornamental trees which lined the way. With his back firmly planted against a tree, as though there existed a sympathetic affinity between the two, sat an athletic Indian with the neck of a black bottle thrust down his throat, while the opposite extremity pointed to the heavens. Between his left forefinger and thumb he held a corn-cob, as a substitute for a stopper. By his side, his blanket hanging in easy folds from his shoulders, stood a tall, fine-looking youth, probably his son, his raven hair falling in masses over his back, with his black eyes fixed upon the elder Indian, as a faithful dog will watch each movement of his intemperate master. One hand supported a rifle, while another was carelessly suspended over his shoulder. There was no change in this group while I remained in sight; they were as immoveable as statues. A little in the rear, lay several "warriors" fast locked in the arms of Bacchus or Somnus, (probably both,) their rifles lying beside them. Near them a knot of embryo chiefs were gamboling in all the glorious freedom of " sans culottes." At a little distance, half concealed by huge baskets apparently just unstrapped from their backs, filled with the motley paraphernalia of an Indian lady's wardrobe, sat, cross-legged, a score of dark-eyed, brown-skinned girls and women, laughing and talking in

their soft, childish language, as merrily as any ladies would have done, whose "lords" lay thus supine at their feet. Half a score of miserable,
starved wretches, "mongrel, whelp and hound,"
which it were an insult to the noble species to term
dogs, wandering about like unburied ghosts " seeking what they might devour," completed the novel
and picturesque *ensemble* of the scene.

On the opposite side of the way was another of a
different character, but not less interesting. Seated
in a circle around their bread and cheese, were half
a dozen as rough, rude, honest-looking countrymen
from the back part of the state, as you could find
in the nursery of New-England's yeomanry. They
are small farmers—own a few negroes—cultivate a
small tract of land, and raise a few bales of cotton,
which they bring to market themselves. Their
carts are drawn around them forming a barricade to
their camp, for here, as is customary among them,
instead of putting up at taverns, they have encamped since their arrival. Between them and
their carts are their negroes, who assume a " cheek
by jowl" familiarity with their masters, while jokes,
to season their homely fare, accompanied by astounding horse-laughs, from ivory-lined mouths that
might convey a very tolerable idea of the crater of
Etna, pass from one group to the other, with perfect good will and a mutual contempt for the nicer
distinctions of colour.

Crossing the narrow bridge, I entered at once
into the body of the city, which is built as compactly within itself and aloof from the suburbs as

though it were separated from them by a wall; and in a few moments, after traversing two sides of a well-built square on fine side walks, I arrived at the "Mansion house," an extensive and commodious brick edifice said to be one of the best hotels in the south west—except Bishop's—agreeably impressed with this, my first *coup d'œil* of a city, so extensively celebrated for the opulence, taste and hospitality of its inhabitants.

XXVI.

A northener's idea of the south-west—Natchez and health—"Broadway" of Natchez—Street scenes—Private carriages—Auction store—Sale of a slave—Manner in which slaves view slavery—Shopping—Fashion—Southern gentlemen—Merchants— Planters—Whip-bearers—Planters' families.

To the northerner, to whom every verdant hill is a magazine of health, every mountain torrent and limpid river are leaping and flowing with life, who receives a new existence as the rays of the summer's sun fall upon his brow, and whose lungs expand more freely and whose pulse beats more strongly under the influence of every breeze, Natchez has been, till within a very short period, associated with miasma and marshes over which the yellow fever, like a demon king, held undisputed sway. This idea is not without foundation. Like

New-Orleans, this city has been the grave of many young and ambitious adventurers. Pestilence has here literally "walked at noonday." The sun, the source and preserver of life and health, in its path over this devoted city, has "become black as sack-cloth," and "the moon that walketh in brightness," shedding her calm and gentle light upon the earth, has been "turned into blood," poisoning the atmos-phere with exhalations of death, and converting the green earth into a sepulchre. But this is a record of the past. The angel of vengeance has gone by, leaving health and peace to exercise their gentle do-minion over this late theatre of his terrible power. No city in our happy country is more blessed with health than is now, this so often depopulated place. For several years past its catalogue of mor-tality has been very much smaller than that of many towns in Vermont and Maine, containing the same number of inhabitants. Even that insatiable de-stroyer, the Asiatic cholera, which has strewn both hemispheres with the bones of its victims, has pass-ed over this city without leaving a trace of his pro-gress, except among the blacks and a few impru-dent strangers. Not a citizen fell a victim to it. If any place demanded a dispensation of mercy it was this—if past misfortunes can challenge an ex-emption from farther infliction.

Main-street is the "Broadway" of Natchez. It extends from the river to the eastern extremity of the city, about half a mile in length, dividing the town into nearly equal portions, north and south. This street is to Natchez what Chartres-street is

to New-Orleans, though on a much smaller scale.
Here are all the banks and most of the dry goods
and fancy stores. Here, consequently, is the centre of business, and, to the ladies, that of attraction;
although the stores are not turned inside out every
morning, to adorn their fronts and create zigzags
on the side-walks, to the great edification of the
shopmen, who are the operators, and the little comfort of gouty or hurrying pedestrians. In passing up
this street, which is compactly built with handsome
brick blocks, generally but two stories in height,
the stranger is struck with the extraordinary number of private carriages, clustered before the doors
of the most fashionable stores, or millineries, rolling through the street, or crossing and recrossing
it from those by which it is intersected, nearly every
moment, from eleven till two on each fair day. But
few of these equipages are of the city : they are
from the plantations in the neighbourhood, which
spread out from the town over richly cultivated
" hill and dale,"—a pleasant and fertile landscape—
far into the interior. Walk with me into this street
about noon on a pleasant day in December. It is
the only one nearly destitute of shade trees ; but
the few it boasts are shedding their yellow leaves,
which sprinkle the broad, regular, and well-con-
structed side-walks, and the warm sun shines down
cheerily and pleasantly upon the promenaders.—
Here, at the corner, surrounded by a crowd, is an
auction store. Upon a box by the door stands a
tall, fine-looking man. But he is *black;* ebony

cannot be blacker. Of the congregation of human beings there, he is the most unconcerned. Yet he has a deeper interest in the transactions of the moment than all the rest—for a brief space will determine whom, among the multitude, he is to call master! The auctioneer descants at large upon his merits and capabilities.—"Acclimated, gentlemen! a first-rate carriage-driver—raised by Col. ——. Six hundred dollars is bid. Examine him, gentlemen—a strong and athletic fellow—but twenty-seven years of age." He is knocked off at seven hundred dollars; and with "There's your master," by the seller, who points to the purchaser, springs from his elevation to follow his new owner; while his place is supplied by another subject. These scenes are every-day matters here, and attract no attention after beholding them a few times; so powerful is habit, even in subduing our strongest prejudices. But the following dialogue, overheard by me, between two well-dressed, smart-looking blacks near by, one seated listlessly upon his coach-box, the other holding the bridle of his master's horse—though brief, contains a volume of meaning, in illustrating the opinions and views of the blacks upon the state of their degraded race.

"You know dat nigger, they gwine to sell, George?"

"No, he field nigger; I nebber has no 'quaintance wid dat class."

"Well, nor no oder gentlemens would. But he's a likely chap. How much you tink he go for?"—

"I a'n't much 'quainted wid de price of such kind o'

peoples. My master paid seven hundred dollar for me, when I come out from ole Wirginney—dat nigger fetch five hun'red dollar I reckon."

" You sell for only seben hun'red dollars !" exclaimed the gentleman upon the coach-seat, drawing himself up with pride, and casting a contemptuous glance down upon his companion : " my massa give eight hundred and fifty silver dollars for me. Gom! I tink dat you was more 'spectable nigger nor dat." At this turn of the conversation the negro was struck off at seven hundred, at which the colloquist of the same price became highly chagrined ; but, stepping upon the stirrup, and raising himself above the crowd, that he might see " the fool massa what give so much for a miserable good-for-nothing nigger, not wort' his corn," consoled himself with the reflection that the buyer was " a man what made no more dan tirty bale cotton ; while my master make tree hun'red, and one of de firs' gemmans too ! "

Thus, though denied the privileges of his desired " caste," by the estimation of his personal value, he aspired to it by a conclusive argument, in the eye of a negro, viz. his master's wealth and rank in society. Can individuals, who are thus affected at the sale of their fellow-men, and who view their state of bondage in this light, feel deeply their own condition, or be very sensitive upon the subject of equal rights ? Yet thus do negroes view slavery. Thus do they converse upon it ; and are as tenacious of the limited privileges, (yet to them unlimited, because they know, and can therefore aspire to no other) which, like flowers, are entwined among the links of their moral bondage.   There is one, proud that his chain weighs down a few more gold pieces than that of his fellow, while the latter is in no less degree mortified at the deficiency in weight of his own.   Do such men "pine in bondage" and "sigh for freedom?"   Freedom, of which they know nothing, and cannot, therefore, feel the deprivation; a freedom of which they have heard only, as the orientals of their fabled genii, but to which generally they no more think of aspiring than the subjects of the caliph to the immortality and winged freedom of these imaginary beings.   These two negroes I have seen repeatedly since, and am assured that they are as intelligent, well informed, and "respectable," as any of their class; none of whom, allowing a very few exceptions, entertain higher or different views of their state as slaves, or of their rank in the scale of human beings.   Do not mistake me : I am no advocate for slavery; but neither am I a believer in that wild Garrisonian theory, which, like a magician's wand, is at once to dissolve every link that binds the slave to his master, and demolish at one blow a system that has existed, still gaining in extent and stability, for centuries.   The familiar French proverb, "imagination gallops while the judgment advances only on a walk," is most applicable to these visionary theorists who would build Rome in a day.

Opposite to the auction store are a cluster of gay carriages, to and from which fair beings, not quite angels, are "ascending and descending," to look

over all the "pretty things" in the richly lined
stores. Was there ever a fancy store that ladies
were not hovering near? "A new store"—"new
goods,"—"less than cost!" What magic words!
What visions of silks and satins, gros de Swiss and
gros de Naples, challys and shawls, Grecian laces
and Paris gloves, with a thousand other charming
etceteras, float before their delighted fancies, in
every form of grace and ornament that the imagination can picture or a refined taste invent. Ladies
are ladies all the world over; and where is the place
in which they do not love "to shop?" In this far
corner of the south and west, you are prepared to
give fashion credit for but few devotees, and those
only partial and half-souled worshippers. But you
must not forget that these are southerners; and the
southerner is never found unfashionable or deficient
in taste. The moving galaxy of grace and beauty
that floats down Chesnut-street, cannot at any time
present more fashionable and elegantly-dressed
promenaders than now enliven the street, or than
that fair bevy of young ladies clustered round yon-
der carriage door, all chattering together, with their
sweet pleasant voices, to a pale, beautiful, and interesting girl within, apparently an invalid. So far
as I can judge, as much of "the ton," in dress and
society, prevails here as in Philadelphia, where
many residents of the city and country spend a portion of every summer—certainly more than at New-
Orleans, which is by far the most unfashionable
city in the United States. The gentlemen of Natchez are less particular in their dress, though much

more punctilious than they were five or six years since, when there was not to be found what would be termed a "fashionable man," (according to the acceptation of the term in New-York) among the residents of this city. And where is the southern gentleman that ever dressed *fashionably?* They dress well and richly, but seldom fashionably. Their garments hang upon them loosely, as though made for larger men; and they wear them with a sort of free and easy air, enviable but inimitable by the stiffer and more formal northerner. The southerner, particularly the planter, would wear with a native and matchless grace the flowing toga of imperial Rome. Though destitute of that fashionable exterior which the tailor supplies, and for which, in general, they have a most sovereign indifference and contempt, they possess—I mean the genuine, native-born, well-educated southerner—an "*air distingué,*" and in the highest degree aristocratic, which is every where the most striking feature of their appearance.

That knot of gentlemen issuing from a plain brick building—one of the banks—is composed of bank directors. Their decisions have elevated or depressed the mercury in many an anxious breast. Two or three faces resemble those one often sees in Wall-street, or on Change, in Boston. The resemblance is so striking that one is quite sure at the first glance that he has seen them there. But no: they are merchants of this city—thorough-going commercial men. The resemblance is only that of a species. Merchants resemble each other every-

where. Their features are strongly marked and
characteristic. It has been said that a Boston merchant may be known all the world over. It has
been proved that a sea-faring life, especially when
commenced in early years, has a tendency to produce a physical change in the organ of vision.
That a mercantile life, long and intently pursued,
has a tendency to stamp a peculiar character upon
the features, is equally certain, in the opinion of
those whose habits of observation may have led
them to such physiognomical investigations. Among
the remainder, are two or three in white blanket
coats, broad-brimmed white hats, with slender riding-
whips in their hands, who will be readily designated
as planters. A circumstance that very soon arrests
the attention of the stranger, is the number of gentlemen with riding-whips in their hands to be met
with in all parts of the city, particularly on days
when any public meeting is held. Every third or
fourth person is thus, to a northerner, singularly
armed. At the north few ride except in gigs. But
here all are horsemen; and it is unusual to see a
gentleman in a gig or carriage. If his wife rides
out, he attends her *à cheval*. Instead of gigs,
therefore, which would fill the streets of a northern
town, saddle-horses, usually with high pummelled
Spanish saddles, and numerous private carriages, in
which are the ladies of the family, drawn by long-
tailed horses, throng the streets and line the outside
of the pavé. At least a third of the persons who
fill the streets are planters and their families from
the country, which every day pours forth its hun-

dreds from many miles around the city, that like a magnet attracts all within its influence.

There are several public buildings in this street of which I shall make more particular mention hereafter. My object now is merely to give you some idea of things as, when presented to it in the novel hues of "first impressions," they strike the eye of a stranger.

XXVII.

First impressions—American want of taste in public buildings—Agricultural bank—Masonic hall—Natchez academy—Education of Mississippians—Cemetery—Theatre—Presbyterian church—Court-house—Episcopal church—Light-house—Hotels—Planters' Houses and galleries—Jefferson hotel—Cotton square.

First impressions, if preserved, before the magnifying medium of novelty through which they are seen becomes dissipated, are far more lively and striking than the half-faded scenes which memory slowly and imperfectly brings up from the past. Yet, if immediately recorded, while the colours are fresh and glowing, there is danger of drawing too much upon the imagination in the description, and exaggerating the picture. On the other hand, if the impressions are suffered to become old and faint, invention is too apt to be called in unconsciously, to fill up and complete the half-forgotten and defective sketch. The medium is safer and more accurate. A period of time sufficiently long should be suffered to elapse, that the mind, by subsequent observation, may be enabled to correct and digest its early impressions, exercise its judgment without a bias, and from more matured experience, be prepared to form its opinions, and make its comparisons with certainty. How far I have attained this desirable medium, the general character and justice of my descriptions must alone determine.

The deficient perception of architectural beauty, in the composition of American minds, has frequently, and with some truth, been a subject upon which foreign tourists love to exercise their castigating pens—weapons always wielded fearlessly and pitilessly against every thing on this side of the Atlantic. The very small number of handsome public buildings in the United States, and the total contempt for order or style which, (with but here and there an honourable exception,) they evince, would give a very plausible foundation for this animadversion, did not Americans redeem their reputation in this point, by the pure and correct taste they universally exhibit in the construction of their private residences. Herein, they are not surpassed by any other nation. Natchez, like most of the minor cities of this country, cannot boast of any public buildings remarkable for harmonious conformity to the rules or orders of architecture. They are, nevertheless, well deserving of notice, highly ornamental to the city, and reflect honour upon the public spirit of its citizens. The Agricultural bank is unquestiona-

bly the finest structure in the city. It has been erected
very recently on the south side of Main-street, presenting a noble colonnaded front, of the modernized
Grecian style; being built somewhat after the model of the United States bank at Philadelphia;
though brick and stucco are here substituted for
marble, and heavy pillars for the graceful column.
It is entered from the street by a broad and spacious flight of steps, leading to its lofty portico, from
which three large doors give admission into its vast
hall, decidedly the finest room south or west of
Washington. The whole structure is a chaste and
beautiful specimen of architecture. It is partially
enclosed by a light, iron railing. To a stranger this
edifice is a striking object, and, contrasted with the
buildings of less pretension around it, will call
forth his warmest admiration. The other banks, of
which there are, in all, three, including a branch of
the United States bank, are plain brick buildings,
undistinguished from the adjoining stores, except
by a colder and more unfurnished appearance, and
the absence of signs. A short distance above this
fine building is the Masonic Hall; a large square
edifice, two lofty stories in height. Its front is
beautifully stuccoed, and ornamented with white
pilasters. The hall is in the second story; a large,
plain, vaulted apartment, almost entirely destitute
of the splendid furniture and rich decorations which
characterise such places at the north. Here ma-
sonry, with its imposing forms, ceremonies, and
honours, is yet preserved in all its pristine glory.
The first story of the building is used as an aca-

demy—the only one in this state. It is a well-conducted institution, and its pupils are thoroughly instructed by competent officers, who are graduates of northern colleges, as are most of the public and private instructors of this state. The number of students is generally large. Those who are destined for professional life, after completing their preparatory course here, usually enter some one of the colleges at the north. Yale, Princeton, and Harvard annually receive several from this state; either from this academy or from under the hands of the private tutors, who are dispersed throughout the state, and from whom a great majority of the planters' sons receive their preparatory education. But on the subject of education in this country, I shall speak more fully hereafter. I could not pass by this institution, which reflects so much honour upon the city, without expressing my gratification at its flourishing condition and high character. It is the more gratifying from being unexpected at the south, which, till very lately, has been wholly dependent upon the northern seminaries or private institutions for the education of her sons. To see here an institution that cannot be surpassed by any of the same rank in other states, must not only be pleasing to the friends of education, but particularly so to the citizens of this state, to whom it is ably demonstrated, by the success of this academy, that literature is not an exotic, though its germs may heretofore have been transplanted from another soil. There is a female seminary also in the city, which, though of a very respectable character, is not so

celebrated and flourishing as many others in the
state.

On the south side of the next square is an old
"burying-ground," crowning an eminence whose
surface is covered with fragments of grave-stones
and dismantled tombs. The street is excavated
through it to its base, leaving a wall or bank of
earth nearly thirty feet in height; upon the verge
of which crumbling tombs are suspended, threaten-
ing to fall upon the passenger beneath. It has not
been used for many years as a place of burial; the
present cemetery being about a mile above the city,
in a delightful spot among the green hills which
cluster along the banks of the river. This old cemetery is a striking but disagreeable feature in the
midst of so fair a city. Adjoining it, on the eastern
side, and nearly at the extremity of the street and
also of the city, stands the theatre; a large, commodious building, constructed of brick, with arched
entrances and perfectly plain exterior. The citizens
of Natchez are not a play-going community; consequently they take little pride in the possession of
a fine theatre. Its interior, however, is well arranged, convenient, and handsomely painted and
decorated. Its boards are supplied, for two or three
months during every season, by performers from
New-Orleans or New-York. Just beyond the theatre is the termination of Main-street, here intersected by another, from which, to the right and left,
fine roads extend into the country—one to Washington, a pleasant village six miles distant, formerly
the seat of government of the territory and the lo-

cation of the public offices; but now a retired, un-assuming and rural spot, boasting of a well-endow-ed college and female seminary—of which, more hereafter. Of the other public buildings of Nat-chez, the Presbyterian church is the finest and most imposing. It stands on a commanding site, over-looking the public square, a pleasant green flat, in the centre of which is the court-house. It is con-structed of bricks, which are allowed to retain their original colour; and surrounded by buff-coloured pilasters of stucco work, which is here generally substituted for granite in facings. It is surmounted, at the west end, by a fine tower of successive sto-ries; on one side of which is a clock, conspicuous from the most distant parts of the city and suburbs. —You are aware, probably, that there are in this country no Congregationalists, so called; Presbyte-rians supply the place of this denomination in the ecclesiastical society of all the south and west. The prevailing denomination, however, in this state, as in all this section of the United States, is that of the Methodists, which embraces men of all classes, including a large proportion of planters. I now merely allude to this and other subjects of the kind, as I intend, in subsequent letters, to treat of them more at large.

The court-house is a fine, large, square building, opposite to the church, surmounted by a cupola. It is surrounded by a beautiful, though not spacious, green. On the streets which bound the four sides of it are situated the lawyers' and public offices, which are generally plain, neat, wooden buildings, from one to two stories in height. Should they be denominated from the state of those who occupy them, they would be correctly designated " bachelors' halls." Shade trees half embower them and the court-house in their rich foliage. Opposite to the south side of the square is the county prison ; a handsome two story brick building, resembling, save in its grated tier of windows in the upper story, a gentleman's private dwelling. There is a fine Episcopalian church in the south-east part of the town, adding much to its beauty. It is built of brick, and surmounted by a vast dome, which has a rather heavy, overgrown appearance, and is evidently too large for the building. It has a neat front, adorned with a portico of the usual brick pillars. There are not many Episcopalians here ; but the few who are of this denomination are, as every where else in the United States, generally of the wealthy and educated class. There is also a Methodist church adjoining the Masonic hall ; a plain, neat building, remarkable only for its unassuming simplicity, like all others of this denomination in America.

The light-house upon the bluff, at the north-west corner of the city, is well deserving of notice, though not properly ranked under the public buildings of Natchez. It is a simple tower, about forty feet in height, commanding a section of the river, north and south, of about twelve miles. But the natural inquiry of the stranger is, " What is its use ?" A light-house on a river bank, three hundred miles from the sea, has certainly no place in the theory of the utilitarian. The use of it its projectors must determine. Were a good telescope placed in its lantern it would make a fine observatory, and become a source of amusement as well as of improvement to the citizens, to whom it is now merely a standing monument, in proof of the proverb, that "wisdom dwelleth not in all men." The hotels are very fine. Parker's, on one of the front squares, near the bluff, is a handsome, costly, and very extensive building, three stories in height, with a stuccoed front, in imitation of granite, and decidedly the largest edifice in the city. Its rooms are large, spacious, and elegantly furnished; suited rather for gentlemen and their families, who choose a temporary residence in town, than for transient travellers and single men, who more frequently resort to the "Mansion-house." This is not so large a structure as the former, though its proprietor is enlarging it, on an extensive scale. It has long been celebrated as an excellent house. Its accommodations for ladies are also very good, their rooms opening into ventilated piazzas, or galleries, as they are termed here, which are as necessary to every house in this country as fire-places to a northern dwelling. These galleries, or more properly verandas, are constructed—not like the New-England piazza, raised on columns half the height of the building, with a flat roof, and surrounded by a railing—but by extending a sloping roof beyond the main building, supported at its verge by slender columns; as the houses are usually of but one story in this country, southerners having a singular aversion to mounting stairs. Such porticoes are easily constructed. No house, particularly a planter's, is complete without this gallery, usually at both the back and front; which furnishes a fine promenade and dining-room in the warm season, and adds much to the lightness and beauty of the edifice.

There is another very good hotel here, equivalent to Richardson's, in New-Orleans, or the Elm-street house in Boston, where the country people usually put up when they come in from the distant counties to dispose of their cotton. It fronts on "Cotton-square," as a triangular area, formed by clipping off a corner of one of the city squares, is termed; which is filled every day, during the months of November, December, and January, with huge teams loaded with cotton bales, for which this is the peculiar market place.

The "City hotel," lately enlarged and refurnished, is now becoming quite a place of fashionable resort.

XXVIII.

Society of Natchez——New-England adventurers—Their prospects—The Yankee sisterhood——Southern bachelors——Southern society—Woman—Her past and present condition—Single combats —Fireside pleasures unknown—A change—Town and country— Characteristic discrepancies.

UNTIL within a very short period, the society of Natchez has exhibited one peculiar characteristic, in the estimation of a northerner, in whose migrating land "seven women," literally fulfilling the prediction, "take hold of one man;" a prediction which has, moreover, been fulfilled, according to the redoubtable and most classical Crockett, in the west; but by no means in this place, or in any of the embryo cities, which are springing up like Jonah's gourd, along the banks of the great "father of waters." The predominance of male population in the countless villages that are dotting the great western valley, rising up amidst the forests, one after another, as stars come out at evening, and almost in as rapid succession, is a necessary consequence of the natural laws of migration. In the old Atlantic and New-England states, the sons, as they successively grow up to manhood, take the paternal blessing and their little patrimony, often all easily packed and carried in a knapsack, but oftener in their heads,

and bend their way to the "great west," to seek
their fortunes, with them no nursery tale, but a
stern and hardly earned reality :—there to struggle
—prosper or fail—with blighted hopes go down to
early graves, or, building a fire-side of their own,
gather around it sons, who, in their declining years,
shall, in their turn, go forth from the paternal roof
to seek beyond the mountains of the Pacific shore
a name, a fire-side, and a home of their own.   And
such is human life !

To this migratory propensity is to be attributed
the recent peculiar state of society in this city, and
throughout the whole western country.   The sons
are the founders of these infant emporiums, but the
daughters stay at home in a state of single blessed-
ness—blessings (?) to the maternal roof, till some
bold aspirants for the yoke of hymen return, after
spying out the land, take them under their migratory wings and bear them to their new home.   But
unluckily for six out of every seven of the fair
daughters of the east, the pioneers of the west feel
disposed to pass their lives in all the solitary dignity
of the bachelor state.   Wrapped up in their specu-
lations, their segars and their "clubs," not even a
second Sabine device could move them to bend their
reluctant necks to the noose.   Those, however,
who do take to themselves "helpmeets," are more
gallant and chivalrous than their Roman predeces-
sors in their mode of obtaining them, not demurring
to travel, like Cœlebs, many hundred leagues to the
land of steady habits, to secure the possession of
some one of its lovely flowers.   The concentrating

of a great number of young gentlemen for a permanent residence in one spot, without a suitable proportion of the gentler sex to enliven and relieve the rougher shades of such an assemblage, must produce a state of society, varying essentially from that in communities where the division is more equal. Hotels, or offices of professional business must be their residences—their leisure hours must be spent in lounging at each other's rooms like college students, (to whose mode of life their's is not dissimilar,) or in the public rooms of the hotels, cafés, or gambling houses. Habits difficult to eradicate are contracted, of dark and fatal consequences to many; and a rude, cavalier bearing is thereby imperceptibly acquired, more congenial with the wild, free spirit of the middle ages, than the refinement of modern times. The bold and rugged outlines natural to the sterner character of man, can only be softened by that refining influence which the cultivated female mind irresistibly exerts upon society. Wherever woman—

"Blessing and blest, where'er she moves,"

has exercised this gentle sway, the ruder attributes of man have been subdued and blended with the soft and lovely virtues so eminently her own. Second to Christianity, of which it is a striking effect, the exalted rank to which man has elevated woman, from that degrading and tyrannical subjugation to which she has in Pagan nations, in all ages, from the pride and ignorance of her *soi disant* "lords," been subjected, has contributed more to the mental and personal refinement, dignity and moral excellence of men, than any other agency that has operated with a moral tendency directly upon the human mind. To the absence of this purifying influence, is to be attributed in a very great degree, that loose, immoral, and reckless state of society, peculiar to all border settlements and new towns, originating generally from communities of men. In such places that mysterious, yet indisputable power, exercised by the other sex upon society, is unknown; and men, throwing the reins upon the necks of their passions, plunge into vice and dissipation, unchecked and unrestrained. In such a state the duello had its origin—that blessed relic of that blessed age, when our thick-skulled ancestors broke each other's heads with mace and battle axe, for "faire ladye's love," or mere pleasant pastime—and a similar state of things will always preserve and encourage it. Hence the prevalence of this practice in the newly settled south and west, where the healthful restraint of female society has been till within a few years unknown. But as communities gain refinement through its influence, this mode of "healing honour's wounds," so unwise, unsatisfactory and sinful, gradually becomes less and less popular—till finally it is but a "theme of the past." To this state of disuse and oblivion it is rapidly advancing in this portion of the southwest, which, according to the theory before advanced, is an indication of the growing refinement, and moral and intellectual improvement of the community. Natchez has been, you are well aware, celebrated for the frequency and sanguinary character of its single combats; and this reputation it has once justly merited. Till within a few years, duels were alarmingly frequent. But more recently public opinion has changed, and the practice is now almost abandoned. The society has emerged from its peculiar bachelor cast, to that social and refined character, which constitutes the charm of well organized and cultivated communities. But a short time since, there were not three married men to ten unmarried. The latter predominating, gave the tone to society, which was, as I have before observed, that of a university, so far as habits and manners were concerned. And the resemblance was still greater, as a large majority of the young men were graduates of northern seminaries, or well informed young merchants. The social or domestic circle, so dear to every New-Englander, in which he delights to mingle wherever he reposes after his wanderings, was neglected or unvalued; and the young ladies, of whom there was found here and there one, (for their appearance in this desert of men was with the unfrequency of " Angel's visits,") were compelled to pine neglected, and

> " To bloom unseen around their lonely hearths,
> And waste their sweetness on the desert air."

Such was the state of society here formerly, varied only, at long intervals, by a public ball at some one of the hotels, got up to kill *ennui*, a plant which, in such a soil, flourishes vigorously. But now " a change has come o'er the spirit of the town." A refined, intellectual, and highly educated class of females, both exotic and natural plants, enrich and diversify the moral features of the former lonely

E 2

and monotonous scene : and as the vine entwining around the oak relieves with lines of grace and beauty its harsh, rugged outlines, so woman here, as every where, has assumed her brilliant sceptre, waved it over the heterogeneous mass, and " bidden it to live."

The society of Natchez, now, is not surpassed by any in America. Originally, and therein differing from most western cities, composed of intelligent and well-educated young men, assembled from every Atlantic state, but principally from New-England and Virginia, it has advanced in a degree proportionate to its native powers. English and Irish gentlemen of family and fortune have here sought and found a home—while the *gentilhomme* of sunny France, and the dark-browed don of " old Castile," dwell upon the green hills that recede gently undulating from the city ; or find, in their vallies, a stranger's unmarbled and unhonoured grave.

The citizens of Natchez are, however, so inseparably connected with the neighbouring planters, that these last are necessarily included in the general term " society of Natchez." The two bodies united may successfully challenge any other community to produce a more intelligent, wealthy, and, I may say, *aristocratic* whole. But I do not much like the term applied to Americans ; though no other word will express so clearly that refinement and elegance to which I allude, and which everywhere indicate the opulence and high breeding of their possessors. This is not so manifest, however, in the external appearance of their dwellings, as it is in their mode or style of living. To this their houses, especially the residences of those who have *made* their wealth, and who yet occupy the same cabins, but little improved, which they originally erected, present a sad contrast. Many of the wealthiest planters are lodged wretchedly; a splendid sideboard not unfrequently concealing a whitewashed beam—a gorgeous Brussels carpet laid over a rough-planked floor—while uncouth rafters, in ludicrous contrast to the splendour they look down upon, stretch in coarse relief across the ceiling.— These discrepancies, however, always characteristic of a new country, are rapidly disappearing; and another generation will be lodged, if not like princes, at least, like independent American gentlemen. —Many of these combinations of the old and new systems still exist, however, of a highly grotesque nature; some of the most characteristic of which I may mention more particularly hereafter.

XXIX.

A Sabbath morning in Natchez—A ramble to the bluff—Louisiana forests—Natchez under the Hill—Slaves—Holidays—Negroes going to church—Negro-street coteries—Market-day—City hotel —Description of the landing—Rail-way—A rendezvous—Neglected Sabbath-bell.

YESTERDAY was the Sabbath; one of those still, bright, and sunny days which poetry and religion have loved to challenge as peculiar to that sacred time. To this beautiful conception, fact, aided somewhat by fancy, does not, however, refuse its sanction. A serene and awful majesty has ever appeared to me as peculiarly belonging to the day of rest. It seems blessed with a holier power than is given to the common days of earth: a more hallowed silence then reigns in the air and over nature —a spirit of sanctity, like a "still small voice," breathes eloquently over the heart, from which better feelings and purer thoughts ascend and hold communion with the unseen world. A spell, like a mantle of heavenly texture, seems thrown over all; to break which, by the light notes of merry music, or the sounds of gay discourse, would seem like profanation. Such was this Sabbath morning. The sun arose in the glory of his southern power, "rejoicing to run his race." Bathed in a sea of his own created light, he poured, with lavish opulence, floods of radiance over nature—illuminating, beautifying, and enriching all on which he shone. I had early rambled to the cliff, to get away from the noise and bustle of the hotel, and to enjoy the luxuriant beauty of the morning. The windows of the dwellings, and the roofs and spires of the town, reflected back the rising sun, whose beams glittered from myriads of dew-drops that spangled the green earth, converting its soft verdure into a carpet, studded with innumerable gems. The city itself reposed, as in a deep sleep, on the quiet hills upon which it rested. The majestic Mississippi was spread out before me like a vast sheet of liquid steel—its unruffled bosom, dotted and relieved here and there by a light skiff, or a huge steamer, booming and puffing far away in the distance ; while the lofty, mural precipices which frowned menacingly over its eastern shore, were reflected from its depth with the accuracy and distinctness of a sub-marine creation. The Louisianian forests, clothing the interminable plains which stretch away to the west, with an almost perennial green, were crested with golden sun-light, and flashing as they waved in the morning breeze, like a phosphorescent sea of mingled green and light. Nature wore her richest garb, and her every feature was eminently beautiful. There was nothing to impair her loveliness, but that fallen, guilty being, who should be a diadem of glory for her brow, and the brightest ornament of her bosom —MAN ! proud and sinful man, desecrating all that is fair and pure wherever he treads—he alone defaced the calm and hallowed character of the scene.

From a row of dilapidated yet inhabited dwellings beneath me, at the base of the cliff, sounds of rude merriment, mingled with the tones of loud dispute and blasphemy, rose with appalling distinctness upon the still air, breaking the Sabbath silence of the hour, in harsh discord with its sacredness. The streets of the lower town were alive with boatmen, draymen, buyers and sellers, horsemen and hacks, and scores of negroes, some wrestling, some fighting, others running foot-races, playing quoits or marbles, selling the products of their little gardens, or, with greater probability, their predatory excursions ; while from all combined, a confused murmur, not unlike the harmony which floated around Babel, rolled upward to the skies—an incense far from acceptable to Him, who has promulgated amid the thunders of Sinai, " Remember the Sabbath day to keep it holy."

In " Natchez under the hill," the Sabbath, as a day of rest and public worship, is not observed according to the strictest letter of the old "blue laws." On that day the stores are kept open and generally filled with boatmen and negroes. With the latter this day is a short jubilee, and, with the peculiar skill of their race, they make the most of it—condensing the occupation and the jollity of seven days into one. It is customary for planters in the neighbourhood to give their slaves a small piece of land to cultivate for their own use, by which, those who are industrious, generally make enough to keep themselves and their wives in extra finery and spending money throughout the year.

They have the Sabbath given them as a holiday, when they are permitted to leave their plantations and come into town to dispose of their produce, and lay in their own little luxuries and private stores. The various avenues to the city are consequently on that day filled with crowds of chatting, 'laughing negroes, arrayed in their Sunday's best, and adroitly balancing heavily loaded baskets on their heads, which, from long practice in this mode of conveyance, often become indurated, like a petrification, and as flat as the palm of the hand, distending at the sides, and elongating in proportion to the depression, causing a peculiar conformation of the skull, which would set phrenology at defiance. Others mounted on mules or miserable-looking plough-horses, in whose presence Rosinante himself would have looked sleek and respectable—burthened with their marketable commodities, jog on side by side, with their dames or sweethearts riding " double-jaded"—as the Yankees term the mode—behind them; while here and there market carts returning from the city, (as this is also market morning) or from the intersecting roads, pour in upon the highway to increase the life, variety, and motley character of its crowd. But this unpleasing picture of a Sabbath morning, has brighter tints to redeem the graver character of its moral shades. Of all that picturesque multitude of holiday slaves, two-thirds, the majority of whom are women, are on their way to church, into whose galleries they congregate at the hour of divine service in great numbers, and worship with an apparent devoutness and attention, which beings who boast intellects of a higher order might not disdain to imitate. The female slaves very generally attend church in this country; but, whether to display their tawdry finery, of which they are fond to a proverb, or for a better purpose, I will not undertake to determine. The males prefer collecting in little knots in the streets, where, imitating the manners, bearing, and language of their masters, they converse with grave faces and in pompous language, selecting hard, high-sounding words, which are almost universally misapplied, and distorted, from their original sound as well as sense to a most ridiculous degree—astounding their gaping auditors "ob de field nigger class," who cannot boast such enviable accomplishments—parading through the streets from mere listlessness, or gathering around and filling the whiskey shops, spending their little all for the means of intoxication. Though negroes are proverbially lovers of whiskey, but few are to be found among them who get drunk, unless on Christmas holidays, when the sober ones are most easily numbered; this is owing to the discipline of plantations, the little means they have wherewith to purchase, and last, though not least, the fear of punishment—that "*argumentum ad corporem*," which leaves a stinging conviction behind it, of the painful effects of "old rye" in the abstract upon the body.

That a market should be held upon the Sabbath in this city, is a "bend sinister" upon its escutcheon. But this custom is defended, even by those who admit its evil tendency, upon the plea "that

meats in this climate will not keep over night."—
This is no doubt the case during a great part of
the year.   A different system of things, in this respect, is desirable ; but the reason just mentioned,
combined with others, peculiar to a southern state
of society, renders any change at present very difficult.

There is, on the whole, with the exception alluded to, very little difference between the observance of the Sabbath here, and that in places of the
same size in New-England ; and the quiet regularity of its Sabbaths, if he could overlook the vast
preponderance of coloured population in the streets
just before church hour, would forcibly remind the
northerner of his own native town. But in the lower
town the face of things very sensibly changes,
though the difference is less perceptible now than
formerly.   A few years since, its reputation was
every way so exceptionable, that, in a very witty
argument, a lawyer of this city demonstrated, that,
so far from being a part and portion of the city proper, it was not even a part or portion of the state !
Where he ultimately consigned it I did not learn.
—It is true the city was not very tenacious of its
rights *quoad* its reprobate neighbour. But more
recently, its superior advantages for heavy grocery
business have induced many merchants, of high
respectability, to remove from the city to this spot,
whose presence has given it a better character.—
So much has it changed from its former reputation,
that where it was once considered disreputable to
reside, there are now extensive stores, kept by gen-

tlemen of excellent character, and a fine hotel,
lately erected, for the convenience of these merchants, (most of whom, like the society which formerly characterised the city, are bachelors) and for
passengers landing from, or waiting for, the steamboats. There is also, I should have remarked in a
former letter, a commodious brick hotel on Main-
street, in the city, under the superintendence of a
young northerner, which, from its location in the
very centre of the city, independent of other qualifications, is a convenient and agreeable temporary
residence for strangers, with the majority of whom
it is a general place of resort. Few towns, whose
inhabitants quadruple those of Natchez, can boast
such fine, commodious, and well-ordered hotels as
this, or a more luxurious *table d'hote* than is daily
spread, between one and two o'clock, in the long
dining-halls of most of them.

The " Landing," which more popular term has
of late superseded the old notorious cognomination,
" Natchez under the Hill," properly consists of
three dissimilar divisions. The northern is composed
mostly of wretched dwellings, low taverns, and
drinking shops, where are congregated free negroes,
more wretched than their brother bondmen, and
poor whites. At the termination of this division are
an excellent steam saw-mill and an oil-mill, where
oil of a superior quality for lamps is extracted from
cotton seed, heretofore a useless article, except for
manure, but now disposed of with considerable profit. About the centre of this northern division is
suspended a strangely-constructed rail-way, spring-

ing from the Levée to the summit of the cliff. It was laid down, or rather built up, a short time since, for the more convenient carriage of cotton to the Landing; but has failed in its object, and is now disused and neglected. Viewed from the Levée, it is a striking feature, rising boldly from the feet of the observer, a mammoth pile of frame-work, at an angle of 45 degrees, and terminating at the height of one hundred and sixty feet, upon the verge of the bluff. The sides are closed up, and a portion is occupied by stores or dwellings, while another part is appropriated for a bowling alley. The noise of the iron-wheeled cars rolling down the steep track, with the roar of thunder, over the heads of the players, must have been a novel accompaniment to the sound of their own balls. The southern division of the Landing consists of one short street, parallel with the river, over which it hangs on one side, while the houses on the other are overhung by a spur of the cliff, which, like an avalanche, threatens every moment to slide and overwhelm it. This street is lined with dancing-houses, tippling-shops, houses of ill-fame, and gambling-rooms.— Here may always be heard the sound of the violin, the clink of silver upon the roulette and faro-tables, and the language of profanity and lewdness : and the revellers, so far from being interrupted by the intervention of the Sabbath, actually distinguish it by a closer and more persevering devotion to their unhallowed pursuits and amusements. The remaining division of the Landing, which lies between the other two, is a short street, extending from the base of the cliff to the Levée, a great part of which it comprises, and along an intersecting street, which skirts the foot of the bluff as far as the rail-way : here are congregated store-houses, boarding-houses, and bachelors' halls—which many of the merchants keep over their own stores, hiring or buying some old black woman to officiate as the representative of Monsieur Ude—the commodious hotel before alluded to, conducted by a " Green Mountain boy," and wholesale and retail grocery and dry goods stores. Neither of these kinds of goods is made, by itself, the sole stock of a dealer, either here or on the hill ; but with the various articles in every kind of commercial dealing they pile their shelves and fill their warehouses; the whole forming a mixed assortment, appropriately adapted to the peculiar wants of their country, town, and steamboat customers. These stores are all kept open upon the Sabbath, on which day there is often more business done than on any other. The blacks, who have no other opportunity of making their little purchases, crowd around the counters—the boatmen trade off their cargoes, and the purchasers store them— steamers are constantly arriving and departing, lading and unlading—and the steam ferry-boat makes its oft-repeated trip from shore to shore—all giving a life, bustle, and variety to the scene, of a very un-sabbath-like character. The merchants plead the necessity of supplying steamers. This is readily admitted ; but it has given rise to a train of unforeseen evils, which have little relation to this basis of the custom. The numerous drinking shops in the other parts of the Landing are, on that day, as much at least, if not more than on other days, filled with a motley assemblage of black, white, and yellow, drinking and carousing.

Nearly two hundred feet below me, as I stood upon the bluff, and within the huge shadow of the cliff, stretched a long, low building, over which proudly waved the star-spangled banner, and to whose inhabitants the sun, already high in the heavens, had not yet risen. From this building issued the sound of bestial revelry, drowning the hum of business and the shouts of boyish merriment. The coarse gray clothing (a shame to our army) of most of those lounging about the door, designated it, in conjunction with the flag over their heads, as a rendezvous—even had not the martial eloquence of a little, half-tipsy, dapper man in a gray doublet, whose voice now and then reached my ear in the intervals of the uproarious proceedings—expatiating to a gaping crowd of grinning Africans—night-capped or bare-headed white females, in slattern apparel and uncombed locks—two or three straight, blanketed, silent Indians—noisy boys and ragged boatmen—upon the glories of a soldier's life, sufficiently indicated its character.

"The sound of the church-going bell" pealed idly over their heads, unheard, or if heard, disregarded; and to the crowds which the eye of an observer could take in from his elevation upon the bluff, the divine institution of the Sabbath is invalid.

XXX.

AFTER a long voyage, the sound of a Sabbath bell, borne over the waves from a white tower, far inland among the green hills of my native land, awed, like a voice from heaven, every spirit on board of our ship, from the commander to the rudest mariner, striking a chord long untouched in many hearts, and awakening associations of inno-cence and childhood, of home and heaven. As one after another, each clear-toned peal rolled so-lemnly over the sea, every footfall was involuntarily hushed, the half uttered jest or oath was arrested on the tongue—the turbulent spirit was quieted and subdued—every rough weather-beaten visage was softened, and for the remainder of that day—long, long after its dying notes had floated like spiritual music over our ship, and died away in the distant "fields of the ocean,"—each one on board felt him-self a better man.

Sensations nearly allied to these were awakened

in my breast, as I stood upon the cliff, the Sabbath morning preceding the date of my last letter, contrasting the calm rich beauty of nature, with the dark scenes of vice, misery and impiety beneath me, by the sudden pealing of the church bell, ringing out its loud melody over the city, awakening the slumbering echoes from

" Tomb and tower, cliff and forest glade,"

and calling man to the worship of his Maker. My thoughts, by a natural association, went backward many a long year, and dwelt upon a sweet sequestered valley, far away among the northern hills, with its chaste temple, whose snow-white slender spire, like the finger of undying hope, pointed man to his home in heaven, where, in early boyhood, we were first taught to worship the Great Being who made us ; to the venerable figure of that silver-headed man of God, whose eloquence, at one time sublime, and full of majesty and power, would strike his hearers with holy dread—at another, soft, persuasive, and artless as the language of a child, diffuse a holy devotion throughout their bosoms, or melt them into tears ; whose audience listened with their hearts, rather than with their ears—so masterly was the intellect, made God-like by religion, which could ring what changes it would, upon the susceptible chords of human sensibility. My reverie of the past, however, was soon interrupted by the rattling of carriages, as they rolled over the noble esplanade between me and the city, from the roads which extend north and south along the banks of the river, on their way to church. I prepared to follow their example. From my position I could look into one of the principal streets of the town, now rapidly filling with well-dressed people, numerous private equipages, and horsemen in great numbers. I soon fell in with the living current, and in a few minutes arrived at the Presbyterian church, situated in the centre and highest part of the city. The approach was literally blockaded by carriages from the suburbs and neighbouring plantations.

The congregation was large, attentive, and so far as I could judge, as exteriorly fashionable as in Boston or New-York. The interior of the building is plain, and vaulted. A handsome pulpit stands opposite the entrance, over which is a gallery for the coloured people. The pulpit is deficient in a sounding-board, that admirable contrivance for condensing the voice, which, in an apartment of vast dimensions, has too great expansion. There was neither organ nor any other instrumental aid to the church music, which, though exclusively vocal, was uncommonly fine—the clergyman himself leading. But the effect was much lessened by the want of that volume and power, which it would gain, were the singers, who are now dispersed over the house in their respective pews, collected into a choir, and placed in the gallery, as is generally customary elsewhere. The discourse was unexceptionable; possessing more originality than is usually found at the present day in compositions of that nature, embellished with considerable beauties of language, and pronounced in a forcible, unimpassioned, yet impressive style of oratory, which I should like to see more adopted in the sacred desk, as eminently fitter for the solemnity of the house of God, than that haranguing declamatory style of headlong eloquence so often displayed in the pulpit.

As I delayed for a minute under the portico of the church, after the services were over, watching, with a stranger's eye, the members of the congregation as they issued from the church and filed off through the several streets to their residences, I felt that I had not, since leaving New-England, beheld a scene which reminded me so forcibly and pleasantly of home. I have, in a former letter, alluded to the prevalence of the Presbyterian church government in Mississippi, to the preclusion of Congregationalists. There is not a resident minister of the latter denomination in this state or in Louisiana. There are only about twenty-four Presbyterian churches in the state, comprising between eight and nine hundred communicants in all; a less number than now composes the late Dr. Payson's church in Portland. The church in Natchez includes about one hundred members, which is the largest number in any one church in the whole state, with two exceptions; one of which is, a Scotch community, about fifty miles in the country east from this city; most of whom, or their fathers before them, emigrating from the land of primitive manners, still retain their national characteristics of simplicity and piety; and that stern, unyielding spirit and Christian devotedness which distinguished the Scottish Presbyterians of "olden time," of whom, though planted in the bosom of an American forest, they are worthy and original representatives. They are a plain, moderately independent, farming community, and sincerely and rigidly devoted to the duties of Christian worship. They have an aged pastor over them, to whom they are devotedly attached; and who is to them, who regard him with the affection of children, indeed a "shepherd and father in Israel." They live like a little band of exiled Waldenses, unsophisticated in their manners, pure and severe in their religion. The Gaelic is spoken among them, and also by many of the other settlers in that portion of the state, who reside in the vicinity of Pearl river; by them also the old popular Gaelic songs are sung, in their original purity and spirit. In the vicinity of this settlement the Presbyterians annually hold a camp meeting. A Presbyterian camp meeting is at least a novelty at the north.

The majority of the ministers of this state are graduates of Princeton college. They form, as do the educated clergy every where, a class of well-informed, intelligent men; though too few in number, and generally placed over congregations too much scattered throughout a large and thinly inhabited extent of country, to command or exercise that peculiar influence upon society which, in more densely populated countries, is so universally possessed by them; and whose elevating, purifying, and moral effect is so readily acknowledged by all classes. So long as this state of society, now peculiar to the south, continues, ministerial influence, in its unadulterated and evangelical power, can hold but limited sway over the heart of the community. Divines are too often looked upon, not as representatives of the Saviour, but merely as intelligent, clever gentlemen, popular and esteemed as they make themselves more or less agreeable and social. A distinguished clergyman in England—where, as you know, the surplice is too often assumed, without any other qualification for the sacred office than the talisman " interest," was termed " a clever, noble fellow," by the neighbouring gentry, for his skill in hunting, and the other lordly sports of English country gentlemen. The manners, customs, amusements, and way of life, of the native born, wealthy, educated planters, have struck me as very similar to those of English gentlemen of wealth and leisure : and it is certain that, generally, many of them would be very apt, like them, to appreciate a clergyman as much for his social qualifications, as for those naturally associated with, and with which he is invested by, his clerical honours.

Here, the Presbyterian clergy, unlike those in the northern states, are generally wealthy. With but a few exceptions, they have, after a short residence in this country, become planters, some of whom have noble annual incomes. After retiring to their plantations they do not—and I mention it with pleasure—altogether resign their ministerial duties. Some of them preach in destitute churches, from time to time ; while others regularly officiate to congregations of their own slaves. One of these clerical planters has erected a neat church upon his plantation, in which he officiates to an assembly of his slaves three Sabbaths in every month; where the worship is conducted with the same regularity, decorum, and dignity, as in other congregations. Some leave the entire management of their estates to overseers, and regularly perform their official duties. But it is difficult for a clergyman to own a rich plantation, without becoming a thorough-going cotton planter. The occupation, with all its ramifications, if not incompatible with his holy office, must necessarily be more or less injurious to the individual, and present a broad target for the shafts of the confessed worshipper of Mammon.

The bugbear reputation of this country for mortality, has long deterred young ministers from filling the places occasionally deserted by their former occupants; many of whom, if they do not resign their office, pass the long summers at the north.— But as no country can well be healthier than this has been, for the last six or seven years, this "health plea" can no longer be offered as an excuse. Indeed, so singularly healthy is this portion of the south-west, that were I required to give it a name, with reference to some one striking characteristic, I should at once call it "Buenos Ayres."* Such, briefly, is the state and condition of the Presbyterian church in this state; which, aside from its form of government, in its formula of faith, and in the

* See a meteorological table and medical report in the appendix —Note C.

rank in society of its members, is equivalent to the Congregational churches in the north.

The peculiar structure of southern society is neither prepared for, nor will it admit of, the exercise of that ecclesiastical influence to which I have above alluded. It is composed, primarily, of wealthy individuals, living aloof from each other on their respective plantations, isolated like feudal chieftains, who, of old, with the spirit of ascetics, frowned defiance at each other, from their castellated rocks : though, do not understand me that planters partake of their belligerent spirit. On the contrary, the reverse is most true of them—for "hospitality" and "southern planter" are synonymous terms. Though there are not more hospitable men in the world than southern gentlemen—though no men can render their houses more agreeable to the stranger—though none are more fascinating in their manners, or more generous in heart—yet they are deficient in that social, domestic feeling, which is the life, excellence, and charm of New-England society, which renders it so dear to every wanderer's heart, and casts around the affections a spell that no power but death can injure or destroy.

The Episcopalian church comprises an infinitely smaller body of members : the few who are of this church, however, are generally opulent planters, merchants, and professional men, with their families. There is but one church of this denomination in the state, which is in this city. I attended worship here the last Sabbath. The house was fa-

shionably but thinly filled. The interior of the
house is plain, though relieved, near the termination
of the southern aisle, by a black marble slab, fixed
in the wall, to the memory of the Rev. Dr. Porter,
late pastor of the church. The pulpit, which is a
miniature forum, is chaste and elegant, and its dra-
pery rich and tastefully arranged. The choir was
full and powerful, whose effect was increased by
a fine-toned organ, the only one in the state; but
whose rich and striking melody must be a powerful pleader, to the ears of amateurs of good church
music, for their more general introduction. The
eloquence of the speaker was engaging, mild, and
gentlemanly. The latter term is very expressive
of his manner, and conciliating pulpit address.—
Though not striking as an orator, his thoughts were
just and pertinent. He

> " Mysterious secrets of a high concern
> And weighty truths—
> Explained by unaffected eloquence."

Contrary to the prevalent opinion at the north,
Roman Catholic influence in this state is entirely
unknown. Formerly there was a Romish church
in this city, ill endowed and seldom supplied with
an officiating priest. This was accidentally destroyed by fire a year or two since; and there is
now no church of that denomination in the state,
and hardly a sufficient number of Catholics to or-
ganize one, did they possess either the spirit or inclination. Such is the peculiar turn of mind of
Mississippians, that they never can be catholicised.

The contiguity of this state to Louisiana, with its French-Roman population, has probably given rise to the opinion above stated, which is as erroneous and unfounded in fact, as is one also very current among northerners, and originating from the same local relation. Obtaining their knowledge of this, among other countries, from Morse's or Cumming's Geography, or other imperfect sources, they have the impression that the French and Spanish languages are much spoken here; whereas they are probably less used here, in mere colloquial intercourse, than in many of the Atlantic states. Maine adjoins Canada; yet who gives Major Downing's fellow-countrymen the credit of speaking French in their daily transactions? It is true that many planters and citizens of Mississippi send their sons to the Catholic seminary at St. Louis, or Bardstown, in Kentucky, and their daughters to the French convents in Louisiana; but this cannot be advanced as any proof of the prevalence of the religion of Rome here, as the same thing is done in New-England, where stand the very pillars of the orthodox faith; and it is done much less frequently now than in former years. The prevailing Christian denomination, as I have before remarked, is that of the Methodists. The excess of their numbers over that of the two other denominations, Presbyterians and Episcopalians, is very great; but having no table of ecclesiastical statistics by me, to which I can refer for greater accuracy, I cannot state correctly the proportions which they bear to each other.—

This denomination embraces all ranks of society, including many of the affluent and a majority of the merely independent planters, throughout the state. —Some of the assemblages here, in the Methodist churches, would remind the stranger rather of a fashionable New-York audience, than a congregation of plain people, soberly arrayed, such as he is accustomed to behold in a Methodist church in New-England. ●Indeed, the Methodists here are generally a widely different class of people from those which compose a northern congregation of the same denomination.

I will conclude my remarks upon the Sabbath, as observed in this city, which was the subject of my last letter, and from which I have so long digressed, by an allusion to a precautionary and wise municipal regulation for freeing the city, before sun-set on the Sabbath, of its army of holiday negroes. At the hour of four the Court-house bell rings out an alarum, long and loud, warning all strange slaves to leave the city. Then commences a ludicrous scene of hurrying and scampering, from the four corners of the town; for wo be to the unlucky straggler, who is found after a limited period within the forbidden bounds ! The penalty of forty stripes, save one, is speedily inflicted, by way of a lesson in the science of discretion. For a lesson, thus administered, few have little relish ; and the subjects thereof, with their heads—the negro's *omnibus*— loaded with their little articles—a pound of this and a pound of that—are, all and singular, soon seen following their noses, with all commendable speed, along the diverging highways, keeping quick time to the tune of " over the hills and far away," to their respective plantations.

———

XXXI.

Catholic burying-ground—Evening in a grave-yard—Sounds of a busy city—Night—Disturbers of the dead—Dishumation of human remains—Mourning cards—A funeral—Various modes of riding—Yankee horsemanship—Mississipian horsemen—Pacers—A plantation road—Residence—The grave—Slaves weeping for their master !—New cemetery.

IN a former letter I have alluded to the old cemetery in the centre of this city, strewed with dismantled tombs, monuments and fragments of gravestones, fenceless and shadeless ; a play-ground for the young academicians, from the adjacent seminary, and a common for the epicurean cow, it stands covering the sides and summit of a pleasantly rounded hill, a monument and a testimony of the characteristic negligence and indifference of Americans for the repositories of their dead.

A few evenings since, as the sun was sinking beneath the level horizon, which was delineated by a line of green foliage, accurately traced along the impurpled western sky, I ascended the slight eminence, upon whose verdant bosom reposes this "city of the dead." Every step through this repository of human ashes, over sunken graves and shattered marble, once reared by the hand of affection or ostentation, forcibly recalled the littleness and vanity of man. The dead slumbered beneath my feet in a marble sleep—cold, silent, and forgotten! From the streets of the city, which on every side closed in this future resting place of its living, the clear laugh, and ringing shout of troops of merry children at their sports, the playful prattle of a group of loitering school girls, the rattling of whirling carriages, from whose windows glanced bright and happy faces, the clattering of horses, the loud conversation of their riders, the tramp of pedestrians along the brick *trottoirs*, the monotonous song of the carman, the prolonged call of the teamster, and the sharp reiterated ringing of his long whip, all mingled confusedly, struck harshly in the clear evening air upon the ear, breaking the silence that should repose over such a scene, and dissipating at once those reflections, which a ramble among the lonely dwellings of the dead is calculated to engender. As I lingered upon the hill, the gradually deepening shadows of evening fell over the town, and subsiding with the day, these sounds, by no means a "concord of enchanting ones," ceased one after the other, and the subdued hum of a reposing city floated over the spot, a strange requiem for its sepultured and unconscious inhabitants. The full moon now rose above the tops of the majestic forest trees, which tower along the eastern suburbs of the city, and poured a flood of mellow light from a southern sky, upon the mouldering ruins encircling the brow of the solitary hill, and glanced brightly upon the roof and towers of the now nearly silent city, which reflected her soft radiance with the mild lustre of polished silver. As I stood contemplating the scene, and yielding to its associations, my attention was drawn to a couple of men ascending the hill from the street. As they approached the crest of the hill, I observed that one of them was equipped with a spade and mattock, and that the other—whose black face glistened in the moonlight like japan, betraying him as a son of Afric— had his head surmounted by a small box. " Resurrectionists," thought I. They stopped not far from me, and the black setting down his box, immediately commenced digging. After observing them for a few minutes I advanced to the spot, and on an inquiry learned that they were disinterring the remains of a gentleman, and those of several members of his family, who had lain buried there for more than thirty years, for the purpose of removing them for re-interment in the new burying-ground north of the town. This cemetery is now wholly disused, and a great number of the dead have been taken up and removed to the new one, but the greater portion still rest, where they were first laid, fresh from among the living; for in all probability the majority who lie there, have neither existing name or friends to preserve their bones from desecration. I was gratified to see that there existed, after so long a period, some remaining affection for the dead displayed in the scene before me. But it

is an isolated instance, and does not palliate the
neglect which is manifested toward the " unknown,
unhonoured, and forgotten," whose bones still moul-
der there, to be " levelled over," when the increase
of the city shall compel the living to construct
their habitations over those of the dead. As I
watched the progress of exhumation, as the grave
was emptied by the brawny arms of the muscular
slave, of load after load of the dark loam, my eye
was attracted by a white object glistening upon the
thrown-up heap by the side of the grave. I raised
it from the damp soil—it was a finger-bone! The
next shovel full glittered with the slender, brittle
fragments of what once was *man !* Not a trace of
the coffin remained, or of the snow-white, scolloped
shroud. The black now threw aside his spade, and
stooping down into the grave, lifted to his companion a round, glaring, white shell, which was once
the temple of the immortal intellect—the tenement
of mind ! A few corroded bones and the half-decay-
ed skull—all that remained of the " human form
divine"—were hastily heaped into the box, the
grave was refilled, and the desecrators of the repose
of the dead departed, as they came, soon to forget
the solemn lesson, which their transient occupation
may have taught them. As I turned away from the
humiliating scene I had just beheld, with a melancholy heart, and a gloom of sorrow drawn over my
feelings, I could not but forcibly recall the words of
the preacher—" that which befalleth the sons of
men, befalleth beasts ; even one thing befalleth
them ; as the one dieth, so dieth the other ; yea, they

have all one breath; so that man hath no pre-
eminence above the beast; for all is *vanity*. All go
unto one place; all are of the dust, and all turn to
dust again."

The Spanish and Roman Catholic custom of
sending printed mourning cards to the relatives and
friends of the deceased, is adopted in this country.
On the death of an individual these tickets are immediately issued and sent throughout the city and
neighbourhood—left indiscriminately, by the carri-
ers, with friends and strangers, at private houses or
in hotels and bar-rooms. While standing yesterday
at the door of the hotel, one of these cards was
placed in my hands by a mulatto slave, who, with
his hands full of them, was distributing them about
the town. It was a beautifully watered sheet, surrounded with a deep mourning body; in the centre
of which were two or three lines of invitation, "to
assist, (*aider*, as the French say) in the funeral
ceremony;" and worded like those often seen inserted in the daily papers of a large city. The use
of these cards is an established custom, and seldom
if ever deviated from. It is at least a feeling one,
and not unworthy of general imitation.

In company with some gentlemen from the hotel,
I attended this funeral, actuated wholly by a stranger's curiosity; for, as well as others of the party,
I was a total stranger to the family of the deceased,
who resided a few miles in the country. Our caval-
cade (for we were all mounted upon those long-
tailed, ambling ponies, to which southerners are so
partial) consisted of six—two Yankees, three south-

erners, and an Englishman. The first rode, as
most Yankees do, awkwardly; for Yankees, at
home, are gig-drivers, not horsemen. Giving too
much heed to the poising of their very erect bodies,
they left their legs to take care of themselves; but
when their attention was drawn, for a moment, to
these members, they would rock upon their saddles,
the very images of "tottering equilibriums," as
Capt. Hall would term them; and fortunate were
they in recovering their nearly forfeited seats again.
—These horses, which advance by first lifting two
legs on one side and then changing to the other, do
not suit brother Jonathan's notions of a riding horse.
So he applies whip and spur, and breaks away into
a long gallop. Then indeed he is in his element.
An Arabian, on being asked what was the best seat
in the world, replied, "The back of a fleet courser."
If the querist had applied to Jonathan, he would
have said, "A galloping nag." Whenever you see
a stranger galloping at the south, you will seldom
err in guessing him to be a Yankee. Our English
friend rode cockney fashion; that is, not much unlike a clothes-pin, or a pair of compasses, astride a
line. Stiff and erect as a Hungarian hussar, he cur-
vetted along the smooth roads, till he had worked
his slight-framed, spirited animal into a fever of excitement, which flung the foam over his rider, as he
tossed his head, swelled his curved neck, and
champed his bit in rage, in vain efforts to spring
away, free from his thraldom; but the rider finger-
ed the slight bridle-rein with the ease and skill of
a master. The southerners of the party rode like

all southerners, admirably, inimitably. They appeared as much at home and at ease in their saddles, as in a well-stuffed arm-chair after dining generously. The Mississippian sits his horse gracefully, yet not, as the riding-master would say, scientifically. He never seems to think of himself, or the position of his limbs. They yield, as does his whole body, pliantly and naturally to the motions of the animal beneath him, with which his own harmonize so perfectly and with such flexibility, that there seems to be but one principle actuating both. He glides easily along upon his pacer, with the bridle thrown upon its neck, or over the high pummel of his handsome Spanish saddle ; talking as unconcernedly with his companions, as though lounging, arm in arm with them, along the streets. He seldom goes out of a pace. If he is in haste, he only paces the faster. Of every variety of gaited animals which I have seen, the Mississippian pacer is the most desirable. I shall, however, have occasion to allude hereafter to southern equestrianism more particularly, and will return from my digression to the funeral.

We arrived at the entrance gate of the plantation after a delightful ride of half an hour, along a fine though dusty road, (for with this impalpable soil it is either paste or powder) bordered with noble forests of oak, black gum, the hoary-coated sycamore, and the rich-leaved, evergreen magnolia, among and around which the grape vine entwined and hung in graceful festoons. Through natural vistas in the wood occasional glimpses could be obtained of white villas, not unfrequently large and elegant, half hidden in the centre of plantations, or among the thick woods which crowned the swelling hills on every side. The road was, like most of the roads here, a succession of gentle ascents and descents, being laid out so as to intersect transversely parallel ridges, themselves composed of isolated hills, gently blending and linking into each other. The country was luxuriant, undulating, and picturesque. The general character of the scenery struck me as remarkably English. The resemblance would be still more striking, did not the taste or convenience of the planters lead them to select the site of their dwellings in the centre of their plantations, or in the depths of their forests, without any reference to the public road, (from which they are most universally concealed) which is always the northern farmer's guide in such a case, thereby giving a solitary character to the road scenery, and detracting much from the general beauty of the country.

The residence to which we were riding was invisible from the road. We passed through a large gate-way, the gate of which, one of our Yankee brethren, who had galloped forward, tried in vain to open, nearly tumbling from his horse in the atttempt, but which one of our southern friends paced up to, and scarcely checking his horse, opened with the merest effort in the world. Winding our way rapidly along a circuitous carriage-way, at one time threading the mazes of the forest, at another, coursing through a cotton field, whitened as though snow had fallen in large flakes and thickly sprinkled its

green surface—now following the pebbly bed of a
deep bayou, with overhanging, precipitous banks,
and now skirting the borders of some brawling rivulet, we arrived in sight of the "house of mourning."
The dwelling, like most in Mississippi, was a long,
wooden, cottage-like edifice, with a long piazza, or
gallery, projecting from the roof, and extending along
the front and rear of the building. This gallery is
in all country-houses, in the summer, the lounging
room, reception room, promenade and dining room.
The kitchen, "gin," stables, out-houses, and negro-
quarters, extended some distance in the rear, the
whole forming quite a village—but more African
than American in its features. We were rather
too late, as the funeral procession was already proceeding to the grave-yard, which was, as on most
plantations, a secluded spot not far from the dwelling, set apart as a family burying-ground. I was
struck with the appearance of the procession. Six
mounted gentlemen in black, preceded the hearse
as bearers. A broad band of white cambric encircled their hats, and streamed away behind in two
pennons nearly a yard in length. A broad white
sash of similar materials was passed over the right
shoulder, from which a pennon of black ribbon flut-
tered, and was knotted under the left side, while
the ends were allowed to hang nearly to the feet.
The hearse was a huge black chest, opening at the
end for the admission of the coffin, which, as I discovered at the grave, was richly covered with black
silk velvet, and studded with a border of gilt nails.
Its top was not horizontal, as you are accustomed to

see them, but raised in the middle like a roof. The
hearse was followed by several private carriages,
gigs, of which a northern procession would consist,
being not much used in this country. An irregular
procession, or rather crowd of slaves in the rear of
all, followed with sorrowful countenances the remains of their master, to his last, long home.

When the heavy clods rattled upon the hollow
sounding coffin, these poor wretches, who had anx-
iously crowded around the grave, burst into one
simultaneous flood of tears, mingled with expressions of regret, sorrow and affection. A group of
slaves lamenting over the grave of their master!
Will not our sceptical countrymen regard this as
an anomaly in philanthropy? Half a dozen slaves
then shovelled for a few moments from the fresh
pile of earth upon the coffin, and a mound soon rose,
where, but a few moments before, yawned a grave!
An appropriate prayer was offered over the dead,
and the procession dispersed at the burial-place.
Such is a plantation burial! In this manner are
consigned to the narrow house, four fifths of the
population of this state. The city and town cemeteries are but little resorted to, for a large proportion of those who breathe their last in town, unless
they are friendless, or strangers, are borne to some
solitary family burial-place in the country for sepul-
ture: there are few families in the towns of Mississippi who have not relatives residing on plantations
in the country.

The grave-yard of Natchez, situated as I have
formerly observed, a little less than a mile north

from the town, on the river road, covers an irregular surface among several small wooded hills, and is surrounded by cotton fields, from which it has been redeemed for its present use. It evinces neither beauty of location, nor taste in the arrangement of its tombs, of which there are but two or three remarkable for elegance or neatness. Its avenues are overgrown with the rank, luxuriant grass, peculiar to grave-yards, varied only here and there by clusters of thorns and briars. The wild and naked features of the spot are occasionally relieved by a shade tree planted by some kindly hand over the grave of a friend; but this occasional testimony of respect will not redeem the cemetery from that negligence and want of taste in this matter with which Americans have been, with too much justice, universally charged by foreigners. In observing the names upon the various head-stones, I noticed that the majority of those who slept beneath, were strangers, mostly from New-England, but many from Europe. Many of them were young. It is thus that the scourge of the south has ever reaped rich, teeming harvests from the north. But those days of terror, it is to be hoped, are for ever past, and that henceforth health will smile over the green hills of this pleasant land, which pestilence has so long blasted with her frowns.

XXXII.

THERE are many causes, both moral and physical, which concur to render the inhabitants of the south dissimilar to those of the north. Some of these may be traced to climate, more to education and local relations, and yet more to that peculiar state of things which necessarily prevails in a planting country and all newly organized states. The difference is clearly distinguishable through all its grades and ramifications, and so strongly marked as to stamp the southern character with traits sufficiently distinctive to be dignified with the term national.

A plantation well stocked with hands, is the *ne plus ultra* of every man's ambition who resides at the south. Young men who come to this country, "to make money," soon catch the mania, and nothing less than a broad plantation, waving with the snow white cotton bolls, can fill their mental vision, as they anticipate by a few years in their dreams of the future, the result of their plans and labours.

Hence, the great number of planters and the few professional men of long or eminent standing in their several professions. In such a state of things no men grow old or gray in their profession if at all successful. As soon as the young lawyer acquires sufficient to purchase a few hundred acres of the rich alluvial lands, and a few slaves, he quits his profession at once, though perhaps just rising into eminence, and turns cotton planter. The bar at Natchez is composed, with but few exceptions, entirely of young men. Ten years hence, probably not four out of five of these, if living, will remain in their profession. To the prevalence of this custom of retiring so early from the bar, and not to want of talent, is to be attributed its deficiency of distinguished names. There is much talent now concentrated at this bar, and throughout the state. But its possessors are young men; and this mania for planting will soon deprive the state of any benefit from it in a professional point of view. As the lawyers are young, the judges cannot of course be much stricken in years. The northerner, naturally associates with the title of "Judge," a venerable, dignified personage, with locks of snow, a suit of sober black, and powdered queue, shoe-buckles, and black silk stockings. Judge my surprise at hearing at the public table a few days since, a young gentleman, apparently not more than four or five and twenty, addressed as "judge!" I at first thought it applied as a mere "*soubriquet*," till subsequently assured that he was really on the bench.

Physicians make money much more rapidly than

lawyers, and sooner retire from practice and assume the planter. They, however, retain their titles, so that medico-planters are now numerous, far out-numbering the regular practitioners, who have not yet climbed high enough up the wall to leap down into a cotton field on the other side. Ministers, who constitute the third item of the diploma'd triad, are not free from the universal mania, and as writing sermons is not coining money, the plantations are like the vocative in Latin pronouns. They, however, by observing the command in Gen. ix. 1, contrive ultimately to reach the same goal. The merchant moves onward floundering through invoices, ledgers, packages, and boxes. The gin-wright and overseer, also have an eye upon this Ultima Thule, while the more wealthy mechanics begin to form visions of cotton fields, and talk knowingly upon the "staple." Even editors have an eye that way !

Cotton and negroes are the constant theme—-the ever harped upon, never worn out subject of conversation among all classes. But a small portion of the broad rich lands of this thriving state is yet appropriated. Not till every acre is purchased and cultivated—not till Mississippi becomes one vast cotton field, will this mania, which has entered into the very marrow, bone and sinew of a Mississippian's system, pass away. And not then, till the lands become exhausted and wholly unfit for farther cultivation. The rich loam which forms the upland soil of this state is of a very slight depth—and after a few years is worn away by constant culture

and the action of the winds and rain. The fields
are then "thrown out" as useless. Every plough-
furrow becomes the bed of a rivulet after heavy
rains—these uniting are increased into torrents, before which the impalpable soil dissolves like ice
under a summer's sun. By degrees, acre after
acre, of what was a few years previous beautifully
undulating ground, waving with the dark green,
snow-crested cotton, presents a wild scene of fright-
ful precipices, and yawning chasms, which are increased in depth and destructively enlarged after
every rain. There are many thousand acres within
twenty miles of the city of Natchez, being the earliest cultivated portions of the country, which are
now lying in this condition, presenting an appearance of wild desolation, and not unfrequently, of
sublimity. This peculiar feature of the country
intrudes itself into every rural prospect, painfully
marring the loveliest country that ever came from
the hand of nature. Natchez itself is nearly isolated by a deep ravine, which forms a natural moat
around the town. It has been formed by "washing," and though serpentine and irregular in its
depth, it is cut with the accuracy of a canal. It is
spanned by bridges along the several roads that
issue from the town.

From the loose and friable nature of this soil,
which renders it so liable to "wash," as is the expressive technical term here, the south-west portion of this state must within a century become
waste, barren, and wild, unless peradventure, some
inventing Yankee, or other patentee may devise a

way of remedying the evil and making the wilderness to "blossom like the rose." A thick bluish green grass, termed Bermuda grass, is used with great success to check the progress of a *wash* when it has first commenced.* It is very tenacious of the soil, takes firm and wide root, grows and spreads rapidly, and soon forms a compact matted surface, which effectually checks any farther increase of the ravines, or "bayous," as these deep chasms are usually termed; though bayou in its original signification is applied to creeks, and deep glens, with or without running water.

* The necessary properties of grasses suited to this climate differ from those required in higher latitudes. They should have deep running roots if erect, to withstand the scorching heat of the sun, or their stems should lie prostrate and cover the ground. This is the peculiarity of grasses in the West Indies and Egypt. The grass peculiar to the last, and well adapted to this country—the cynosurus Ægyptus—grows in South Carolina and Georgia, and is highly esteemed. Among the small variety of grasses cultivated here, is the Washita winter grass, perennial, and the Natchez winter grass, an annual. The latter is a phalaris, not known at the north. It is a rich grass and very succulent. There is a variety of this grass termed striped grass, cultivated in yards at the north, which is unknown here, and which from its peculiar properties is excellent to bind banks, and would be of great service on plantations where there are bayous. The Bermuda grass has large succulent leaves and runners, and is better adapted to this climate than any other. Lucerne and esparcette have the same properties, but have never been tried. The white clover of Kentucky, known by the name of Buffalo clover, is also admirably adapted, upon the above principles, to this soil and climate. Hay as an article of culture is unknown here. White clover is abundant upon the commons. There are several grasses peculiar to this country unknown at the north; but they are never transplanted from the fields and woods, and are scarcely known and never cultivated. There is properly but *one plant* in the south, if planters are to draw up the botanical catalogue, and that is the *cotton plant !*

When this state was first settled, tobacco was exclusively cultivated as the grand staple. But this plant was found to be a great exhauster of the soil; cotton rapidly superseded its culture, and it was shortly banished from the state, and found a home in Tennessee, where it is at present extensively cultivated. It has not for many years been cultivated here. Planters have no room for any thing but their cotton, and corn, on their plantations, and scarcely are they willing to make room even for the latter, as they buy a great part of their corn, annually, from the Kentucky and Indiana flat boats at the " Landing."

Among northerners, southern planters are reputed wealthy. This idea is not far from correct —as a class they are so; perhaps more so than any other body of men in America. Like our Yankee farmers they are tillers of the soil. "But why" you may ask, "do they who are engaged in the same pursuits as the New-England farmer, so infinitely surpass him in the reward of his labours?" The northern farmer cannot at the most make more than three per cent. on his farm. He labours himself, or pays for labour. He *must* do the first or he cannot live. If he does the latter, he can make nothing. If by hard labour and frugal economy, the common independent Yankee farmer, such as the traveller meets with any where in New-England, lays up annually from four to seven hundred dollars, he is a thriving man and " getting rich." His daughters are attractive, and his sons will have something " handsome" to begin the world with. But the

southern farmer can make from fifteen to thirty
per cent. by his farm. He works on his plantation
a certain number of slaves, say thirty, which are to
him what the sinewy arms of the Yankee farmer are
to himself. Each slave ought to average from
seven to eight bales of cotton during the season,
especially on the new lands. An acre will generally average from one to two bales. Each bale
averages four hundred pounds, at from twelve to
fifteen cents a pound. This may not be an exact
estimate, but it is not far from the true one. Deducting two thousand and five hundred dollars for
the expenses of the plantation, there will remain the
net income of eleven thousand dollars. Now suppose this plantation and slaves to have been purchased on a credit, paying at the rate of six hundred dollars apiece for his negroes, the planter
would be able to pay for nearly two-thirds of them
the first year. The second year, he would pay for
the remainder, and purchase ten or twelve more ;
and the third year, if he had obtained his plantation
on a credit of that length of time, he would pay for
that also, and commence his fourth year with a
valuable plantation, and thirty-five or forty slaves,
all his own property, with an increased income for
the ensuing year of some thousands of dollars.
Henceforward, if prudent, he will rank as an opulent
planter. Success is not however always in proportion to the outlay or expectations of the aspirant for
wealth. It is modified and varied by the wear and
tear, sickness and death, fluctuations of the market,
and many other ills to which all who adventure in

the great lottery of life are heirs. In the way above alluded to, numerous plantations in this state have been commenced, and thus the wealth of a great number of the opulent planters of this region has originated. Incomes of twenty thousand dollars are common here. Several individuals possess incomes of from forty to fifty thousand dollars, and live in a style commensurate with their wealth. The amount is generally expressed by the number of their negroes, and the number of " bales" they make at a crop. To know the number of either is to know accurately their incomes. And as this is easily ascertained, it is not difficult to form a prompt estimate of individual wealth.

To sell cotton in order to buy negroes—to make more cotton to buy more negroes, " ad infinitum," is the aim and direct tendency of all the operations of the thorough-going cotton planter; his whole soul is wrapped up in the pursuit. It is, apparently, the principle by which he " lives, moves, and has his being." There are some who "work" three and four hundred negroes, though the average number is from thirty to one hundred. "This is all very fine," you say, " but the slaves!—there's the rub." True; but without slaves there could be no planters, for whites will not and cannot work cotton plantations, beneath a broiling southern sun.— Without planters there could be no cotton; without cotton no wealth. Without them Mississippi would be a wilderness, and revert to the aboriginal possessors. Annihilate them to-morrow, and this state and every southern state might be bought for a song.

I am not advocating this system; but destroy it—and the southern states become at once comparative ciphers in the Union. Northerners, particularly Yankees, are at first a little compunctious on the subject of holding slaves. They soon, however, illustrate the truth contained in the following lines, but slightly changed from their original application. With half-averted eyes they at first view slavery as

> " ——— A monster of such horrid mien,
> That to be hated needs but to be seen:
> But seen too oft, familiar with her face,
> They soon endure—and in the end embrace."

Many of the planters are northerners. When they have conquered their prejudices, they become thorough, driving planters, generally giving themselves up to the pursuit more devotedly than the regular-bred planter. Their treatment of their slaves is also far more rigid. Northerners are entirely unaccustomed to their habits, which are perfectly understood and appreciated by southerners, who have been familiar with Africans from childhood; whom they have had for their nurses, play-fellows, and " bearers," and between whom and themselves a reciprocal and very natural attachment exists, which, on the gentleman's part, involuntarily extends to the whole dingy race, exhibited in a kindly feeling and condescending familiarity, for which he receives gratitude in return. On the part of the slave, this attachment is manifested by an affection and faithfulness which only cease with life. Of this state of feeling, which a southern life and education can only give, the northerner knows nothing. Inexperience leads him to hold the reins of government over his novel subjects with an unsparing severity, which the native ruler of these domestic colonies finds wholly unnecessary. The slave always prefers a southern master, because he knows that he will be understood by him. His kindly feelings toward, and sympathies with slaves, as such, are as honourable to his heart as gratifying to the subjects of them. He treats with suitable allowance those peculiarities of their race, which the unpractised northerner will construe into idleness, obstinacy, laziness, revenge, or hatred. There is another cause for their difference of treatment to their slaves. The southerner, habituated to their presence, never fears them, and laughs at the idea. It is the reverse with the northerner : he fears them, and hopes to intimidate them by severity.

The system of credit in this country is peculiar. From new-year's to new-year's is the customary extension of this accommodation, and the first of January, as planters have then usually disposed of their crops, is a season for a general settlement throughout every branch of business. The planters have their commission merchants in New-Orleans and Natchez, who receive and ship their cotton for them, and make advances, if required, upon succeeding crops. Some planters export direct to Liverpool and other ports, though generally they sell or consign to the commission merchants in Natchez, who turn cotton into gold so readily, that one verily would be inclined to think that the philosopher's stone might be concealed within the bales. A planter often commences with nothing, or merely an endorser—buys land and negroes, and, in the strong phraseology of Crockett, "goes ahead." In a few years he becomes opulent. Others, however, (as was the case with the old settlers especially) and young men at the present time, with little means, commence with a piece of wild land, and five or six, or perhaps not more than two negroes—and go on strengthening and increasing, adding acre to acre, negro to negro, bale to bale, till wealth crowns their labours. Many of the oldest and wealthiest planters began in this manner, when they had to dispute possession of the soil with the Spaniard, the wild beast of the forest, or wilder Indian. They are now reaping the rewards of their youthful toil, in the possession of sons and daughters, lands and influence, and all the luxuries and enjoyments which wealth commands. Their sons, more fortunate in their youth than their sires, receive, from the paternal bounty, plantations and negroes, and at once, without previous toil or care, assume the condition of the refined and luxurious planter. So you perceive that a Yankee farmer and a southern planter are birds of a very different feather.* Now in this sad, idolatrous world, where Mammon is worshipped on millions of altars, the

* I have lying before me a letter, bearing date July 1, 1806, from a distinguished German botanist; in which, at the close of an article upon the plants of this country, he inquires of Wm. Dunbar, Esq. to whom the letter is addressed, "if the cotton plant has ever been tried in Mississippi ? *It seems to promise much!*" Mississippi planters of the present day will certainly coincide with this gentleman in his opinion.

swelling hills and noble forests of the south must
certainly be "where men ought to worship." If
the satirical maxim, "man was made to make money," is true, of which there can be no question—
the mint of his operations lies most temptingly between the "Father of waters" and the arrowy
Pearl. And men seem to feel the truth of it—or of
the maxim of Bacon, that "territory newly acquired
and not settled, is a matter of burthen rather than
of strength;" for they are spreading over it like a
cloud, and occupying the vast tracts called "the
Purchase," recently obtained from the Indians, previous to their removal to the west. The tide of
emigration is rapidly setting to the north and east
portions of the state. Planters, who have exhausted their old lands in this vicinity, are settling and
removing to these new lands, which will soon become the richest cotton growing part of Mississippi.
Parents do not now think of settling their children
on plantations near Natchez, but purchase for them
in the upper part of the state. Small towns, with
"mighty names," plucked from the ruins of some
long since mouldered city of classic fame and memory, are springing up here and there, like mush-
rooms, amidst the affrighted forests. Sixteen new
counties have lately been created in this portion of
the state, where so recently the Indian tracked his
game and shrieked his war-whoop; and as an agricultural state, the strength and sinew of Mississippi
must be hereafter concentrated in this fresher and
younger portion of her territory.

XXXIII.

An excursion—A planter's gallery—Neglect of grounds—Taste and economy—Mississippi forests—The St. Catherine—Cotton fields—Worm fences—Hedges—The pride of China—The magnolia tree and flower—Plantation roads—White cliffs—General view of a plantation.

A FEW days since, in company with a northern friend, I made an excursion to an extensive plantation two hours' ride from the city. We left the hotel at an early hour, exchanging our mattresses— the universal southern bed—for more luxurious seats in elastic Spanish saddles, upon delightfully cradling pacers, and proceeded through one of the principal streets, already alive with pedestrians and horsemen; for, in a southern climate, evening and morning constitute the day—the day itself being a " noon of indolence," where ice and shade are the only blessings to be devoutly wished. Ambling along at an easy gait toward the great southern road, leading to New-Orleans, we passed, just on the confines of the country, the residence of the Presbyterian clergyman, and one of the most charming retreats I have yet seen in the vicinity of Natchez, whose suburbs are peculiarly rich in tasteful country seats. Our eyes lingered over the luxuriant shrubbery clustering about the edifice, entwining around its columns and peeping in at the windows. Clumps of foliage, of the deepest green, were enamelled with flowers of the brightest hues; and every tree was an aviary, from which burst the sweetest melody. What a spot for the student! Among flowers and vines and singing birds! What a freshness must they fling around his heart! What a richness must clothe even the language of sermons composed in such pleasant shades—the cool wind loaded with fragrance, leaping from among the trees upon the brow, and playing refreshingly among the hair!

Leaving, to the right, the romantic fort Rosalie, rearing its green parapets in strong relief against the sky—a prominent object amid the slightly elevated surface of the surrounding country—we turned into one of those pleasant roads which wind in all directions through the rich scenery of this state. The first mile we passed several neat dwellings, of the cottage order; one of which, with a gallery in front, and surrounded by a smooth, green slope, was the residence of the Episcopalian clergyman. It was a chaste and pretty mansion, though not so luxuriantly embowered as the abode of the clergyman above alluded to. A huge colonnaded structure, crowning an abrupt eminence near the road, struck our eyes with an imposing effect. It was the abode of one of the wealthiest planters of this state; who, like the majority of those whose families now roll in their splendid equipages, has been the maker of his fortune. The grounds about this edifice were neglected; horses were grazing around the piazzas, over which were strewed saddles, whips, horse blankets, and the motley paraphernalia with which planters love to lumber their galleries. On nearly every piazza in Mississippi may be found a wash-stand, bowl, pitcher, towel, and water-bucket, for general accommodation. But the southern gallery is not constructed, like those at the north, for ornament or ostentation, but for use. Here they wash, lounge, often sleep, and take their meals.— Here will the stranger or visiter be invited to take a chair, or recline upon a sofa, settee, or form, as the taste and ability of the host may have furnished this important portion of a planter's house. I once called on a planter within an hour's ride of Natchez, whose income would constitute a fortune for five or six modest Yankees. I entered the front yard—a green level, shaded with the relics of a forest—the live oak, sycamore, and gum trees—through a narrow wicket in a white-washed paling, the most common fence around southern dwellings. In the front yard were several sheep, colts, calves, two or three saddle and a fine pair of carriage-horses, negro children, and every variety of domestic fowl. The planter was sitting upon the gallery, divested of coat, vest, and shoes, with his feet on the railing, playing, in high glee, with a little dark-eyed boy and two young negroes, who were chasing each other under the bridge formed by his extended limbs. Three or four noble dogs, which his voice and the presence of his servant, who accompanied me to the house, kept submissive, were couching like leopards around his chair. A litter of young bull-headed pups lay upon a blanket under a window opening into a bed-room, white with curtains and valances; while a domestic tabby sat upon the window-sill, gazing musingly down upon the rising generation of her hereditary foes, perhaps with reflections not of the most pleasing cast. A hammock, suspended between an iron hook driven into the side of the house and one of the slender columns which supported the sloping roof of the gallery, contained a youth of fourteen, a nephew of the planter, fast locked in the embraces of Morpheus; whose *aid-de-camp*, in the shape of a strapping negress, stood by the hammock, waving over the sleeper a long plume of gorgeous feathers of the pea-fowl—that magnificent bird of the south, which struts about the ground of the planter, gratifying the eye with the glorious emblazonry upon his plumage by day, and torturing the ear with his loud clamours by night. A pair of noble antlers was secured to one of the pillars, from whose branches hung broad-brimmed hats, bridles, a sheep-skin covering to a saddle, which reposed in one corner of the piazza, a riding whip, a blanket coat or capote, spurs, surcingle, and part of a coach harness. A rifle and a shot-gun with an incredibly large bore, were suspended in beckets near the hall entrance; while a couple of shot-pouches, a game-bag, and other sporting apparatus, hung beside them. Slippers, brogans, a pillow, indented as though recently deserted, a gourd, and a broken "cotton slate," filled up the picture, whose original, in some one or other of its features, may be found in nearly every planter's dwelling in this state.

There are many private residences, in the vicinity of Natchez, of an equally expensive character with the one which furnished the above description, whose elegant interiors, contrasting with the neglected grounds about them, suggest the idea of a handsome city residence, accidentally dropped upon a bleak hill, or into the midst of a partially cleared forest, and there remaining, with its noble roof grasped by the arms of an oak, and its windows and columns festooned by the drooping moss, heavily waving in the wind. Thus are situated many of the planters' dwellings, separated from the adjacent forests by a rude, white-washed picket, enclosing around the house an unornamented green, or grazing lot, for the saddle and carriage-horses, which can regale their eyes at pleasure, by walking up to the parlour windows and gazing in upon handsome carpets, elegant furniture, costly mantel ornaments, and side-boards loaded with massive plate; and, no doubt, ruminate philosophically upon the reflection of their figures at full-length in long, richly-framed mirrors. Very few of the planters' villas, even within a few miles of Natchez, are adorned with surrounding ornamental shrubbery walks, or any other artificial auxiliaries to the natural scenery, except a few shade trees and a narrow, gravelled avenue from the gate to the house. A long avenue of trees, ornamenting and sheltering the approach to a dwelling, is a rare sight in this state, though very frequently seen in Louisiana. Yet, in no region of the south can fine avenues of beautiful trees be made with such facility as in Mississippi. No state surpasses this in the beauty, variety, and rapid growth of its ornamental shade trees; the laurel, sycamore, locust, oak, elm, and white bay, with the "pride of China,"—the universal shade tree in the south-west—arrive here at the most perfect maturity and beauty. Every plantation residence is approached by an avenue, often nearly a mile in length; yet so little attention is paid to this species of ornament and comfort, in a climate where shade is a synonym for luxury, that scarcely one of them is shaded, except where, in their course through a forest, nature has flung the broad arms of majestic trees across the path.

The peculiarity of the dwellings of planters, evinced in hiding the prettiest cottage imaginable under the wild, gnarled limbs of forest trees, fringed with long black moss, like mourning weeds, which hangs over the doors and windows in melancholy grandeur, may be traced, very naturally, to the original mode of life of most of the occupants, who, though now opulent, have arisen, with but few exceptions, from comparative obscurity in the world of dollars. Originally occupying log huts in the wilderness, their whole time and attention were engaged in the culture of cotton; and embellishment, either of their cabins or grounds, was wholly disregarded. When they became the lords of a domain and a hundred slaves; for many retain their cabins even till then—ostentation, as they saw the

elegancies of refined society displayed around them
—necessity, for fear of being entombed in the ruins
of their venerable log palaces—or a desire for
greater comfort—razed the humble cabin, and reared upon its site the walls of an expensive and beautiful fabric. Here the planter stops. The same causes
which originally influenced him to neglect the improvement of his grounds, still continue to exist;
and though he may inhabit a building that would
grace an English park, the grounds and scenery
about it, with the exception of a paling enclosing
a green yard, are suffered to remain in their pristine rudeness.   Thus far, and with few exceptions,
no farther, have the wealthiest planters advanced.
Here they have taken a stand; and a motive cause,
equal to that which led to the first step from the
cabin to the more elegant mansion, must again operate, or the finest villas in Mississippi will, for many
years to come, be surrounded, on one or more sides,
with the native forests, or stand in unpicturesque
contiguity with ploughed fields, cattle-pens, and the
several interesting divisions of a farm-yard.

You will judge, from this state of things, that the
Mississippi planters are not a showy and stylish
class, but a plain, practical body of men, who, in
general, regard comfort, and conformity to old habits, rather than display and fashionable innova-
tions; and who would gaze with more complacency
upon an acre of their domain, whitened, like a new-
ly-washed flock, with cotton, than were it spread
out before them magnificent with horticulture, or
beautifully velveted with green.   Still planters are

not destitute of taste ; it is their principle to make
it yield to interest. " What a fine park you might
have around your house," once remarked an English gentleman to a planter in this state, as he surveyed the finely undulating fields here and there
sprinkled with an oak, extending on every side
around the dwelling.

" Very true," replied the southron, " but these
few acres yield me annually from ten to twelve
bales of cotton : this would be too great a sacrifice
for the mere gratification of the eye."

" Still very true," replied the Englishman, " but
this sense could be gratified without any sacrifice.
Your plantation consists of eight or nine hundred
acres, and not one half is under cultivation ; a portion of that now uncultivated might be substituted
for this." To this the planter answered, that the
soil about his house would produce more to the
acre than the other, by at least one bale in every
ten, having been long under cultivation ; and that
merely as a matter of taste, though no one admired
a fine park or lawn more than himself, he could
not devote it to this object.

This principle of the land economist, so devoutly
reverenced, will long preclude that desirable union
of taste and interest, which is the combined result
of wealth attained and enjoyed. The last state men
cannot be said to be in, who, however wealthy, never relax their exertions in adding to their incomes ;
which is, and ever will be the case with the planter,
and indeed every other man, so long as he can, by
his efforts, annually increase his revenue ten or

twenty thousand dollars. To the immense profit which every acre and the labour of every slave yield the planter, and to no other cause, is to be referred the anomalous result manifested in neglecting to improve their estates : for an acre, that will yield them sixty dollars per annum, and a slave, whose annual labour will yield from two to five hundred dollars, are, by the laws which regulate the empire of money, to be appropriated to the service of interest, to the entire exclusion of the claims of taste.

About a mile from Natchez, we passed, close by the road-side, a family cemetery, whose white paling was bursting with shrubbery. No mausoleum gratefully relieving the eye, rose amid the luxuriant foliage, enshrining the affection of the living or the memory of the dead. On the opposite side of the road stood a handsome mansion, though without that noble expanse of lawn which is the finest feature in the grounds of an English country residence. Instead of a lawn, a small unimproved court-yard intervened between the house and the road. Winding round an extensive vegetable garden, attached to the house, which is the only dwelling for more than ten miles immediately on the road, we travelled for an hour, either over a pleasantly rolling country, with extensive cotton fields, spreading away on either hand ; or beneath forest trees, which, in height and majesty, might vie with the " cedars of Lebanon." There is a grandeur in the vast forests of the south, of which a northerner can form no adequate conception. The trees spring from the ground into the air, noble columns, from fifty to a hundred feet in height, and, expanding like the cocoa, fling abroad their limbs, which, interlocking, present a canopy almost impervious to the sun, and beneath which wind arcades of the most magnificent dimensions. The nakedness of the tall shafts is relieved by the luxuriant tendrils of the muscadine and woodbine twining about them, in spiral wreaths, quite to their summit, or hanging in immense festoons from tree to tree. In these woods horsemen can advance without obstruction, so spacious are the intervals between the trees, so high the branches above them, and so free from underwood is the sward. Of such forest-riding the northerner knows nothing, unless his lore in tales of Italian banditti may have enabled him to form some idea of scenes with which his own country refuses to gratify him. So much do the northern and southern forests differ, that a fleet rider will traverse the latter with more ease than the woodman can the former.

Cut from the shaft of a southern forest tree, a section forty or fifty feet in length, and plant the mutilated summit in the earth, and its stunted appearance would convey to a Mississippian a tolerably correct idea of a forest tree in New-England; or add to the low trunk of a wide spreading northern oak, the column abstracted from its southern rival, and northerners would form from its towering altitude, a tolerable idea of a forest tree in Mississippi. Hang from its heavy branches huge tassels of black Carolina moss, from two to six feet in length—suspend from limb to limb gigantic festoons of vines, themselves but lesser trees in size, and clothe its trunk with a spiral vestment of leaves, as though a green serpent were coiled about it, and you will have created a southern tree in its native majesty. Imagine a forest of them lifting their tops to heaven and yourself bounding away upon a fleet horse beneath its sublime domes, with a noble stag, flying down its glades like a winged creature, while the shouts of hunters, the tramp of horses, and the baying of hounds echo through its solemn corridors, and then you will have some faint idea of the glory of a southern forest and the noble character of its enjoyments.*

Between three and four miles from Natchez we crossed the St. Catharine, a deeply bedded and narrow stream, winding through a fertile tract of country in a very serpentine course, for nearly thirty leagues before it empties into the Mississippi, twenty miles below Natchez. This stream is celebrated in the early history of this state, and still possesses interest from the Indian traditions with which it is associated. In numerous villages, formerly scattered along its banks, and spread over the beautiful hills among which it meanders, but not a vestige of which now remains, it is supposed, on the authority both of oral and written history, that more than two hundred thousand Indians but a few

* The forests of Mississippi consist of oak, ash, maple, hickory, sweet gum, cypress, (in the bottoms) yellow poplar, holly, black and white flowering locusts, pecan, and pine on the ridges, with a countless variety of underwood, ivy, grape vines, (vitis silvestris) papaw, spice-wood, and innumerable creepers whose flexile tendrils twine around every tree.

degrees removed from the refinements of civilized
life, dwelt peaceably under their own vine and fig-
tree. But where are they now? "Echo answers
—Where!"

Between five and six miles from town the road
passed through the centre of one of the most
extensive plantations in the county. For more than
a mile on either side, an immense cotton field spread
away to the distant forests. Not a fence, except
that which confined the road, (always degraded, in
the parlance of the country, when running between
two fences, to a "lane,") was to be seen over the
whole cultivated surface of a mile square. The absence of fences is a peculiarity of southern farms.
As their proprietors cultivate but one article as a
staple, there is no necessity of intersecting their
lands by fences, as at the north, where every farm is
cut up into many portions, appropriated to a variety of productions. To a northern eye, a large extent of cultivated country, without a fence, or
scarcely a dwelling, would present a singular appearance; but a short residence in the south will
soon render one familiar with such scenery where
no other meets the eye. The few fences, however,
that exist on plantations, for defining boundaries,
confining public roads, and fencing in the pasture
lands—which, instead of broad green fields as in
New-England, are the woods and cane-brakes—are
of the most unsightly kind. With a gently undulating surface and a diversity of vale and wood scenery unrivalled, the natural loveliness of this state is
disfigured by zigzag, or Virginia fences, which

stretch along the sides of the most charming roads, surround the loveliest cottages, or rudely encroach upon the snowy palings that enclose them, and intersect the finest eminences and fairest champaigns. The Yankee farmer's stone and rail fences are bad enough, but they are in character with the ruder features of his country; but the worm fences and arcadian scenery of the south are combinations undreamed of in my philosophy. These crooked lines of deformity obtruding upon the eye in every scene —the numerous red banks and chasms caused by the "wash," and Congo and Mandingo nymphs and swains, loitering around every fountain, rambling through the groves, or reclining in the shades, are in themselves sufficient to unruralise even "Araby the blest." Yet with all these harsh artificial features, there is a picturesqueness—a quiet beauty in the general aspect of the scenery, not unfrequently strengthened into majesty, so indelibly stamped upon it by nature that nothing less than a rail-road can wholly deface it.

On the plantation alluded to above, through which lay our road, I noticed within the fence a young hedge, which, with an unparalleled innovation upon the prescriptive right of twisted fences, had recently been planted to supersede them. In a country where the "chickasaw rose," which is a beautiful hedge thorn, grows so luxuriantly, it is worthy of remark that the culture of the hedge, so ornamental and useful as a field-fence, is altogether neglected. Planters would certainly find it eventually for their interest, and if generally adopted, the scenery of this state would rival the loveliest sections of rural England. Delaware, without any striking natural beauties, by clustering green hedges around her wheat-fields and farm-houses, has created an artificial feature in her scenery which renders her naturally tame aspect extremely rural, if not beautiful. The hedge, however, will not be introduced into this state to the exclusion of the rail-fence, until the pine woods, dwindled here and there to a solitary tree, refuse longer to deform in the shape of rails, a country they were originally intended to beautify.

The "quarters" of the plantation were pleasantly situated upon an eminence a third of a mile from the road, each dwelling neatly white-washed and embowered in the China tree, which yields in beauty to no other. This, as I have before remarked, is the universal shade tree for cabin and villa in this state. It is in leaf about seven months in the year, and bears early in the spring a delicate and beautiful flower, of a pale pink ground slightly tinged with purple. In appearance and fragrance it resembles the lilac, though the cluster of flowers is larger and more irregularly formed. These after loading the air with their fragrance for some days, fall off, leaving green berries thickly clustering on every branch. These berries become yellow in autumn, and long after the seared leaf falls, hang in clusters from the boughs, nor finally drop from them until forced from their position by the young branches and leaves in the succeeding spring. The chief beauty of this tree consists in the richness and

arrangement of its foliage. From a trunk eight or
ten feet in height, the limbs, in the perfect tree,
branch irregularly upward at an angle of about 45°
or 50°. From these, which are of various lengths,
slender shoots extend laterally, bearing at their ex-
tremities a thick tuft of leaves. These slender
branches radiate in all directions, each also terminating in fine feathery tufts, which, being laid one
over the other like scales on armour, present an
almost impenetrable shield to the rays of the sun.
These young shoots throughout the season are constantly expanding their bright parasols of leaves,
and as they are of a paler hue than the older leaves,
which are of a dark purple green, the variegated
effect, combined with the singularly beautiful arrangement of the whole, is very fine. The rapid
growth of this tree is remarkable. A severed limb
placed in the ground, in the winter, will burst forth
into a fine luxuriant head of foliage in the spring.
From a berry slightly covered with soil, a weed, not
unlike the common pig-weed, in the rapidity of its
growth and the greenness of its stalk, shoots up
during the summer four or five feet in height. During the winter its stalks harden, and in the spring, in
a brown coat, and with the dignity of a young tree,
it proudly displays its tufts of pale, tapering leaves.
In three or four summers more it will fling its limbs
over the planter's cottage—and cast upon the ground
a broad and delightful shade. Divest a tree of the
largest size of its top, and in the spring the naked
stump will burst forth into a cloud of foliage. Such
is the tree which surrounds the dwellings and bor-

ders the streets in the villages of the south-west—
the "vine" and the "fig tree" under which every
man dwells.

About two leagues from Natchez the road entered
an extensive forest, winding along upon a ridge
thickly covered with the polished leaved magnolia
tree (M. grandiflora)—the pride of southern forests.
This tree is an evergreen, and rises from the ground
often to the height of seventy feet, presenting an exterior of ever-green leaves, and large white flowers.
Its leaves appearing like "two single laurel-leaves
rolled into one," are five or six inches in length, of
a dark green colour, the under side of a rich brown,
and the upper beautifully glazed, and thick like
shoe leather. The flower is magnificent. In June
it unfolds itself upon the green surface of the immoveable cone in fine relief. When full blown it
is of a great size; some of them cannot be placed
in a hat without crushing them. Its petals are a
pure white, shaped and curved precisely like a
quarter-section of the rind of an orange, and nearly
as thick, and perfectly smooth and elastic. They
are frequently used by boarding-school misses to
serve as *billets doux*, for which, from their fragrance and unsullied purity, they are admirably
fitted. They are so large that I have written upon
one of them with a lead pencil in ordinary hand-
writing, a stanza from Childe Harold. It must be
confessed that the writing as well as the material is
of a very ephemeral kind; but for this reason the
material is perhaps the more valuable when pressed
into the service of Don Cupid. They are so fra-

grant that a single flower will fill a house with the most agreeable perfume; and the atmosphere for many rods in the vicinity of a tree in full flower is so heavily impregnated, that a sensation of faintness will affect one long remaining within its influence.

The remainder of our ride was through a fine forest, occasionally opening into broad cotton fields. Once on ascending a hill we caught, through a vista in the woods over broad fields, a glimpse of the cypress forests of Louisiana, spread out like a dark sea to the level horizon. The Mississippi rolled through the midst unseen. As we rode on we passed roads diverging to the right and left from the highway, leading to the hidden dwellings of the planters. A large gate set into a rail fence usually indicates the vicinity of a planter's residence in the south—but the plantation roads here turned into the forests, through which they romantically wound till lost in their depths. Any of these roads would have conducted us to the villa of some wealthy planter. There can be little ostentation in a people who thus hide their dwellings from the public road. Jonathan, on the other hand, would plant his house so near the highway as to have a word from his door with every passenger. Deprive him of a view of the public road, and you deprive him of his greatest enjoyment—the indulgence of curiosity. About nine miles from town the forest retreated from the road, and from the brow of a hill, the brown face of a cliff rose above the tops of the trees about a league before us. To the eye so long accustomed to the unvarying green hue of the scenery—the

rough face of this cliff was an agreeable relief. It
was one of the white cliffs alluded to in a former
letter. Shortly after losing sight of this prominent
object, we turned into a road winding through the
woods, which conducted us for a quarter of an
hour down and up several precipitous hills, across
two deep bayous, through an extensive cotton field
in which the negroes were industriously at work
without a "driver" or an "overseer," and after winding a short distance bordered by young poplars
round the side of a hill, passed through a first, then
a second gateway, and finally brought us in front of
the dwelling house of our host, and the termination
of our interesting ride.

XXXIV.

Horticulture—Chateaubriand—A Mississippi garden and plants—
A novel scene—Sick slaves—Care of masters for their sick—Shamming—Inertness of negroes—Burial of slaves—Negro mothers—A
nursery—Negro village on the Sabbath—Religious privileges of
slaves—Marriages—Negro "passes"—The advantages of this regulation—Anecdote of a runaway.

IN America, where vegetation is on a scale of
magnificence commensurate with her continental
extent—it is remarkable that a taste for horticulture should be so little cultivated. In the southern
United States, nature enamels with a richness of
colouring and a diversity of materials which she has

but sparingly employed in decorating the hills and valleys of other lands. The grandeur of the forests in the south, and the luxuriance of the shrubs and plants, have no parallel. But southerners tread the avenues, breathe the air, and recline under the trees and in the arbours of their paradise, thankfully accepting and enjoying their luxurious boon, but seldom insinuating, through the cultivation of flowers, that nature has left her work imperfect. There are, it is true, individual exceptions. One of the finest private gardens in the United States, which has suggested these remarks, is in the south, and within two hours ride of Natchez. But as a general rule, southerners, with the exception of the cultivation of a few plants in a front yard, pay little regard to horticulture. So in New-England, a lilac tree between the windows, a few rose bushes and indigenous plants lining the walk, and five or six boxes or vases containing exotics standing upon the granite steps on either side of the front door, constitute the sum of their flower plants and the extent to which this delightful science is carried. The severity of northern winters and the shortness of the summers, may perhaps preclude perfection in this pleasing study, but not excuse the present neglect of it. The English, inhabiting a climate but a little milder, possess a strong and decided horticultural taste —England itself is one vast garden made up of innumerable smaller ones, each, from the cluster of shrubbery around the humblest cottage to the magnificent park, that spreads around her palaces, displaying the prevailing national passion.

Though southerners do not often pursue horticulture as a science, yet they are passionately fond of flowers. At the south, gentlemen, without the charge of coxcombry or effeminacy, wear them in the button-holes of their vests—fair girls wreathe them in their hair, and children trudge to school loaded with bouquets. The south is emphatically the land of flowers; nature seems to have turned this region from her hand as the *chef d'œuvre* of her skill. Here, in the glowing language of Chateaubriand, are seen "floating islands of Pistia and Nenuphar, whose yellow roses spring up like pavilions; here magnificent savanas unfold their green mantles, which seem in the distance to blend ther verdure with the azure of the skies. Suspened on the floods of the Mississippi, grouped on rocks and mountains and dispersed in valleys, trees of every odour, every shape, every hue, entwine their variegated heads, and ascend to an immeasurable height; bignonias, vines, and colocynths, wind their slender roots around their trunks, creep to the summit of their branches, and passing from the maple to the tulip tree and alcea, form a thousand bowers and verdant arcades; stretching from tree to tree they often throw their fibrous arms across rivers and erect on them arches of foliage and flowers. Amidst these fragrant clusters, the proud magnolia raises its immoveable cone, adorned with snowy roses, and commanding the whole forest, meets with no other rival than the palm-tree, whose green leaves are softly fanned by refreshing gales." The race here now is for wealth; in good time the passion will change, and men, tired of contesting for the prize in the game of life, which they have won over and over again, will seek a theatre on which to display their golden laurels; and where are men more fond of displaying their wealth than on their persons, equipage, and dwellings? Horticulture, the taste in such cases earliest cultivated, will then shed its genial influence over the valley of the south-west, and noble mansions and tasteful cottages, around which forests now gloomily frown, or rude fields spread their ploughed surfaces, will be surrounded by noble grounds enriched by the hand of taste from the lavish opulence of the forests and savanas. The garden alluded to at the commencement of this letter, is situated upon the plantation, an excursion to which was the subject of my last. As this is said to be the finest garden in Mississippi, to which all others more or less approximate, in the character of their plants, style, and general arrangement, I would describe it, could my pen do adequate justice to the taste of its proprietor, or the variety and beauty of the plants and flowers. Among them—for I will mention a few—which represented every clime, were the cape myrtle, with its pure and delicately formed flower, the oak geranium, the classical ivy, and the fragrant snow-drop. The broad walks were, as usual in southern gardens, bordered by the varnished lauria mundi, occasionally relieved by the cape jessamine, slender althea, and dark green arbor vitæ. The splendidly attired amaryllis, the purple magnolia, the Arabian and night-blooming jessamines, the verbenum, or lemon-scented geranium,

with the majestic aloe, that hoary monarch of the
garden, which blooms but once in a century, the
broad-leaved yarra, or caco, the fragrant snow-drop,
and the sweet-scented shrub and oleander, with
countless other shrubs and flowers, breathing forth
the sweetest fragrance, gratified the senses, and
pleased the eye wherever it was turned. There
spread the cassia, a creeping plant, bearing a pink
flower, and admirably adapted to bind the soil of
this region, to prevent its " washing," by the texture of its thickly matted shoots, its tenacity to the
soil, and the density of its foliage, all which combined, render it a secure shield laid over the surface
of the ground; box-trees, in luxuriant, dark green
cones, two or three feet high, were interspersed
among the loftier shrubs at the angles of the several
avenues, which were lined with diminutive hedges
of this thickly-leaved plant. In the centre of the
main avenue, which, on account of the inclination
of the garden, was a terraced walk, terminating in
an artificial pond, was a large diamond-shaped bed
of violets enamelled with blue and green, from
which arose a cloud of fragrance that floated over
the whole garden, gathering rich tributes from a
hundred flowers of the sweetest perfume and loveliest hues. Around this pond, were crescents of
shrubs and trees, among which the melancholy
weeping willow drooped its graceful tendrils over
the water.* Beyond this little lake, the primeval

* The weeping willow is less luxuriant in this climate than in
latitude 40 °. It is not however cultivated in this state as it is in
Pennsylvania, where it arrives at the greatest perfection. There is a

forests, which on every side bounded the prospect,
rose majestically on the summit of a high hill, in
front, affording a striking contrast to the Hesperian
elegancies spread around the observer.

Arbours of the lauria mundi, and pleasant alcoves
invited to repose or meditation; and thickly shaded
walks, wound on either side of the principal walk
which they occasionally intersected, in graceful serpentine lines, bordered by the eglantine, or Scotch

willow which grows on the banks of the Mississippi, whose roots
become as dry as tinder, after the periodical swell has subsided, but
which vegetates afresh as soon as it is watered by the next inunda-
tion.   This property of dying and returning again to vegetative existence, is not peculiar to this willow; other plants possess the same
singular property, though this exceeds all others in magnitude.   The
plants of that description known to botanists, are all water mosses
except two species of ducksmeat—the "lemna minor" and the "lemna gibba."   These are but minute vegetables floating on the surface
of stagnant water, without taking root in the pond.   They may be
dried in the hot sun and then kept in a deal box for two or three
years, after which they will revive, if placed in spring, river or rain
water.   There is at the north a kind of natural paper, resembling
the coats or strata of a wasp's nest in colour and consistency, which
is formed of the sediment of ponds, that become dry in hot weather.
If a piece of this paper-like substance be put in a glass of fresh water
and exposed to light, it loses its dirty-white colour in a few minutes
and assumes a lively green.   This sudden and unexpected change
is occasioned by a number of aquatic mosses, constituting a part of
the materials of the paper or sediment in question, and belonging to
the genus "Conferra;" for these minute vegetables may be said to
be in the state of suspended animation, while they remain dry; but
the presence of water restores them to their natural functions by its
animating virtue.

So long retaining the principle of life, these curious plants, as
well as the two species above mentioned, may be transported to any
distant country in a torpid condition, where they might again be
animated.   The same remark will apply to the Mississippi willow
which suggested these observations.

rose, the monthly rose—the flower-pot plant of the north—which here grows in luxuriant hedges, from six to ten feet high. The moss, and wild rose, the last a native, in which the creative power of horticulture annually unfolds new beauties, the dwarf cape jessamine, the Washita willow, with its pretty flower, the laurustina, hypiscus, and citronelle, or fragrant lemon grass, the tea-tree, three feet high, with orange and lemon trees, bending under their golden fruit, and a guava tree, the only one in fruit in the state, clustering with its delicious apple, presented on every side the most delightful offerings to the senses. But I must beg your indulgence for intruding upon you a botanical catalogue of plants in a southern garden, which Pomona, envying the fair divinity presiding there, might sigh to make her empire. Besides this exception to my general philippic in the former part of this letter, against the practical floral taste of Mississippians, there are a few others sufficiently beautiful to atone for the prevailing deficiency of which I have spoken. Clifton, an elegant villa near Natchez, and one of the finest residences in the state, for the beauty of its grounds, and the extent of the prospect from its lofty galleries, boasts a garden of almost unrivalled beauty, and rich in the number and variety of its shrubs and plants. There are three or four other gardens, buried like gems in the centre of old plantations, which, in horticultural wealth and display, nearly rival those above mentioned. I record these instances with pleasure, as indicating the existence of that fine taste, in the germ at least, which refinement, opulence, and leisure, will in time unfold and ripen into maturity.

While standing upon the gallery in the evening, enjoying the various busy scenes and confused sounds peculiar to a plantation at the close of day, my attention was drawn to a lugubrious procession, consisting of seven or eight negroes approaching the house from the "quarters," some with blankets thrown like cloaks over their shoulders, their heads bandaged, and moving with a listless gait of inimitable helplessness. One after another they crawled up and presented themselves, before the open passage in the gallery. Seeing such a sad assembly I approached them with curiosity, while their master, notified of their arrival, came out to examine into the state of this his walking hospital. Of all modifications of the "human face divine," that of the sick negro is the most dolorous. Their miserable, abject, hollow-eyed look has no parallel. The negro is not an Adonis in his best estate. But he increases his natural ugliness by a laxity of the muscles, a rolling of the eye and a dropping of the under jaw, when ill, which give his face a most ludicrously wo-begone appearance. The transparent jet-black hue of his skin altogether disappears, leaving the complexion a dingy brown or sallow, which in no slight degree increases the sadness of his physiognomy. Those who are actually ill generally receive every attention that humanity—not "interest"—dictates. It has been said that interest is the only friend of the slave; that without this lever applied to the feelings of the master, he would never be in-

fluenced to care for his slaves either in health or in
sickness.   However true this may be in individual
instances, a vast number of cases have come within
my knowledge, which have convinced me that as a general censure this charge is unmerited. Planters, particularly native planters, have a kind of affection for
their negroes, incredible to those who have not observed its effects.   If rebellious they punish them—
if well behaved they not unfrequently reward them.
In health they treat them with uniform kindness, in
sickness with attention and sympathy.   I once
called on a native planter—a young bachelor, like
many of his class, who had graduated at Cambridge
and travelled in Europe—yet northern education
and foreign habits did not destroy the Mississippian. I
found him by the bed side of a dying slave—nur-
sing him with a kindness of voice and manner, and
displaying a manly sympathy with his sufferings
honorable to himself and to humanity.   On large
plantations hospitals are erected for the reception
of the sick, and the best medical attendance is provided for them.   The physicians of Natchez derive
a large proportion of their incomes from attending
plantations.   On some estates a physician perma-
nently resides, whose time may be supposed sufficiently taken up in attending to the health of from
one to two hundred persons.   Often, several plantations, if the " force" on each is small, unite and employ one physician for the whole.   Every plantation
is supplied with suitable medicines, and generally
to such an extent, that some room or part of a
room in the planter's house is converted into a small

apothecary's shop. These, in the absence of the physician in any sudden emergency, are administered by the planter. Hence, the health of the slaves, so far as medical skill is concerned, is well provided for. They are well fed and warmly clothed in the winter, in warm jackets and trowsers, and blanket coats enveloping the whole person, with hats or woolen caps and brogans. In summer they have clothing suitable to the season, and a ragged negro is less frequently to be met with than in northern cities.

The attendance which the sick receive is a great temptation for the slaves to "sham" illness. I was dining not long since in the country where the lady— a planter's daughter, and the wife and mother of a planter—sent from the table some plates of rich soup and boiled fowl to "poor sick Jane and her husband," as she observed in her reply to one who inquired if any of her "people" were unwell. A portion of the dessert was also sent to another who was convalescent. Those who are not considered ill enough to be sent to the hospital, are permitted to remain in their houses or cabins, reporting themselves every evening at the "great hus," as they term the family mansion. The sombre procession alluded to above, which led to these remarks, consisted of a few of these invalids, who had appeared at the gallery to make their evening report. On being questioned as to their respective conditions, a scene ensues that to be appreciated, must be observed.

"What ails you, Peter?" "Mighty sick, master." * "Show me your tongue :" and out, inch by inch, projects a long tongue, not unlike the sole of his shoe in size and colour, accompanied by a groan from the very pit of the stomach. If the negro is actually ill, suitable medicine is prescribed, which his master or the physician compels him to swallow in his presence. For, sick or well, and very fond of complaining, they will never take " doctor's stuff," as they term it, but, throwing it away as soon as they are out of sight, either go without any medicine, or take some concoction in repute among the old African beldames in the " quarters," by which they are sickened if well, and made worse if ill, and present themselves for inspection the next evening, by no means improved in health. They are fond of shamming, or " skulking," as sailors term it, and will often voluntarily expose themselves to sickness, in order to obtain exemption from labour.

There is no animal so averse to labour, even to the most necessary locomotion, as the African. His greatest enjoyment seems to be a state of animal inactivity. Inquire of any ordinary field negro why he would like to be free, if he ever happened to indulge the wish, and he will reply, " because me no work all day long." It is well known that the " lazzaroni" of Italy, the gauchos who infest Buenos Ayres, and the half-bloods swarming in the streets of all South American cities, will never labour, unless absolutely obliged to do so for the purpose of sustaining existence, and then only for the tempo-

* The negro seldom is heard to say " massa ;" they generally say *master*, distinctly.

rary supply. I once applied to a half-naked gaucho, who, with his red *capote* wound about his head, was dozing in the sun on the *plaza*, to carry a portmanteau. Slowly raising the heavy lids of his large glittering eyes, he took two pieces of money, of small value, from the folds of his red sash, and held them up to my view, murmuring, with a negative inclination of his head—" Tengo dos reales, señor;" thereby implying, " I will take mine ease while my money lasts—no more work till this is gone." By such a feeling is this class of men invariably governed. Individuals of them I have known to work with great industry for a day or two, and earn a few dollars, when they would cease from their usual labour, and, until their last penny was expended, no remuneration would prevail on them to carry a trunk across the square. From my knowledge of negro character at the south, however elevated it may be at the north, I am convinced that slaves, in their present moral condition, if emancipated, would be lazzaroni in every thing but colour. Sometimes a sham patient will be detected ; although, to make their complaints the more specious, they frequently discolour the tongue. This species of culprit is often punished by ridicule and exposure to his fellows, whose taunts on such occasions embody the purest specimens of African wit. Not unfrequently these cheats are punished by a dose from the medicine chest, that effectually cures them of such indispositions. Latterly, since steaming has been fashionable, a good steaming has been known to be an equally effective prescription.

When a negro dies, his remains are placed in a
coffin and decently interred. Labour is often entirely suspended on the plantation, and the slaves
are assembled in their Sunday clothes to attend the
funeral. Divine service is sometimes performed in
the little chapel on the plantation, at which not only
the slaves but the members of the white family are
present. A Presbyterian clergyman recently informed me that he had been sent for by a native
planter, to attend the funeral of one of his slaves
and preach his funeral sermon. He went, though
twelve miles distant from his residence, and remarked that he was never present on a more interesting occasion. On most plantations females are
allowed a month's cessation from field labour, before
and after confinement. But it cannot be denied that
on some plantations nothing but actual confinement
releases them from the field ; to which the mother
soon after returns, leaving an infant a few days old
at the " quarters," which she is permitted to visit
three or four times in the day. Sometimes, when
a little older, infants are brought into the field, under the care of an old nurse, to save the time which
the mothers would otherwise consume in walking
to and from the " quarters." Once, on riding through
a plantation, I noticed, under a China tree, which
shaded the shelter-house—a rude building, in the
centre of extensive cotton fields, in which negroes
seek shelter on the approach of a storm—a group
of infants and children, whose parents I discovered
at work more than half a mile distant. Several
little fellows, not two years old, and as naked as

young frogs, were amusing themselves in rolling
over the grass, heedless of the occasional warning
of their *gouvernante*, "Take care de snake."—
Slung from a limb in a blanket reposed two others,
very snugly, side by side, mumbling corn bread;
while, suspended from the tree, in a rude cradle,
were three or four more of this band of nurslings,
all in a pile, and fast asleep. I am indebted to this
scene for a correct application of the nursery song,
which I had never before been able exactly to understand, commencing—

> "Rock a bye, baby, upon the tree top,
> When the wind blows the cradle will rock;
> When the bough breaks the cradle will fall,
> And down tumbles baby, cradle and all."

These little candidates for "field honours," are
useless articles on a plantation during the first five
or six years of their existence. They are then
made to take the first lessons in the elementary
part of their education. When they have learned
their manual alphabet tolerably well, they are placed
in the field to take a spell at cotton-picking. The
first day in the field is their proudest day. The
young negroes look forward to it, with as much rest-
lessness and impatience as school-boys to a vaca-
tion. Black children are not put to work so young
as many children of poor parents at the north. It
is often the case that the children of the domestic
servants become pets in the house, and the play-
mates of the white children of the family. No
scene can be livelier or more interesting to a
northerner, than that which the negro quarters of a

well regulated plantation present, on a Sabbath morning, just before church hour. In every cabin the men are shaving and dressing—the women, arrayed in their gay muslins, are arranging their frizzly hair, in which they take no little pride, or investigating the condition of their children's heads —the old people neatly clothed are quietly conversing or smoking about their doors, and those of the younger portion, who are not undergoing the infliction of the wash-tub, are enjoying themselves in the shade of the trees or around some little pond, with as much zest as though " slavery" and " freedom" were synonymous terms. When all are dressed and the hour arrives for worship, they lock up their cabins, and the whole population of the little village proceeds to the chapel, where divine worship is performed, sometimes by an officiating clergyman, and often by the planter himself, if a church member. The whole plantation is also frequently formed into a Sabbath class, which is instructed by the planter or some member of his family; and often such is the anxiety of masters that they should perfectly understand what they are taught—a hard matter in the present state of African intellect—that no means calculated to advance their progress are left untried. I was not long since shown a manuscript catechism, drawn up with great care and judgment by a distinguished planter, on a plan admirably adapted to the comprehension of negroes. The same gentleman, in conjunction with two or three neighbouring planters, employs a Presbyterian clergyman, formerly a missionary among the Choctaws at the Elliott station before their dispersion, to preach to the slaves, paying him a salary for his services. On those plantations which have no chapel, and no regular worship on the Sabbath, negroes are permitted to go to the nearest town to church; a privilege they seldom know how to appreciate, and prefer converting their liberty into an opportunity for marketing or visiting. Experience, however, has convinced planters that no indulgence to their slaves is so detrimental as this, both to the moral condition of the slave, and the good order of the plantation, for there is no vice in which many of them will not become adepts, if allowed a temporary freedom from restraint, one day in seven. Hence this liberty, except in particular instances, is denied them on some estates; to which they are confined under easy discipline during the day, passing the time in strolling through the woods, sleeping, eating, and idling about the quarters. The evenings of the Sabbath are passed in little gossipping circles in some of the cabins, or beneath the shade of some tree in front of their dwellings, or at weddings. The negroes are usually married by the planter, who reads the service from the gallery—the couple with their attendants standing upon the steps or on the green in front. These marriages, in the eye of the slave, are binding. Clergymen are sometimes invited to officiate by those planters who feel that respect for the marriage covenant, which leads them to desire its strict observance, where human legislation has not provided for it. On nuptial occasions the negroes partake of fine suppers, to which the ladies add many little delicacies, and handsome presents of wearing apparel to the married pair. When the negroes desire a clergyman to perform the ceremony for them, planters seldom refuse to comply with their request.

When negroes leave the plantation, for whatever purpose, whether to attend church, class meeting or market, visit their husbands, wives, or sweethearts, or are sent on errands, they must carry with them a written permission of absence from their master, stating the object for which his slave leaves his plantation, the place or places to which he is going, and the time to which his absence is limited. This written authority is called a " pass," and is usually written somewhat after this form :

"Oakland — June — 18—

" Pass J —— to Natchez and back again by sunset," or " E —— has permission to visit his wife on Mr. C ——'s plantation, to be absent till 9 o'clock."

In such fluctuating property as slaves, it often happens that husband, wife, and children may all belong to different owners ; and as negroes belonging to different plantations intermarry, such a provision, which is a state law, is necessary to preserve discipline, and embrace within the eye or knowledge of the master, every movement of his slave. Were slaves allowed to leave the estates without the knowledge of their masters, during a certain portion of every week, an immense body of men in the aggregate, consisting of a few from every plantation in the state, would be moving among the plantations, at liberty to plan and execute any mischief they might choose to set on foot. If negroes leave the plantation without a "pass," they are liable to be taken up by any white person who suspects them to be runaways, and punishment is the consequence. The law allows every white man in town or country this kind of supervision over negroes; and as there are always men who are on the lookout for runaways, for the purpose of obtaining the reward of several dollars for each they can bring back to his master, the slave, should he leave the plantation without his "pass"—the want of which generally denotes the runaway—is soon apprehended. You will see that this regulation is a wise legal provision for the preservation both of private and public security. An anecdote connected with this subject was recently related to me by a planter whose slave was the hero. "A gentleman," said he, "met one of my negroes mounted on horseback, with a jug in his hand, riding toward Natchez. Suspecting him from appearances to be a runaway, he stopped him and asked for his "pass." The slave unrolled first one old rag—an old rag is a negro's substitute for a pocket—and then another without success. "I 'spec' me loss me pass, master." "Whom do you belong to?" "Mr. ——," giving the wrong person. "Where are you going?" "To Natchez, get whiskey, master." At the moment, my brand upon the horse struck the eye of the gentleman; "You are a runaway, boy—you belong to Mr. D ——." Instantly the negro leaped from his horse, cleared the fence, and fled through the woods like a deer toward home. The gentleman on arriving at his own house, sent a servant to me with the horse which the runaway had deserted. I immediately assembled the whole force of the plantation and not one of the negroes was missing; the culprit having managed to arrive at the plantation before I could receive any intimation of his absence. I tried a long time to make the guilty one confess, but in vain. So at last, I tried the effect of a *ruse*. "Well, boys, I know it is one of you, and though I am not able to point out the rogue, my friend who detected him will recognize him at once. So you must walk over to his house. Fall in there—march!"

"They proceeded a short distance, when I ordered a halt. "Mind, boys, the guilty one shall not only be punished by me, but I will give every 'hand' on the plantation the liberty of taking personal satisfaction, for compelling them to take a walk of three miles.—So, march!" They moved on again for about a quarter of a mile, when they came to a full stop—deliberated a few moments and then retraced their steps. "Hie! what now?" "Why, master, Bob say he de one." Bob, who it seems had confessed to his fellow-slaves as the best policy, now stepped forward, and acknowledged himself to be the runaway."

XXXV.

THE morning after my arrival at the plantation, which suggested the subject of my last letter, two gentlemen, with their guns and dogs, arrived at the house, to proceed from thence, according to a previous arrangement, on a deer hunt. This noble and attractive game abounds in the "bottoms" and river hills in this region; though the planters, who are in general passionately fond of hunting, are fast thinning their numbers. The branching antlers of a stag, as in the old oaken halls of England, are found fixed, in some conspicuous station, in almost every planter's habitation—trophies of his skill, and testimonials of his attachment to the chase.

Having prepared our hunting apparatus, and assembled the dogs, which, from their impatient movements, evidently needed no intimation of our design, we mounted our horses, and, winding through the cotton fields, entered a forest to the south, and proceeded, in fine spirits, toward the "drive," four or five miles below, as the hunting station is tech-

nically termed by deer hunters. There were, ex-
clusive of a servant, four in our party. One of them,
my host, formerly an officer in the navy, having,
some years since, left the service, and settled himself down as a cotton planter, presented in his person the anomalous union, in Mississippi, of the sail-
or and farmer : for in this state, which has little intercourse directly with the sea, sailors are rare birds.
Till recently a ship could not be seen by a Mississippian without going to New-Orleans, or elsewhere
out of the state : but since Natchez became a port
of entry, and ships have ascended here, the citizens
who flocked in from all the country round, to gaze
upon them, are a little more *au fait* to this branch
of nautical knowledge. It would be difficult to say
which predominates in this gentleman, the bluff and
frank bearing of the sailor, or the easy and independent manner of the planter. In the management of his plantation, the result of his peculiar
economy has shown, that the discipline with which
he was familiar in the navy, with suitable modifications, has not been applied unsuccessfully to the
government of his slaves. What a strange inclination sailors have for farming ! Inquire of any New-
England sea-captain the ultimatum of his wishes,
after leaving the sea—for sailors in general follow
the sea as the means of securing them a snug
berth on shore—and he will almost invariably reply—" a farm." Another of our party was a
planter, a native of Mississippi, and the son of a
gentleman whose philosophic researches have greatly contributed to the advancement of science. He

was a model of a southern planter—gentlemanly, companionable, and a keen hunter. The government of his plantation, which is one of the finest in the state, is of a parental rather than an imperious character. He rules rather by kindness than severity, and his slaves obey from the principle of a desire to please, rather than from fear. And the result of his discipline has fully overthrown the sweeping assertion, which it is the fashion to repeat and believe, that " the more kindly slaves are treated the worse they are." A favourite theory of philanthropists, in relation to master and slave, is more practically illustrated on the estate of this gentleman, than the most sanguine of its framers could have anticipated. As I have, in a former letter, alluded to that branch of the domestic economy of this plantation, relating to the religious privileges of the slaves, and shall again have occasion to refer to its discipline, I will pursue the subject here no farther.

The third individual of our party was a gentleman originally from New-Jersey; a state which has contributed many valuable citizens to Mississippi. But he had been too long in the south to preserve his identity as a Jersey man. The son of a distinguished barrister, he had been a lawyer himself; but, like all professional men, who have remained here a short time, he had taken his third degree as a cotton planter. He is a gentleman of fine taste and a chastened imagination; and besides some beautiful tales, contributed to the periodicals, he is the author of that delightful story, the " Fawn's leap," published in the Atlantic Souvenir of 1830. The literary world will have reason to feel regret, in which the subject of my remark will, no doubt, be far from sympathising, that fortune has placed him among her *protegés*. He possesses an independent property, and resides on an estate called " Woodbourne," eight or nine miles from Natchez. With true Mississippi taste, he has placed his handsome villa in the midst of a forest; but the majestic beauty of the lofty trees, as surveyed from the gallery, and the solemn grandeur of the primeval forests which inclose his dwelling on all sides, struck me, at the moment, as far superior to any display of art in ornamental grounds, and nearly unhinged my predilection for artificial scenery. In this charming retirement, and in the quiet enjoyment of private life, he has laid aside the gown of the author to assume the capote of the planter, and become an indefatigable devotee to the lordly pleasures of the chase. Few men, who hunt merely *en amateur*, and especially, few literary men, can boast that they have killed twenty-seven deer, and been at the death of fifty-two—yet this gentleman can do so with truth : and a row of notches, cut in his hunting-horn, which I found suspended from an antler in the gallery of the house we had just left, recorded the fact. Besides this gentleman, there are but few individuals who are known out of this state as cultivators of literature. Mississippi is yet too young to boast of her authors, although she is not deficient in men of talent and learning. But the members of the learned professions are too much involved in schemes of wealth to have leisure or inclination for the cultivation of general literature.

Half way through the forest into which we entered on leaving the plantation, we came to a rude dwelling, inhabited by a ruder old hunter, who was to officiate as "driver." He accompanied us with his dogs for a while, and then turned aside into the woods to surround the deer in their place of resort and drive them toward the river, between which and them we were to take our "stands," for the purpose of intercepting them, as they dashed by to the water. For if alarmed while feeding upon the high grounds back from the Mississippi, they at once bound off to the shelter of the swamps or bottoms near the river—and the skilful hunter, whose experience teaches him by what paths they will seek to gain the lowlands where the hounds cannot follow them, takes his stand with his rifle behind some tree by which he is tolerably sure the deer will pass, and as the noble and terrified animal bounds past him, he levels the deadly rifle with unerring aim, and buries a bullet in his heart.

Emerging from the forest a mile or two above our hunting ground, we came suddenly upon an amphitheatre of naked hills nearly surrounded by forests of dark pine. Winding through romantic defiles thickly bordered with cedars, we gradually ascended to the summit of the highest of this cluster of treeless hills, when all at once the Mississippi, rolling onward to the sea, burst upon our sight in all its majesty. There is a grand and desolate character in those naked cliffs which hang in huge terraces over the river, to the perpendicular height of three hundred feet. The view from their summits is one of the most sublime and extensive in the south-west. To the north and south the broad river spreads away like a long serpentine lake, its western shore presenting a plain, clothed even to the horizon with a boundless forest, with a plantation here and there breaking the uniformity of its outlines, near the water's edge.

After a farther ride of a mile, over a hilly road through woods alternately exposing and hiding the river, we arrived at the "deer-stand,"—a long ridge nearly parallel with the river, and covered with a very open forest with a low "bottom," between the ridge and the water, and an extensive "drive," or forest frequented by deer, extending two miles inland. Our "driver" with the whole pack, had turned off into the "drive" some time before, and having examined the ground, we took our "stands" about a hundred yards apart, each behind a large tree commanding an opening, or avenue, through which the deer were expected to pass. Several of these "stands," and many more than we could occupy, were on the ridge, all of which should have been occupied to insure a successful issue to our sport. A few moments after we had taken our stands, and while listening for the least token of the "driver's" presence in the depths of the forest —the distant baying of dogs, in that peculiar note with which they open when they have roused their game, fell faintly upon our ears. The chorus of canine voices, however, soon grew louder and more

violent—and as they awoke the echoes of the
forests, and came down upon us like a storm—my
heart leaped and the blood coursed merrily in my
veins.   All at once the deep voices of the hounds
ceased as though they were at fault; but after a
few moments' pause, a staunch old hunter opened
again far to the right, and again the whole pack
were in pursuit in full cry, and the crashing of trees
and under-brush directly in front of us about a quarter of a mile in the wood, with the increased roar of
the pack, warned us to be ready.   The next moment the noise moved away to the right, and all at
once, with a crash and a bound, a noble stag, with
his head laid back upon his shoulders, crossed our
line at the remotest stand, and disappeared in the
thick woods along the river.   The dogs followed
like meteors.   Away to the left another crashing
was heard, and a beautiful doe leaped across the
open space on the ridge, and was lost in the thicket.
The sounds of affrighted deer, passing through the
forest at a great distance, were occasionally heard,
but these soon died away and we only heard the
wild clamour of the dogs, which the driver, who
was close at their heels, in vain essayed to recall by
sounding his horn long and loud, and sending its
hoarse notes into the deepest recesses of the wood.

After a great deal of trouble, by whipping, coax-
ing, and driving, nearly all the dogs were again collected, as it was in vain to pursue the deer to their
retreats.   Some of the old hunters slowly coming
in at the last, laid themselves down by us panting
and half dead with fatigue.   By and by the driver

again started into the "drive" with the dogs; but
an engagement for the evening, precluding my participation in a renewal of the spirit-stirring scene,
I reluctantly left my agreeable party who were out
for the day, and proceeded homeward. They returned late at night with, I believe, a single deer as
the reward of their patience and unwearied spirits,
two most important virtues in a thorough-bred deer-
hunter. Uncommon nerve and great presence of
mind are also indispensable qualifications. "Once,"
remarked a hunting gentleman to me, "while waiting at my stand the approach of a buck, which
sometime before seeing him I had heard leaping
along in immense bounds through the thicket—-his
sudden appearance in an open space about a hundred yards in front, bearing down directly toward
me at fearful speed, so awed and unnerved me for
the moment, that although my rifle was levelled at
his broad breast, I had not the power to pull the
trigger, and before I could recover myself the noble
creature passed me like the wind." Yet this gentleman was a tried hunter, and on other occasions
had brought down deer as they came toward him at
full speed, at the distance of from sixty to a hundred yards.

On my return from the hunting ground, I lingered
on the romantic cliff we had crossed in the morning, delighted at once more beholding scenery that
reminded me of the rude features of my native state.
Dismounting from my horse, which I secured to the
only tree upon the cliff, I descended, after many hair-
breadth escapes a ravine nearly two hundred feet in

depth, which conducted me to the water side and near the mouth of the beautiful St. Catharine, which, after a winding course of more than eighty miles, empties itself into the Mississippi through an embouchure ten yards wide, and as accurately defined as the mouth of a canal. Near this spot is a silver mine lately re-discovered, after the lapse of a third of a century. Its history, I believe, is this. Some thirty or forty years ago, a Spaniard who had been a miner in Mexico, passing down the Mississippi, discovered ore which he supposed to be silver. He took a quantity of it into his pirogue, and on arriving at a planter's house on the banks of the river in Louisiana, tested it as correctly as circumstances would admit, and was satisfied that it was pure silver. He communicated the discovery to his host, gave him a few ingots of the metal and took his departure. What became of him is not known. The host from year to year resolved to visit the spot, but neglected it, or was prevented by the intrusion of more pressing employments, till four or five years since. He then communicated the discovery to a Mexican miner, an American or an Englishman, who stopped at his house, and to whom, on hearing him speak of mines, he showed the masses he had received so many years before from the Spaniard. The man on examining them and ascertaining the metal to be pure silver, became at once interested in the discovery, obtained the necessary information to enable him to find the spot, and immediately ascended the river. On arriving at the cliffs he commenced his search, and after a few days discovered the vein, in one of the lowest strata of the cliffs. He found it difficult, however, to engage the neighbouring planters in his scheme of working it, for what planter would exchange his cotton fields for a silver mine ? Yet they treated him with attention, and seconded his efforts by lending him slaves. More than a hundred weight of the ore was obtained, and sent on to Philadelphia to undergo the process of fusion. It probably is not rich enough for amalgamation, as it contains a superior bulk of iron pyrites, blende, lead and earthy matter. The amount of pure silver procured from the ore has not been ascertained, the result of the process not having yet been made known. I obtained several pieces, which make a very pretty show in a cabinet, and this is probably the highest honour to which it will be exalted, at least till the surface of the earth refuses longer to bear ingots of silver, in the shape of the snowy cotton boll.

The peculiar features of these cliffs are a series of vast concavities, or inverted hollow cones, connected with each other by narrow gorges, whose bottoms are level with the river, and surrounded by perpendicular and overhanging walls of earth, often detached, like huge pyramids, and nearly three hundred feet in height. There are five clusters of these cliffs in this state, all situated on the eastern shore of the Mississippi, from forty to one hundred miles apart, of which this is the most important in height and magnitude, as well as in grandeur and variety of scenery. They are properly the heads or terminations of the high grounds of the United States—the *antennæ* of the Alleghanies.* The hypothesis that they were promontories in past ages, with the waves of the Mexican Gulf breaking at their bases, has had the support of many scientific men. This opinion carries with it great probability, when the peculiar qualities of the Mississippi are considered in relation to its "forming effects." These effects are a consequence of the general truth of the proposition, that every mechanical destruction will be followed by a mechanical formation; hence the masses separated by the waters of the Mississippi, will be again deposited on the surface of the land, or its shores, about its mouth, and on the bottom of the sea. You are aware that one twelfth of the bulk of this vast volume of water is earth, as ascertained by its depositing that proportion in the bottom of a glass filled with the water. During the flood the proportion is greater, and the earthy particles are as dense as the water can hold in suspension. The average velocity of the current below the Missouri, is between one and two miles an hour, and it is calculated that it would require four months to discharge the column of water embraced between this point and its delta. Bearing constantly within its flood a mass of earth equal to one twelfth of its whole bulk, it follows that it must bear toward the sea, every four years, more than its cubical bulk of solid earth. Now where is this great column of earth deposited? Has it been rolling onward for centuries, without any visible ef-

* There are five more cliffs above this state, between it and the mouth of the Ohio; and one on the western shore of the Mississippi at Helena, Arkansas.

fects ? This will not be affirmed, and experience
proves the contrary in the hourly mechanical depo-
sitions of the ochreous particles of this river, in its
noble convexities, its extensive bottoms, and the
growing capes at its mouth.   But a small portion of
the turbid mixture has been deposited in the bed of
the river, particularly in its southern section, as moving water will not deposit at any great depth.*

* The following extract from a private letter in the author's possession, bearing date New Orleans 28th April, 1804, contains some
interesting facts, relative to the depth of the lower Mississippi, and
other characteristics of this river, which were obtained by the writer
from actual observation.

" In Nov. 1800, when there was scarcely any perceptible current,
in company with Mr. Benj. Morgan and Capt. Roger Crane, I set
off from just above the upper gate of this city and sounded the
river, at every three or four boats' length, until we landed opposite to
M. Bernody's house on the right bank of the river. The depth of
water increased pretty regularly: viz. 10. 12. 13. 15. 17. 19. and
20 fathoms. The greatest depth was found at about 120 yards from
Bernody's shore. This operation was accurately performed; and
as the river rises about twelve feet on an average at this place, the
depth at high water will be twenty two fathoms. A M. Dervengé,
whose father was chief pilot in the time of the French, informed
me that his father often told him that a little way below the English
Turn there was fifty fathoms of water ; and M. Laveau Trudo said
that about the upper Plaquemine, there was sixty fathoms, or three
hundred and sixty feet.

In the year 1791, during five days that I lay at the Balize, I
learned from M. Demaron Trudo, who was then commandant of
that place, that there was about three feet difference between the
high and low waters. From the best information I have been able
to collect, there is a declension of eight or nine feet from the natural
banks of the river at this city, to the banks upon which is the site
of the house where the Spanish commandant lived before they
removed up to Plaquemine, at the distance of about three leagues
from the sea. There is a gradual slope or descent of the whole
southern region of the Mississippi river, from the river Yazoo, in

Now when the general appearance and geological features of the South-West, including the south part of Mississippi and nearly the whole of Louisiana, are observed with reference to the preceding statements, the irresistible conviction of the observer is, that the immense plain now rich with sugar and cotton fields, a great emporium, numerous villages and a thousand villas, was formed by the mechanical deposits of the Mississippi upon the bed of the

lat. 32 ° 30´ N. to the ocean or Gulf of Mexico. The elevation of the bluff at Natchez is about 200 feet; at St. Francisville, seventy miles lower, it is a little more than 100 feet ; at Baton Rouge, about thirty miles lower, it is less than 40 feet, at New Orleans, according to the above statement eight feet, and at the Balize less than two feet. This vast glacis, at a similar angle of inclination, extends for some leagues into the Gulf of Mexico, till lost in the natural bed of the ocean.

The river, whose current is said to be the most rapid at the period when it is about to overflow its banks, runs in its swiftest vein or portion about five miles an hour. I allude to the line of upper current, and not to the mass, which moves much slower than the surface. The average velocity of the river when not in flood is not above two miles an hour. This is easily ascertained, by the progression and regular motion of its swells, and not by its apparent motion.

In November, 1800, as before observed, the motion of the stream was so sluggish as to be scarcely perceptible. A vessel that then lay opposite the Government House, advanced against it with a light breeze. I was told by a respectable lady, Mdme. Robin, who lives about six leagues below the city, that the water of the river was so brackish that she was obliged to drink other water, and that there were an abundance of porpoises, sharks, mullet, and other sea-fish, even above her plantation, nearly one hundred miles from the Gulf. The citizens thought the water brackish opposite the town. It looked quite green like sea-water, and when held to the light was quite clear. Although I did not think it brackish, I found it vapid and disagreeable. This is a phenomenon of rare occurrence, and not satisfactorily accounted for."

ocean, precisely as they are now building up fields into the Mexican Gulf. Do not understand me that the present fertile surface of this region was the original bed of the ocean, but that it rose out of it, as the coral islands come up out of the sea, by the gradual accumulation of deposits. The appearance of these inland promontories or cliffs, which suggested these remarks, and the fact that the highlands of the south-west, all terminate along the southern border of this region, from fifty to one hundred miles from the sea, leaving a broad alluvial tract between, and presenting a well defined *inland* sea-board, go far to strengthen the opinion I have adopted.

The chain of cliffs along the eastern shore of the Mississippi, have a parallel chain opposite to them on the other side of the great savana, skirted by the Mississippi, about forty miles distant. This savana or valley gradually widens to the south until near the mouth of the river, where it is increased to one hundred and forty or fifty miles in breadth. It is this great valley which is of mechanical formation, and its present site was in all probability covered by the waters of a bay similar to the Chesapeake, extending many leagues above Natchez to the nearest approximation of the cliffs on either side, where alone must have been an original mouth of this great river. Where the spectator, in looking westward from these bluffs; now beholds an extensive and level forest, in ages past rolled the waters of the Mexican sea—and where he now gazes upon a broad and placid river flow

N 2

ing onward to mingle with the distant ocean, the
very waves of that ocean rolled in loud surges,
dashed against the lofty cliffs, and kissed the pebbles at his feet.

———

XXXVI.

THOUGH not much given to theorising, I have
been drawn into some undigested remarks in my
last letter, upon a theory, which is beginning to
command the attention of scientific men, to which
the result of geological researches daily adds weight,
and to which time, with correct observations and
farther discoveries, must add the truth of demon-
stration.

This letter I will devote to a subject, naturally
arising from the preceding, perhaps not entirely
without interest—I mean the physical geography
and geology of this state. In the limits of a letter
it is impossible to treat this subject as the nature of
it demands, yet I will endeavour to go so far into its
detail, as to give you a tolerable idea of the general
features of the region.

Besides the cliffs, or great head-lands, alluded to
in my last letter, frowning, at long intervals, over
the Mississippi, serrated ridges, formed of continuous hills projecting from these points, extend in various directions over the state. These again branch
into lower ridges, which often terminate near the
river, between the great bluffs, leaving a flat space
from their base to the water, from a third of a mile
to a league in breadth.   These flats, or "bottoms,"
as they are termed in western phraseology, are inundated at the periodical floods, increasing, at those
places, the breadth of the river to the dimensions
of a lake.   The forest-covered savana, nearly forty
miles across, through which the Mississippi flows,
and which is bordered by the mural high lands or
cliffs alluded to in my last letter, is also overflowed
at such seasons ; so that the river then becomes, in
reality, the breadth of its valley.   The grandeur of
such a spectacle as a river, forty miles in breadth,
descending to the ocean between banks of lofty
cliffs, too far distant to be within each other's horizon, challenges a parallel.   But, as this vast plain
is covered with a forest, the lower half of which
only is inundated, the width of the river remains
as usual to the eye of the spectator on the cliffs,
who will have to call in the aid of his imagination
to realize, that in the bosom of the vast forest out-
spread beneath him rolls a river, to which, in breadth,
the noble stream before him is but a rivulet.   The
interior hills, or ridges, mentioned above, are usually covered with pine ; which is found only on
such eminences, and in no other section of the south

or west, except an isolated wood in Missouri, for more than fifteen hundred miles. The surface of the whole state is thus diversified with hills, with the exception of an occasional interval on the borders of a stream, or a few leagues of prairie in the north part of the state, covered with thin forests of stunted oaks. These hills rise and fall in regular undulations, clothed with forests of inconceivable majesty, springing from a rich, black loam, peculiarly fitted to the production of cotton; though, according to a late writer on this plant, " it flourishes with equal luxuriance in the black alluvial soil of Alatamaha and in the glowing sands of St. Simon's.*

The general features of this state have suggested the idea of an immense ploughed field, whose gigantic furrows intersect each other at various angles. —Imagine the hills, formed by these intersections, clothed with verdure, whitened with cotton fields, or covered with noble woods, with streams winding along in the deep ravines, repeatedly turning back upon their course, in their serpentine windings, before they disembogue into the Mississippi on the west, or the Pearl on the east, and you will have a rude though generally correct idea of the bolder features of this state.

A " plain," or extensive level expanse, which is not a marsh, forms, consequently, no part of its scenery, hill and hollow being its stronger characteristics. For a hilly country it presents one striking peculiarity. The surface of the forests, viewed

* It has been said that cotton will thrive as well in a sandy soil, with a *sea* exposure, as in a rich loam in the interior.

from the bluffs, or from some superior elevation in
the interior, presents one uniform horizontal level,
with scarcely an undulation in the line to break the
perspective.   Particularly is this observable about
a mile from Natchez, from the summit of a hill on
the road to the village of Washington.   Here an
extensive forest scene lies east of the observer, to
appearance a perfect level.   But as he travels over
hill and through ravine, anticipating a delightful
prairie to lie before him, over which he may pace,
(or *canter*, if he be a northerner) at his ease, he will
find that the promised plain, like the *mirage* before
the fainting Arabian, for ever eludes his path.

There is another remarkable feature in this country, peculiar to the whole region through which the
lower Mississippi flows, which I can illustrate no
better than by resorting to the idea of a ploughed
field.   As many of these intersecting furrows, or
ravines, terminate with the ridges that confine them,
near the river, with whose medium tides they are
nearly level, they are inundated by the periodical
effluxes, which, flowing up into the land, find a passage through other furrows, and discharge into some
stream, that suddenly overflows its banks ; or winding sluggishly through the glens, cut deep channels
for themselves in the argillaceous soil, and through
a chain of ravines again unite with the Mississippi,
after having created, by their surplus waters, numerous marshes along their borders, and leaving
around their course innumerable pools of stagnant
water, which become the home of the lazy alliga-

tor,* and the countless water-fowls which inhabit these regions. These inlets are properly bayous. They radiate from the Mississippi, in the state of Louisiana, in countless numbers, forming a net-work of inlets along its banks for fifty miles on either side, increasing in numbers and size near its mouth; so that, for many leagues above it, an inextricable tissue of lakes and inlets, or bayous, form communications and passes from the river to the Gulf,† "accessible," says Flint, "by small vessels and bay-craft, and impossible to be navigated, except by pi-

---

* The alligator is found on the shores of the lower Mississippi, in bayous and at the mouths of creeks. It is seldom seen far above 32° north latitude. There has been much dispute as to the identity of the crocodile and alligator, nor are naturalists yet united in their opinions upon this point. The opinion that they belong to the same species is supported by the systema natura, as it came from the hand of Linneus, but it is positively contradicted in the last edition of this work, published by Professor Gmelin.

† "The experienced savage or solitary voyager, descending the Mississippi for a thousand miles, paddles his canoe through the deep forests from one bluff to the other. He moves, perhaps, along the inundated forests of the vast interval through which the Mississippi flows, into the mouth of White river. He ascends that river a few miles, and by the Grand Cut-off moves down the flooded forest into Arkansas. From that river he finds many *bayous*, which communicate readily with Washita and Red river; and from that river, by some one of its hundred bayous, he finds his way into the Atchafalaya and the Teche; and by this stream to the Gulf of Mexico, reaching it more than twenty leagues west of the Mississippi. At that time this is a river from thirty to a hundred miles wide, all overshaded with forests, except an interior strip of little more than a mile in width, where the eye reposes upon the open expanse of waters visible between the forests, which is the Mississippi proper."

lots perfectly acquainted with the waters." The entrance of some of these bayous, which are in the vicinity of Natchez, is fortified against the effluxes of the river by *levées*, constructed from one high-land to another; and by this means the bottom lands in the rear are protected from the overflow, and, when cultivated, produce fine crops of cotton. Inundations are also caused when the Mississippi is high, by its waters flowing up into the small rivers and creeks, whose natural level is many feet below the high water mark, till they find a level.—The water of these streams is consequently forced back upon itself, and, rising above its banks, over-flows all the adjacent country. This "back-water," as it is termed, is more difficult to be resisted by le-vées than the effluxes of the bayous; and for the want of some successful means of opposing its force, some of the finest "bottom lands" in the state remain uncultivated, and covered with water and forest.

The smaller rivers and streams in this state are wild and narrow torrents, wholly unlike those pla-cid streams which flow through New-England, lined with grassy or rocky banks, and rolling over a stony bottom, which can be discerned from many feet above it, through the transparent fluid. Here the banks of the streams are precipices, and entirely of clay or sand, and cave in after every rain, which suddenly raises these torrents many feet in a few minutes; and such often is their impetuosity, that if their banks are too high to be inundated, they cut out new channels for themselves; and a planter may, not improbably, in the morning after a heavy rain, find an acre or more added to his fields from an adjoining estate; to be repaid, in kind, after another rain. In the dry season the water of these streams—which, with the exception of three or four of the large ones, are more properly conduits for the rain water that falls upon the hills, than permanent streams—is tolerably clear, though a transparent sheet of water larger than a spring, whether in motion or at rest, I have not seen in this state. After a rain they become turbid, like the Mississippi, impetuous in their course, and dangerous to travellers. Few of these streams are covered with bridges, as their banks dissolve, during a rain, almost as rapidly as banks of snow—so light is the earth of which they are composed—and the points from which bridges would spring are soon washed away. The streams are therefore usually forded; and as their beds are of the finest sand, and abound in quicksands, carriages and horses are often swallowed up in fording them, and lives are not unfrequently lost.

The roads throughout the state, with the exception of these fords, are very good, winding through fine natural scenery, past cultivated fields, and pleasant villages.

In the neighbourhood of these streams, on the hills, and in the vales throughout the state, springs of clear cold water abound. There is a deep spring on the grounds attached to Jefferson College in this state, whose water is so transparent, that to the eye, the bottom appears to be reflected through no other medium than the air. The water is of a very mild temperature in the winter, and of an icy coolness in the summer. The spring is in a deep glen, surrounded by lofty trees, one of which, from its shape, branching from the root into two trunks, and uniting again in an extraordinary manner by a transverse limb, thirty feet from the ground, is called "St. Catharine's Harp," and is one among the natural curiosities of that vicinity. In the interior of the state are several mineral springs, which of late years have become very fashionable resorts for those who do not choose, like the majority of Mississippians, to spend their summers and money at the Kentucky, Virginian, or New-York springs. The waters of most of these springs are chalybeate, with a large proportion of sulphuric acid combined with the iron. The most celebrated are the Brandywine, romantically situated in a deep glen in the interior of the state, and the Bankston springs, two hour's ride from the capital. The constituent qualities of the waters, as ascertained by a recent chemical analysis, are sulphate of magnesia, sulphate of soda and sulphur, which exist in such a state of combination as to render the waters not disagreeable to the taste, yet sufficiently beneficial to the patient. They are said to act favourably upon most of the diseases of the climate, such as affections of the liver, bowels, cutaneous and chronic diseases, congestive and bilious fevers, debility, and numerous other ills "that flesh is heir to." The location is highly romantic and healthy. In the words of another—"the circumjacent country is for several miles covered with forests, of which pine is the principal growth; its surface is elevated and undulating, entirely free from stagnant waters, and other local causes of disease. The site of the springs is not inferior in beauty to any spot in the southern country. They are situated in a narrow plane, surrounded, on one side by an almost perpendicular bluff from which they flow, on the other, by a gentle declivity, dividing itself into two twin ridges; which, after describing a graceful curve, unite again at a point on which stands the principal building, one hundred feet in length, and on either of these ridges, is built a row of new and comfortable apartments. Through the centre of the grove, a path leads from the principal building to the spring, forming at all hours of the day, a delightful promenade. The water at the fountain, is exceedingly cool and exhilarating. A dome supported by neat columns, rises above the fountain, which, with the aid of the surrounding hills and overhanging forest, renders it at all times impervious to the sun. The roads, which during the summer season are always good, communicate in various directions with Port Gibson, Vicksburg, Jackson, Clinton, and Raymond, affording at all times good society. The forest abounds with deer and other game, the chase of which will afford a healthy amusement to those who may be tempted to join in it."

The mineral waters in the state are chiefly sulphurous and chalybeate, with the exception, I believe, of one or two of the saline class.

In the vicinity of these springs, and also on most of the water courses in the state, and, with but an exception or two, in these places alone, are found the only stones in the state. Rock is almost unknown. I have not seen even a stone, within fifteen miles of Natchez, larger than the third part of a brick, and those that I have seen were found in the pebbly bed of some stream. There is a stratum of pebbles from one to three feet thick extending through this state. It is variously waved, sometimes in a plane, and at others forming various angles of inclination, and at an irregular depth from the surface, according to the thickness of the superimposed masses of earth which are composed of clay, loam, and sand. This stratum is penetrated and torn up by the torrents, which strew their beds with the pebbles. There is no rock except a species of soft sand-stone south of latitude 32° north, in this state, except in Bayou Pierre, (the stony bayou) and a cliff at Grand Gulf, forty miles above Natchez. This last is composed of common carbonate of lime and silex, but the quantity of each has not been accurately determined.

The sand-stone alluded to above, is in the intermediate state between clay and stone, in which the process of petrifaction is still in progress. In the north-east portion of the state, this species of stone, whose basis is clay, is found in a more matured state of petrifaction. Perfect gravel is seldom met with here, even in the stratum of pebbles before mentioned. These resemble in properties and colour, the clay so abundant in this region; a great proportion of the gravel is composed of a petrifaction of clay and minute shells, of the mollusca tribe.

I have found in the dry bed of the St. Catharine's, pebbles, entirely composed of thousands of the most delicately formed shells, some of which, of singularly beautiful figures, I have not before met with. Concave spiral cones, the regular discoid volute, cylinders, a circular shell, a tenth of an inch in diameter, formed by several concentric circles, and a delicate shell formed by spiral whorls, with fragments of various other minute shells, principally compose them. The variety of shells in this state is very limited. All that have been found here have their surfaces covered with the smooth olive-green epidermis, characteristic of fresh water shells, and are all very much eroded. Agates of singular beauty have also been discovered, and minute quartz crystals are found imbedded in the cavities of pebbles composed of alumina and grains of quartz. Mica and feldspar I have not met with. About two years ago, on the plantation of Robert Field, Esq. in the vicinity of the white cliffs, a gentleman picked up from the ground a large colourless rock crystal, with six sided prisms and a pyramidal termination of three faces. Curiosity led him to examine the spot, and after digging a few minutes beneath the surface, he found three more, of different sizes, two of them nearly perfect crystals, but the third was an irregular mass of colourless transparent quartz. This is the only instance of the discovery of this mineral in the state, and how these came to be on that spot, which is entirely argillaceous and at a great distance from any rocks or pebbles, is a problem. Pure flint is not found in this state, yet the

plough-share turns up on some plantations, numerous arrow-heads, formed of this material, and there
is also a species of stone, artificially formed, in size
and shape precisely resembling the common wedge
for cleaving wood, with the angles smoothly rounded. They are found all over the south-western
country, and the negroes term them "thunder bolts;"
but wiser heads have sagely determined their origin
from the moon. Planters call them spear-heads,
for which they were probably constructed by the
aborigines. The stone of which they are made is
not found in this country. Some of them I believe
are composed of mica and quartz. Many of them
are a variety of the mica and of a brown colour,
sometimes inclining to green, and highly polished.
I have seen some on a plantation near Natchez, of
an iron black colour resembling polished pieces of
black marble.

The several strata which compose this state are
an upper layer of rich black loam from one to three
feet thick, the accumulation of centuries, and a second stratum of clay several feet in thickness, beneath which are various substrata of loam and sand,
similar to that which constitutes the islands and "bottoms" of the Mississippi. With the exception of the
Yazoo, which flows through a delightful country rich
in soil and magnificent with forests, along whose
banks the Mississippians are opening a new theatre for the accumulation of wealth, and where villages spring up annually with the yearly harvest—
and the Pearl—a turbid and rapid torrent whose
banks are lined with fine plantations and beautiful

villages--this state boasts no rivers of any magnitude ;
and these, when compared with the great Mississippi, are but streams ; and in their chief characteristics
they nearly resemble it.

But I have gone as far into geology as the limits
of a letter writer will permit. A volume might be
written upon the physical features of this country,
without exhausting a subject prolific in uncommon
interest, or half surveying a field, scarcely yet examined by the geologist.*

* A bed of lime-stone has been recently discovered on the shore
at Natchez below high water mark, two hundred feet lower than
the summit level of the state of Mississippi. There are some extraordinary petrifactions in the north part of this state, among which
is the fallen trunk of a tree twenty feet in length, converted into solid rock. The outer surface of the bark, which is in contact with the
soil, is covered as thickly as they can be set, with brilliant brown
crystals resembling garnets in size and beauty.

Thin flakes of the purest enamel, the size of a guinea and irregularly shaded, have been found in the ravines near Natchez. In the
same ravines mammoth bones are found in great numbers, on the
caving in of the sides after a heavy rain.

XXXVII.

Topography—Natchez—Washington—Seltzertown—Greenville
—Port Gibson—Raymond—Clinton—Southern villages—Vicksburg—Yeomen of Mississippi—Jackson—Vernon—Satartia—Benton—Amsterdam—Brandon and other towns—Monticello—Manchester—Rankin—Grand Gulf—Rodney—Warrenton—Woodville
—Pinckneyville—White Apple village.

In my last letter I alluded to the geological features of Mississippi, the peculiarities of its soil and
rivers, or streams, and the characteristics of its
scenery.   In this I will give you a brief topographi-
cal description of the state, embracing its principal
towns and villages.   Were I confined to the details
of the tourist, in my sketches, you might follow me
step by step over hill and dale, through forest and
"bottom," to the several places which may form the
subject of the first part of this letter.   But a short
view of them, only, comes within my limits as a
letter-writer.   For the more minute information I
possess upon this subject I am indebted to a gentleman,* whose scientific and historical researches
have greatly contributed to the slender stock of information upon this state—its resources, statistics,
and general peculiarities.

Although I have said a great deal of Natchez,
under this head something may be communicated

* Henry Vose, Esq., of Woodville.

upon which I have not touched in my remarks upon that city. Natchez is one hundred and fifty-five miles from New-Orleans by land, and two hundred and ninety-two by water. It contains a population of about three thousand, the majority of whom are coloured. The influx of strangers—young merchants from the north, who have within the last four years, bought out nearly all the old standing merchants—numerous mechanics, and foreign emigrants—is rapidly increasing the number, and in five years, if the rail-road already surveyed from this city to the capital, a distance of one hundred and nine miles, is brought into operation, it will probably contain twice the present number of souls. Under the Spanish government vessels came up to Natchez; and in 1803 there was, as appears by a publication of Col. Andrew Marschalk, of Mississippi, a brisk trade kept up between this and foreign and American ports which suddenly ceased, after a few years' continuance, on account of the obstacles interposed by the Spaniards. In 1833, this trade was revived by some enterprizing gentlemen of Natchez, and cotton is now shipped directly to the northern states and Europe, from this port, instead of being conveyed by steamboats to New-Orleans and there reshipped. There are two oil mills in this city worked by steam. The oil is manufactured from cotton-seed, which heretofore was used as manure. This oil is said to be superior to sperm oil, and the finest paint oil. Similar manufactories are established in New-Orleans, and I think, also, in Mobile. The material of which this oil is made is so abundant that it will in all probability in a very few years supersede the other oils almost entirely. The "cake" is in consistency very much like that of flax-seed. It is used, in equal parts with coal, for fuel, and burns with a clear flame, and a fire so made is equally warm as one entirely of coal.

A Bethel church is to be erected this year under the hill, the erection of which on this noted spot, will be the boldest and most important step Christianity has taken in the valley of the Mississippi. There are four occasionally officiating Methodist ministers here, one of the Presbyterian, and one of the Episcopalian denominations. There are eighteen physicians and surgeons, and sixteen lawyers, the majority of whom are young men. There is a weekly paper, with extensive circulation, and three others are about to be established. There are five schools or seminaries of learning—three private, and two public—a flourishing academy for males, and a boarding-school for young ladies, under the care of very able teachers. There are also a hospital and poor-house, and a highly useful orphan asylum. There are no circulating libraries in the city, nor I believe in the state. There are three banks one of which—the Planter's bank—has branches in seven different towns in the state. Steamboats were first known at Natchez in 1811-12.

Washington, six miles north-east from Natchez, with a charming country between, through which winds one of the worst carriage-roads in the west, not even excepting the delightful rail-roads from

Sandusky to Columbus, in Ohio, is a corporation one mile square, containing about four hundred inhabitants, of all sizes and colours. It contains a fine brick hospital and poor-house in one building, two brick churches, one of the Baptist, and the other of the Methodist denomination. The first has recently settled a preacher, the other has long had a stationed minister, who regularly officiates in the desk. There is a Presbyterian clergyman residing in the place, whose church is five miles distant in the country, in a fine grove on one of the highest elevations in the state. The inhabitants of the village are principally Methodists, a majority of which sect will be found in nearly every village in the south-west.

Jefferson College, the oldest and best endowed collegiate institution in the state, is pleasantly situated at the head of a green on the borders of the village. It is now flourishing; but has for several years been labouring under pecuniary embarrassments, which are now, by a generous provision of Congress, entirely removed, and with a fund of nearly two hundred thousand dollars, it bids fair to become a useful and distinguished institution. There is also a female seminary in a retired part of this village, which was handsomely endowed by Miss Elizabeth Greenfield, of Philadelphia, a member of the society of Friends, from whom it is denominated the Elizabeth Academy. It is one of the first female institutions in this state, and under the patronage of the Methodist society.

Washington is one of the oldest towns in the state,

was formerly the seat of government, under the territorial administration, and once contained many more inhabitants than any other place except Natchez, in the territory. It was nearly depopulated by the yellow fever in 1825, from the effects of which it has never recovered. The public offices, with the exception of the Register's and Receiver's offices, are removed to Jackson. The town possesses no resources, and is now only remarkable for its quiet beauty, the sabbath-like repose of its streets, and its pure water, and healthy location, upon the plane of an elevated table land, rising abruptly from the St. Catharine's, which winds pleasantly along by one side of the village with many romantic haunts for the student and "walks" for the villagers, upon its banks. There is a post office in the village, through which a triweekly mail passes to and from Natchez. The route of the rail-road will be through this place, when it will again lift its head among the thriving villages of the Great Valley.

Seltzertown, containing a tavern and a blacksmith's shop (which always form the nucleus of an American village) is six miles from Washington and twelve from Natchez. It is remarkable only for the extensive scenery around it, and the remarkable Indian fortifications or temples in its vicinity. These will form the subject of another letter.

Greenville, on the road from Natchez, passing through the two former places, is twenty-one miles from that city. It is delightfully situated in a little green vale, through which winds a small stream. The plain is crossed by the rail-road, which here becomes a street, bordered by two rows of dilapidated huses, overgrown with grass and half buried in venerable shade trees. From the prison with its dungeons fallen in, and its walls lifting themselves sullenly above the ruins by which they are enclosed, to the tavern with its sunken galleries, and the cobbler's shop with its doorless threshold, all were in ruins, a picture of rural desolation exhibiting the beau ideal of the "deserted village." Greenville was formerly a place of some importance, but other towns have grown up in more eligible spots, for which this has been deserted by its inhabitants. One does not meet with a lovelier prospect in this state, than that presented to the eye on descending from the hill south and west of the valley, into the quiet little vale beneath, just before the going down of the sun. The air of peace and quiet which reigns around the traveller, will perhaps remind him of the valley whose description has so delighted him while lingering over the elegant pages of Rasselas.

Forty two miles from Natchez is Port Gibson, one of the most flourishing and beautiful towns in the south. It is only second to Natchez in the beauty of its location, the regularity of its streets, the neatness of its dwellings, and the number and excellence of its public buildings. It is but seven miles by land from the Mississippi, with which it communicates by a stream, called Bayou Pierre, navigable for keel and flat boats, and, in high floods, for steamboats, quite to the village. It is very healthy, and has seldom been visited by epidemics. It contains about one thousand souls. The citizens were once distinguished for their dissipation, if not profligacy; but they are now more distinguished for their intelligence and morality as a community. There is no town in the south which possesses so high a standard of morals as Port Gibson. This reformation is the result of the evangelical labours of the Presbyterian clergyman of that place; who, with untiring industry and uncommon energy, combined with sterling piety, in a very few years performed the work and produced the effect of an age.

There are a Presbyterian and a Methodist church in the town, with their respective clergymen. It contains also a branch bank, court-house, gaol, post-office, and one of the finest hotels in the state. A weekly paper, called the " Correspondent," and very ably edited, is published here. The society of the village and neighbourhood is not surpassed by any in the state. There are some very pretty country seats in the vicinity, the abodes of planters of intelligence and wealth; and the country around is thickly wooded, with fine plantations interspersed; and the general features of the scenery, though tame, are beautiful. The road from Natchez to Port Gibson is through a rich planting country, pleasantly undulating, with alternate forest and field scenery on either hand. But beyond Port Gibson the country assumes a more rugged aspect, and is less beautiful. The road, for the first few miles, winds among woods and cotton fields; but, after crossing Bayou Pierre, at a ford, called "Grindstone Ford," where the first rock is seen, in coming north from the Mexican Gulf, the forest is for many miles

unbroken.   I cannot express the strange delight I
experienced as the iron heels of my horse first rung
upon the broad rocky pavement, when ascending the
bank of this stream from the water.   No one but a
northerner, the bases and crests of whose native
hills are of granite, and who has passed two years
or more in the stoneless soil of this region, can duly
appreciate such emotions from such a cause.

For forty seven miles from Port Gibson, the road
winds through a "rolling" country, two thirds of
which is enveloped in the gloom of the primeval
forests, and then enters the little village of Raymond, situated in an open space among the lofty
forest trees which enclose it on all sides.   Raymond has been planted and matured to a handsome
village, with a fine court-house, several hotels, and
neat private dwellings, within five years.   The society, like that of most new towns in this state, is
composed of young men, merchants, lawyers, and
physicians, the majority of whom are bachelors.   The
village is built around a pleasant square, in the centre
of which is the court-house, one of the finest public
buildings in this part of the state.   It contains about
four hundred inhabitants, not one fifth of whom are
females.

Beyond Raymond the country is less hilly,
spreading more into table lands, which in many
places are marshy.   A ride of eight miles through
a rudely cultivated country, in whose deep forests
the persecuted deer finds a home, often bounding
across the path of the traveller, will terminate at
Clinton, formerly Mount Salus, one of the prettiest

and most flourishing villages in the state. It is situated upon a cluster of precipitous hills, contains some good buildings, and is a place of much business, which a rail-road, now in projection to the Mississippi, will have a tendency greatly to increase. There is a Methodist church in the village, and a small society of Presbyterians. The most flourishing female seminary in the state is located in the immediate vicinity, under the superintendence of a lady, formerly well known in the literary world of New-York, as the authoress of one or two works, and a contributor to the columns of the " Mirror" when in its infancy. There is also a college in this place, but it is not of long standing or very flourishing. The system adopted in this country, of combining an academy with a college, though the state of education may require some such method, will always be a clog to the advancement of the latter. There is a Spanish proverb, "manacle a giant to a dwarf and he must stoop," which may have yet a more extensive application, and the truth of which this system is daily demonstrating. Here are a land office and a printing office, which issues a weekly paper. There are many enterprising professional men and merchants in the village from almost every state in the Union, but they are generally bachelors, and congregate at the hotels, so that for the number of inhabitants the proportion of families and dwellings is very small. When a number of high-spirited young men thus assemble in a little village, a code of honour, woven of the finest texture and of the most sensitive materials, will naturally

be established.   This code will have for its basis—
feeling.   It will be constantly appealed to, and its
adjudications sacredly observed.   To the decisions
of such a tribunal, may be traced the numerous *af-
faires d'honneur* which have occurred in the south
during the last twenty years, most of which originated in villages composed principally of young
gentlemen.   There is something striking to the eye
of a northerner, on entering one of these south-
western villages.   He will find every third build
ing occupied by a lawyer or a doctor, around whose
open doors will be congregated knots of young men,
en deshabille, smoking and conversing, sometimes
with animation, but more commonly with an air of indifference.   He will pass by the stores and see them
sitting upon the counters or lounging about the doors.
In the streets and bar-rooms of the hotels, they will
cluster around him, fashionably dressed, with sword
canes dangling from their fingers.   Wherever he
turns his eyes he sees nothing but young fellows.
Whole classes from medical and law schools, or
whole counting-houses from New-York or Boston,
seem to have been transported *en masse* into the little
village through which he is passing.   An old man,
or a gray hair, scarcely relieves his vision.   He will
be reminded, as he gazes about him upon the youthful faces, of the fabled village, whose inhabitants
had drunk at the fountain of rejuvenescence.   Women he will find to resemble angels, more than he
had believed; for "few and far between," are their
forms seen gliding through the streets, blockaded
by young gentlemen, and "few" are the bright eyes

that beam upon him from galleries and windows. If he stays during the evening, he may pass it in the noisy bar-room, the billiard-room, or at a wine-party. If he remains a "season," he may attend several public balls in the hotel, where he will meet with beautiful females, for whom the whole country, with its villages and plantations for twenty miles round, has been put under contribution. One of the most fashionable assemblies I have attended in the south-west, I was present at, one or two winters since, in the village of Clinton.

This village contains about four hundred inhabitants, and is thirty-five miles from Vicksburg, its port, on the Mississippi. Vicksburg is about two miles below the Walnut hills, one of the bluffs of the Mississippi, and five hundred from the Balize. It contains nearly two thousand inhabitants. Thirty thousand bales of cotton, about one eighth of the whole quantity shipped by the state at large, are annually shipped from this place. In this respect it is inferior only to Natchez and Grand Gulf, the first of which ships fifty thousand. There is a weekly paper published here, of a very respectable character, and well edited, and another is in contemplation. There are also a bank, with two or three churches, and a handsome brick court-house, erected on an eminence from which there is an extensive view of the Mississippi, with its majestic steamers, and humbler flat boats, "keels" and "arks," and of the vast forests of the Louisiana shore, which every where, when viewed from the Mississippi side of the river, exhibits the appearance of an ocean whose

surface, even to the level horizon, is thickly covered
with the tops of trees in full foliage, like the golden
isles of sea weed floating in the southern seas.

There is no town in the south-west more flourishing than Vicksburg. It is surrounded by rich
plantations, and contains many public-spirited individuals; whose co-operation in public enterprises
is opening new avenues of wealth for the citizens,
and laying a broad and secure foundation for the
future importance of the town. It is already a
powerful rival of Natchez: but the two places are
so distant from each other, that their interests will
always revolve in different circles. The situation
of this town, on the shelving declivity of a cluster
of precipitous hills, which rise abruptly from the
river, is highly romantic. The houses are scattered
in picturesque groups on natural terraces along
the river, the balcony or portico of one often overhanging the roof of another. Merchandise destined
for Clinton is landed here, and hauled over a hilly
country to that place, a distance of thirty-five miles.
Cotton is often conveyed to Vicksburg, and other
shipping places, from a distance of one hundred
miles in the interior. The cotton teams, containing
usually ten bales, are drawn by six or eight yoke
of oxen, which accomplish about twenty miles a
day in good weather. The teamsters camp every
night, in an enclosure formed by their waggons and
cattle, with a bright fire burning; and occasionally
their bivouacs present striking groups for the pencil. The majority of these teamsters are slaves;
but there are many small farmers who drive their

own oxen, often conveying their whole crop on one waggon. These small farmers form a peculiar class, and include the majority of the inhabitants in the east part of this state. With the awkwardness of the Yankee countryman, they are destitute of his morals, education, and reverence for religion. With the rude and bold qualities of the chivalrous Kentuckian, they are destitute of his intelligence, and the humour which tempers and renders amusing his very vices. They are in general uneducated, and their apparel consists of a coarse linsey-woolsey, of a dingy yellow or blue, with broad-brimmed hats ; though they usually follow their teams barefooted and bare-headed, with their long locks hanging over their eyes and shoulders, giving them a wild appearance. Accost them as they pass you, one after another, in long lines, cracking their whips, which they use instead of the goad—perhaps the turn-out of a whole district, from the old, gray-headed hunter, to the youngest boy that can wield the whip, often fifteen and twenty feet in length, including the staff—and their replies will generally be sullen or insulting. There is in them a total absence of that courtesy which the country people of New-England manifest for strangers. They will seldom allow carriages to pass them, unless attended by gentlemen, who often have to do battle for the high-way. Ladies, in carriages or on horseback, if unattended by gentlemen, are most usually insulted by them. They have a decided aversion to a broad-cloth coat, and this antipathy is transferred to the wearer. There is a species of warfare kept up between them and the citizens of the shipping ports, mutually evinced by the jokes and tricks played upon them by the latter when they come into market; and their retaliation, when their hour of advantage comes, by an encounter in the back woods, which they claim as their domain. At home they live in log-houses on partially cleared lands, labour hard in their fields, sometimes owning a few slaves, but more generally with but one or none.— They are good hunters, and expert with the rifle, which is an important article of furniture in their houses. Whiskey is their favourite beverage, which they present to the stranger with one hand, while they give him a chair with the other. They are uneducated, and destitute of the regular administration of the gospel. As there is no common school system of education adopted in this state, their children grow up as rude and ignorant as themselves; some of whom, looking as wild as young Orsons, I have caught in the cotton market at Natchez, and questioned upon the simple principles of religion and education which every child is supposed to know, and have found them wholly uninformed. This class of men is valuable to the state, and legislative policy, at least, should recommend such measures as would secure religious instruction to the adults, and the advantages of a common education to the children, who, in thirty years, will form a large proportion of the native inhabitants of Mississippi.

About three miles from Clinton, on the main road to the capital, is situated " New Forest," a cotton

plantation, owned and recently improved by two
enterprising young gentlemen from Hallowell, in
Maine. They are the sons of one of the most eminent and estimable medical gentlemen in New-
England; whose pre-eminent success in the management of an appaling and desolating epidemic,
a few years since, acquired for him a proud and
distinguished name, both at home and abroad.—
New Forest is spread out upon the elevated ridges
which separate the waters of the Chitalusa, or Big
Black, and Pearl rivers; and pleasantly situated
in one of the richest and healthiest counties, on a
line with the projected rail-road, and in the immediate neighbourhood of the capital of the state—it
will soon become one of the most valuable and
beautiful " homesteads" to be seen in the south.

Besides the proprietors of this estate, there are
several other young gentlemen from Maine, residing
in Mississippi, who, with the characteristic energy
and perseverance of northerners, are steadily advancing to wealth and distinction.

Jackson, the capital of the state, is in latitude
32° 17′, and in longitude 13° 07′ west of Washington. It is one hundred and eight miles north-east
of Natchez, and forty-five miles east of Vicksburg,
on the Mississippi. It lies on the right bank of
Pearl river; which, after a southerly course, and
dividing the state into two nearly equal parts, empties into Lake Borgne, in the Gulf of Mexico. This
river is navigable two hundred miles from its mouth,
and steamboats have been as far as Jackson. But
the torrent is rapid, and the obstructions to naviga-

tion are very numerous.   There are many pleasant and thriving villages on its banks, and a rich country of plantations spreads away on either side.   The great rail-road from New-Orleans to Nashville will run near and parallel with this river for a great distance, and will monopolize, for the former market, all that branch of the cotton trade which is now attached to the ports on the Mississippi above mentioned.   Jackson was but recently selected as the seat of government of this state.   Its site was chosen for its central position alone, without any reference to its resources, or any other aids to future importance, than it might derive from being the state capital.   It is built upon a level area, half a mile square, cut out .from the depth of the forest which surrounds it.   It is a quarter of a mile from the Pearl, which is concealed by the forests ; a steep, winding path through which leads to the water side, where the turbid current darts by, a miniature resemblance of the great river rolling to the west of it.   There are a branch bank in this place, and a plain, two-storied brick edifice, occupied by the legislature and courts of justice.   Three newspapers are published here, which, like all others in this state, are of a warmly political character.   A handome state house is now in the progress of erection, and many private and public buildings are going up in various parts of the town.   There is a steam saw-mill near the village, for water privileges are unknown in this region of impetuous streams ; and several other avenues of wealth and public benefit are opening by the enterprising citizens.—

During the intervals of the sessions of the legislature and supreme court, Jackson is a very uninteresting village ; but during the sessions of these bodies, there is no town in the state which, for the time, presents so lively and stirring a scene.

Vernon is a pleasant village situated on a rapid and navigable stream, which often winds through wild and romantic scenery. Steamboats ascend to this place during part of the year. It is rapidly improving and filling with many young men, some of whom, possessing both talent and industry, are natives of this state. It is worthy of remark that those communities composed principally of young Mississippians, are distinguished by much less dissipation and adherence to the code of honour formerly alluded to, than such as are formed of young men principally from the northern and Atlantic southern states. The young Mississippian is not the irascible, hot-headed, and quarrelsome being he has been represented, although naturally warm-hearted and full of generous feelings, and governed by a high sense of honour. He is seldom a beau or a buck in the city-acceptation of those terms, but dresses plainly—as often in pantaloons of Kentucky jean, a broad brimmed white hat, brogans and a blanket coat, as in any other style of vesture. Nevertheless he knows how to be well-dressed, and the public assemblies of the south-west boast more richly attired young gentlemen than are often found in the assembly-rooms of the Atlantic cities. He is educated to become a farmer—an occupation which requires and originates plainness of manners

—and not to shine in the circles of a city. He prefers riding over his own, or his father's estate, wrapped in his blanket coat, to a morning lounge in Broadway enveloped in a fashionable cloak. He would rather walk booted and spurred upon the "turf," the "exchange" of southern planters, than move, shod in delicate slippers, over the noiseless carpet of the drawing-room. His short handled riding-whip serves him better than the slender rattan—his blanketed saddle is his cabriolet—the road between his plantation and a cotton market, his "drive"—and the noble forests on his domain—the home of the stag and deer—he finds when he moves through their deep glades, with his rifle in his hand, better suited to his tastes than the "mall," or Hyde Park, and he will be ready to bet a bale of cotton that the sport which they afford him is at least an equivalent to shooting cock-sparrows from a thorn bush on a moor.

Satartia is on the left side of the river Yazoo, fourteen miles from Vernon and thirty-five by land from Vicksburg. The village is pleasantly situated near the water, contains ten or fifteen stores, a tavern, and several dwelling houses, with a post-office. From ten to twelve thousand bales of cotton are annually shipped here. It promises to be one of the largest shipping ports in north Mississippi.

Benton, on the Yazoo, twenty-two miles to the north of Vernon, is a growing place, and issues a weekly newspaper. The rich country around is rapidly settling, and in the course of twenty years it will be one of the wealthiest portions of this state. Amsterdam, within steamboat navigation, on a deep creek, sixteen miles from Vicksburg, is a thriving town. Columbia, on the east bank of the Pearl, is accessible by steamboats, and Columbus, on the Tombeckbee, some hundred miles above Mobile, is a flourishing town. There is here a printing press which issues a weekly paper. Steamboats occasionally ascend to this place from Mobile. There are besides, east of the Pearl river, Brandon, so called in honour of the ex-governor; Winchester, Westville, Pearlington, and Shieldsborough—the latter in the southern extremity of the state on Lake Borgne, within forty miles of New-Orleans—most of which are thriving villages. One of the most flourishing towns on the Pearl is Monticello, about ninety miles east of Natchez.

Manchester, on the Yazoo, has been but recently settled. It is very flourishing, contains many stores and dwellings, and ships from twelve to fifteen thousand bales of cotton annually. It is seventy-six miles from the mouth of the Yazoo, on the Mississippi. Twenty-five miles from this village is Rankin, within three miles of steamboat navigation, and rapidly rising into importance. There are many other villages in this new region yet in embryo, but which must grow with the country into wealth and distinction.

Grand Gulf, about forty-five miles above Natchez, on the Mississippi, situated on a natural terrace, receding to a wooded crescent of hills on the north and east, and just above a dangerous eddy which gives the name to the town, is the third town of commercial importance in the state. It was settled five years ago, and the present year about forty-five thousand bales of cotton were shipped from this port. It contains about nine hundred inhabitants. A rail-road is projected to Port Gibson eight miles back from the river, and to the interior, which will benefit both places. Within sight of the village, and a short distance above it, is the only cliff of rocks in this region. Mississippians and Louisianians should do pilgrimage there. In the vicinity of this town Aaron Burr surrendered to General Mead, and the detachment ordered out to arrest him.

Rodney is a pleasant town twenty miles above Natchez, on the river. It is a place of commercial importance, and ships annually many thousand bales of cotton. Its inhabitants are enterprising and intelligent.

Warrenton, nine miles below Vicksburg, is the only other village between Natchez and the latter place.

The most important settlement south of Natchez is Woodville, a beautiful village, built around a square, in the centre of which is a handsome court-house. Various streets diverge from this public square, and are soon lost in the forests, which enclose the village. There are some eminent lawyers who reside here, and the neighbourhood is one of the wealthiest and most polished in the state. Governor Poindexter resided till recently at a neat country seat a short ride from Woodville, striking only for its quiet cottage-like beauty. Dr. Carmichael, president of the board of medical censors of this state, and formerly a surgeon in the revolutionary army, and the late Governor Brandon, reside also in the neighbourhood, but still more distant in the country. One of the most eminent lawyers of this place is a native of Portland, who has also distinguished himself as an occasional contributor to the annuals. One of the first lawyers in Vickburg, if not in the state, is a native of Maine, and a graduate of Bowdoin. He is this year a candidate for congress; though with that juvenility, which characterises southern athletæ in every intellectual arena, he scarcely yet numbers thirty summers.

There are three churches in Woodville; a Methodist, Episcopalian, and Baptist. A weekly paper is published here, conducted with talent and editorial skill. The court-house, which is a substantial and handsome structure of brick, contains a superior clock. A market-house and a gaol are also numbered among the public buildings. There is a branch of the Planters' bank here, and an academy for boys and another for girls, established within a mile of the village, are excellent schools. Woodville is about eighteen miles from the Mississippi. Its port is Fort Adams, formerly mentioned. A railroad is in contemplation, between Woodville and St. Francisville, La. twenty-nine miles distant, on the river, which will render the communication easy and rapid to New-Orleans. This village contains about eight hundred inhabitants, and is one of the healthiest in Mississippi. During a period of eighteen months—according to Mr. Vose, to whose accurate and elaborate researches I am indebted for much of my information upon the topography of this state—out of one hundred and forty-four men, of whom he kept an account for that length of time, only three died, and two of these were killed.

Fayette, a very neat and pleasant village, containing a handsome court-house and church, is twenty-five miles east of Natchez. It is the most rural and New-England like village, except Port Gibson, in the state. Meadville, to the south, is a small retired place, containing a post-office.

Kingston, on the road from Natchez to Woodville, originally settled by a colony from New-Jersey, is a small village, containing a church, post-office, two or three stores, and several dwelling-houses. This and Pinckneyville, a few miles south of Woodville, the latter merely a short street, lined by a few dwelling-houses and stores, are the only places south of Natchez, besides those already mentioned, of any importance. The site of White Apple village, the capital of the Natchez tribe, and the residence of "Great Sun," chief of the chiefs of that interesting nation, is pointed out to the traveller, on the river road to Woodville from Natchez. A few mounds, with the usual remains of spear and arrow heads, beads, and broken pottery only exist, to mark the spot. Fragments of gold lace and Spanish weapons have been found in the neighbourhood, with many other traces of the march of the Spanish army through this country.

I will conclude my long letter with an allusion

to the only remaining place of any importance.—
About eighteen miles to the east of Woodville are
the "Elysian Fields!" "Shade of Achilles," you
exclaim, "are the Elysü Campi of thy ghostly wanderings discovered in a Mississippian forest?" Nevertheless they are here, and the great problem is
solved. Some have placed these regions in the sun,
some in the moon, and others in the middle region
of the air; and others again in the centre of the
earth, in the vicinity of Tartarus, and probably in
the neighbourhood of the "incognita terra" of Capt.
Symmes. By many, and this was the vulgar opinion, they were supposed to lie among the Canary
isles : but, march of mind! more modern and wiser heads have discovered their position nearly on
the confines of Louisiana and Mississippi. Here
the traveller will behold beautiful birds with gorgeous plumage—for splendidly enamelled birds enrich, with their brilliant dyes, the forests of the
south—and his ear will drink in the sweetest melody from the feathered myriads—such as would
have tempted even " pius Æneas" to linger on his
way : but this, alas ! is all that his imagination will
recognize of Elysium. Trojan chiefs he will find
metamorphosed into Mandingo negroes, who, in
lieu of managing " war-horses," and handling arms,
are guiding, with loud clamour, the philosophic
mule, or wielding the useful hoe. Nymphs gathering flowers, "themselves the fairer," he will find
changed into Congo sylphs, whose zoneless waists
plainly demonstrate the possibility of the quadra-
ture, who with skilful fingers gather the milk-white

cotton from the teeming stalks. A few buildings, of an ordinary kind, and a post-office, surrounded by cotton fields and woods, make up the sum of this celestial abode for departed heroes.

———

XXXVIII.

Coloured population of the south—Mississippi saddle and horse caparisons—Ride through the city—Chain gang—Lynch law— Want of a penitentiary—Difficulties in consequence—Summary justice—Boating on the Mississippi—Chain gang and the runaway —Suburbs—Orphan asylum—A past era.

FOR the tourist to give sketches of the south without adverting to the slave population, would be as difficult, as for the historian to write of the early settlement of America without alluding to the aborigines. I shall, therefore, in this and two or three subsequent letters, discursively, as the subject is suggested to me, introduce such notices of the relative and actual condition of the slaves in this state, as may have a tendency to correct any prejudices, which as a New-Englander you may have imbibed, and set you right upon a subject, which has been singularly misrepresented. With slavery in the abstract, my remarks have nothing to do. Southerners and northerners think alike here—but I wish to present the subject before you precisely, as during a long residence in Mississippi it has constantly been presented to me—not to give you *ex parte* facts, and those from the darkest side of the picture—recording the moan here, and omitting the smile there—remembering the sound of the lash, and forgetting that of the violin—painting the ragged slave, and passing by his gayly-dressed fellow—but to state facts impartially and fearlessly, leaving you to draw your own conclusions.

Aware of the nature of the ground, upon which I am about to venture, I trust that I shall approach a subject upon which the sons of the chivalresque south are naturally so sensitive—involving as it does, a right so sacred as that of property—without those prejudices with which a northerner might be supposed fore-armed. Among the numerous important subjects with which the public mind within a few years past has been agitated, no one has been so obscured by error, and altogether so little understood as this.

In my letters from New-Orleans, there was but little allusion to this subject, as I then possessed very slight and imperfect knowledge of it. But the broad peculiarities of slavery, and the general traits of African character differ not materially, whether exhibited on the extensive sugar fields of Louisiana, or on the cotton plantations of Mississippi. The relative situations, also, of the slaves are so much alike, that a dissertation upon slavery as it exists in one state, can with almost equal precision be applied to it as existing in the other. All my remarks upon this subject, however, are the result only of my observations in the state of Mississippi.

" Will you ride with me into the country ?" said a young planter as we rose from the *table d'hote* of the Mansion house. " I am about purchasing a few negroes, and a peep into a slave-mart may not be uninteresting to you." I readily embraced the opportunity thus presented of visiting a southern slave market ; and in a few minutes our horses were at the door—long-tailed pacers with flowing manes and slender limbs. One of them was caparisoned with the deep concave Spanish saddle I have so often mentioned, with a high pummel terminating in a round flat head—and covered with blue broadcloth, which hung nearly to the stirrup, and, extending in one piece far behind, formed ample housings. The other horse bore an ordinary saddle, over which was thrown a light blue merino blanket several times folded, and secured to the saddle by a gayly-woven surcingle. Southerners usually ride with a thick blanket, oftener white than coloured, thus bound over their saddles, forming a comfortable cushion, and another placed between the saddle and the back of the horse. These blankets are considered indispensable in this climate. They are not always of the purest white, and the negroes, whose taste in this as well as in many other things might be improved, usually put them on awry, with a ragged corner hanging down in fine contrast with the handsome saddle, and in pleasant companionship with the cloth skirts of the rider. These little matters, however, the southerner seldom notices. If well mounted, which he is always sure to be, the " keeping" of the *ensemble* is but a secondary affair.

The saddle blankets are often unstrapped by the rider, in case of rain, and folded about him after the manner of the Choctaws. This custom of wearing blankets over the saddle originated with the old pioneers, who carried them to sleep on, as they camped in the woods.

Crossing Cotton Square—the chief market place for cotton in the city—we in a few minutes entered upon the great northern road leading to Jackson, the capital of this state, and thence to Washington, the seat of the general government. Near the intersection of this road with the city streets, a sudden clanking of chains, startled our horses, and the next instant a gang of negroes, in straggling procession, followed by an ordinary looking white man armed with a whip, emerged from one of the streets. Each negro carried slung over his shoulder a polished iron ball, apparently a twenty-four pounder, suspended by a heavy ox chain five or six feet in length and secured to the right ancle by a massive ring. They moved along under their burthen as though it were any thing but comfortable—some with idealess faces, looking the mere animal, others with sullen and dogged looks, and others again talking and laughing as though "Hymen's chains had bound them." This galley-looking procession, whose tattered wardrobe seemed to have been stolen from a chimney-sweep, was what is very appropriately termed the "Chain gang," a fraternity well known in New-Orleans and Natchez, and valued for its services in cleaning and repairing the streets. In the former city however there is one for whites as well as blacks, who may be known by their parti-coloured clothing. These gangs are merely moving penitentiaries, appropriating that amount of labor, which at the north is expended within four walls, to the broader limits of the city. In Natchez, negro criminals only are thus honoured—a " coat of tar and feathers" being applied to those white men who may require some kind of discipline not provided by the courts of justice. This last summary process of popular justice, or more properly excitement, termed " Lynch's law," I believe from its originator, is too much in vogue in this state. In the resentment of public as well as private wrongs, individuals have long been in the habit of forestalling and improving upon the decisions of the courts, by taking the execution of the laws into their own hands. The consequence is, that the dignity of the bench is degraded, and justice is set aside for the exhibition of wild outbreaks of popular feeling. But this summary mode of procedure is now, to the honour of the south, rapidly falling into disuse, and men feel willing to yield to the dignity of the law and acquiesce in its decisions, even to the sacrifice of individual prejudices. That " border" state of society from which the custom originated no longer exists here—and the causes having ceased which at first, in the absence of proper tribunals, may have rendered it perhaps necessary thus to administer justice, the effect will naturally cease also—and men will surrender the sword of justice to the public tribunals, erected by themselves.

The want of a penitentiary has had a tendency to

keep this custom alive in this state longer than it would otherwise have existed. When an individual is guilty of any offence, which renders him amenable to the laws, he must either be acquitted altogether or suffer death. There is no intermediate mode of punishment, except the stocks, whipping, branding and cropping—the last two are seldom resorted to now as legal punishments, and the others are regarded as too light an expiation for an offence which merited a seven years' imprisonment. Therefore when a criminal is acquitted, because his guilt is not quite sufficient to demand the sacrifice of his life, but enough to confine him to many years' hard labour in a state's prison—popular vengeance, if the nature of his guilt has enlisted the feelings of the multitude—immediately seizes upon him, and the poor wretch expiates his crime, by one of the most cruel systems of justice that human ingenuity has ever invented. When a criminal is here condemned to death, whose sentence in other states would have been confinement for a limited period, there is in public feeling sometimes a reaction, as singularly in the other extreme. Petitions for his pardon are circulated, and, with columns of names appended, presented to the governor, for here there can be no commutation of a sentence of death.— There must be a free, unconditional pardon or the scaffold. Sometimes a criminal under sentence of death is pardoned by the governor, thinking his crime not sufficiently aggravated to be atoned for by his life, which may often be the case in a state

where eleven crimes are punishable with death.*
In such instances the criminal, unless escorted beyond the reach of popular resentment, receives from
the multitude a commutation of his sentence, which,
through the tender mercies of his judges, is more
dreadful than death itself. Death indeed has in two
or three instances terminated the sufferings of these
victims of public feeling ; sometimes they have been
placed upright in a skiff with their arms pinioned
behind them, and a jug of whiskey placed at their
feet, and thus thrown upon the mercy of the Mississippi, down which under a burning sun, naked and
bareheaded they are borne, till rescued by some
steamer, cast upon the inhospitable shores, or buried
beneath the waves. This act, inhuman as it may
appear, does not indicate a more barbarous or inhuman state of society than elsewhere. It is the consequence of a deficiency in the mode and means of
punishment. Was there but one sentence passed
upon all criminals in sober New-England, and that
sentence, death, humanity would lead to numerous
acquittals and pardons, while popular feeling, when
it felt itself injured, refusing to acquiesce in the total
escape of the guilty, would take upon itself to in-
flict that punishment which the code had neglected
to provide. A penitentiary in this state would at

* The capital crimes of this state are, murder, arson, robbery,
rape, burglary, stealing a slave, stealing or selling a free person
for a slave, forgery, manslaughter, second offence—horse stealing, second offence—accessories, before the fact, to rape, arson, robbery and burglary.

once do away this custom, which however necessary it may appear in the opinion of those who adhere to it, can never be defended.

The " chain gang," which led to this digression, consists of insubordinate negroes and slaves, who, having run away from their masters, have been taken up and confined in jail, to await the reclamation of their owners ; during the interval elapsing between their arrest and the time of their liberation by their masters, they are daily led forth from the prison to work on the streets, under the charge of an overseer.   This punishment is considered very degrading, and merely the threat of the Calaboose, or the " ball and chain," will often intimidate and render submissive the most incorrigible.

" Hi ! Bill—dat you in ball and chain ?" said, as we passed by, a young slave well dressed and mounted on his master's fine saddle-horse ; " I no tink you eber runaway—you is a disgrace to we black gentlemen—I neber 'sociate wid you 'gain."

Bill, who was a tall, good-looking mulatto, the coachman of a gentleman near town, and of course, high in the scale of African society—seemed to feel the reproof, and be sensible of his degradation ; for he hung his head moodily and in silence.   The other prisoners, however, began to vituperate the young horseman, who was glad to escape from their Billingsgate missiles, by quickening his speed.

When a runaway is apprehended he is committed to jail, and an advertisement describing his person and wearing apparel, is inserted in the newspaper for six months, if he is not claimed in the interim ;

at the expiration of which period he may be sold at auction, and the proceeds, after deducting all expenses, go to the use of the county. Should the owner subsequently claim and prove his property, the amount paid into the treasury, on account of the sale, is refunded to him. An owner, making his claim before the six months have expired, and proving his property before a justice of the peace, is allowed to take him away on producing a certificate to that effect from the justice, and paying the expenses incurred in the apprehension and securing of his slave. All runaways, or suspected runaways, may lawfully be apprehended, and carried before a justice of the peace, who at his discretion may either commit them to jail, or send them to the owner, and the person by whom the arrest was made, is entitled to six dollars for each, on delivering him to his master.

The road, for the first mile after leaving town, passed through a charming country, seen at intervals, and between long lines of unpainted, wretched looking dwellings, occupied as " groggeries," by free negroes, or poor emigrants. The contrast between the miserable buildings and their squalid occupants, and the rich woodlands beyond them on either side, among whose noble trees rose the white columns and lofty roofs of elegant villas, was certainly very great, but far from agreeable. On a hill a short distance from the road the " Orphan Asylum" was pointed out to me, by my companion, as a monument of the benevolence and public spirit of the ladies of Natchez. Shortly after the prevalence of a great epidemic in this city, seven-

teen years ago, which left many children orphans,
and destitute, a few distinguished ladies formed
themselves into a society for their aid, obtained
bountiful subscriptions, for on such occasions hearts
and purses are freely opened, gathered the parent-
less children scattered throughout the city, and
placed them in this asylum, where all destitute orphans have since found a home.   The institution is
now in a flourishing state, and is under the patronage of several ladies of great respectability.   Some
distance beyond the asylum, to the left, a fine view
of groves and green hills, presenting a prospect
strikingly resembling English park scenery, terminated in the roofs and columns of a " southern
palace" rising above rich woods and ever-green foliage—the residence of the family of a late distinguished officer under the Spanish *regime*.   These
massive structures, with double colonnades and
spacious galleries, peculiar to the opulent southern
planter, are numerous in the neighbourhood of
Natchez, but they date back to the great cotton era,
when fortunes were made almost in a single season.
Magnificence was then the prevailing taste, and the
walls of costly dwellings rose, as the most available
means of displaying to the public eye the rapidly
acquired wealth of successful speculators.   But
times are now somewhat changed.   The rage for
these noble and expensive structures has passed
away, and those which are now seen, rear themselves among magnificent groves—monuments only
of the past, when the good old customs of Virginia
characterized the inhabitants.   These were for the

most part gentlemen of education, or officers of the army—for those were military times. This was the day of dinner parties and courtly balls—an era to which the gentlemen, who participated in them, now look back with a sigh. Perhaps no state—not even Virginia herself, which Mississippi claims as her mother country—could present a more hospitable, chivalrous, and high-minded class of men, or more cultivated females than this, during the first few years, subsequent to its accession to the Union.

XXXIX.

Slave mart—Scene within—File of negroes—"Trader"—Negro feelings—George and his purchaser—George's old and new wife—Female slaves—The intellect of the negro—A theory—An elderly lady and her slaves—Views of slaves upon their condition—Separation of kindred among slaves.

HAVING terminated my last letter with one of my usual digressions, before entering upon the subject with which I had intended to fill its pages, I will now pursue my original design, and introduce you into one of the great slave-marts of the south-west.

A mile from Natchez we came to a cluster of rough wooden buildings, in the angle of two roads, in front of which several saddle-horses, either tied or held by servants, indicated a place of popular resort.

"This is the slave market," said my companion, pointing to a building in the rear; and alighting, we left our horses in charge of a neatly dressed yellow boy belonging to the establishment. Entering through a wide gate into a narrow court-yard, partially enclosed by low buildings, a scene of a novel character was at once presented. A line of negroes, commencing at the entrance with the tallest, who was not more than five feet eight or nine inches in height—for negroes are a low rather than a tall race of men—down to a little fellow about ten years of age, extended in a semicircle around the right side of the yard. There were in all about forty. Each was dressed in the usual uniform of slaves, when in market, consisting of a fashionably shaped, black fur hat, roundabout and trowsers of coarse corduroy velvet, precisely such as are worn by Irish labourers, when they first "come over the water;" good vests, strong shoes, and white cotton shirts, completed their equipment. This dress they lay aside after they are sold, or wear out as soon as may be; for the negro dislikes to retain the indication of his having recently been in the market. With their hats in their hands, which hung down by their sides, they stood perfectly still, and in close order, while some gentlemen were passing from one to another examining for the purpose of buying. With the exception of displaying their teeth when addressed, and rolling their great white eyes about the court—they were so many statues of the most glossy ebony. As we entered the mart, one of the slave merchants—for a "lot" of slaves is usually accompanied, if not owned, by two or three individuals—approached us, saying "Good morning, gentlemen! Would you like to examine my lot of boys?[*] I have as fine a lot as ever came into market."— We approached them, one of us as a curious spectator, the other as a purchaser; and as my friend passed along the line, with a scrutinizing eye—giving that singular look, peculiar to the buyer of slaves as he glances from head to foot over each individual —the passive subjects of his observations betrayed no other signs of curiosity than that evinced by an occasional glance.   The entrance of a stranger into a mart is by no means an unimportant event to the slave, for every stranger may soon become his master and command his future destinies.   But negroes are seldom strongly affected by any circumstances, and their reflections never give them much uneasiness.   To the generality of them, life is mere animal existence, passed in physical exertion or enjoyment.   This is the case with the field hands in particular, and more so with the females than the males, who through a long life seldom see any other white person than their master or overseer, or any other gentleman's dwelling than the "great hus," the "white house" of these little domestic empires in which they are the subjects.   To this class a change of masters is a matter of indifference;—they are handed from one to another with the passiveness of a purchased horse.   These constitute the lowest rank of slaves, and lowest grade in the scale of the human species.   Domestic and city slaves form classes of a

* Male slaves of any age under forty are always denominated boys.

superior order, though each constitutes a distinct class by itself. I shall speak of these more fully hereafter.

"For what service in particular did you want to buy?" inquired the "trader of my friend, "A coachman." "There is one I think may suit you, sir,' said he; "George, step out here." Forthwith a light-coloured negro, with a fine figure and good face, bating an enormous pair of lips, advanced a step from the line, and looked with some degree of intelligence, though with an air of indifference, upon his intended purchaser.

"How old are you, George?" he inquired. "I don't recollect, sir, 'zactly—b'lieve I'm somewere 'bout twenty-dree.'" "Where were you raised?" "On master R——'s farm in Wirginny." "Then you are a Virginia negro." "Yes, master, me full blood Wirginny." "Did you drive your master's carriage?" "Yes, master, I drove ole missus' carage, more dan four year." "Have you a wife?" "Yes, master, I lef' young wife in Richmond, but I got new wife here in de lot. I wishy you buy her, master, if you gwine to buy me."

Then came a series of the usual questions from the intended purchaser. "Let me see your teeth —your tongue—open your hands—roll up your sleeves—have you a good appetite? are you good tempered? "Me get mad sometime," replied George to the last query, "but neber wid my horses." "What do you ask for this boy, sir?" inquired the planter, after putting a few more questions to the unusually loquacious slave. "I have held him at one thousand dollars, but I will take nine hundred and

seventy-five cash.   The bargain was in a few minutes concluded, and my companion took the negro
at nine hundred and fifty, giving negotiable paper
—the customary way of paying for slaves—at four
months.   It is, however, generally understood, that
if servants prove unqualified for the particular service for which they are bought, the sale is dissolved.
So there is in general perfect safety in purchasing
servants untried, and merely on the warrant of the
seller.   George, in the meanwhile, stood by, with
his hat in his hand, apparently unconcerned in the
negotiations going on, and when the trader said to
him, " George, the gentleman has bought you ; get
ready to go with him," he appeared gratified at the
tidings, and smiled upon his companions apparently
quite pleased, and then bounded off to the buildings
for his little bundle.   In a few minutes he returned
and took leave of several of his companions, who,
having been drawn up into line only to be shown to
purchasers, were now once more at liberty, and
moving about the court, all the visiters having left
except my friend and myself.   " You mighty lucky,
George" said one, congratulating him, " to get sol so
quick." Oh, you neber min', Charly," replied the
delighted George ; " your turn come soon too."

    " You know who you' master be—whar he live ?"
said another.   " No, not zactly ; he lib on plantation some whar here 'bout."   After taking leave of
his companions, George came, hat in hand, very
respectfully, to his purchaser, and said, " Young
master, you never be sorry for buy George ; I make
you a good servant.   But—beg pardon, master—

but—if master would be so good as buy Jane—"
" Who is Jane ?"—" My wife, since I come from
Wirginny. She good wife and a good girl—she
good seamstress an' good nurse—make de nice
shirts and ebery ting."

" Where is she, George ?" " Here she be, master," said he, pointing to a bright mulatto girl, about
eighteen, with a genteel figure and a lively countenance, who was waiting with anxiety the reply of
the planter. Opposite to the line of males was also
a line of females, extended along the left side of
the court. They were about twenty in number,
dressed in neat calico frocks, white aprons and
capes, and fancy kerchiefs, tied in a mode peculiar
to the negress, upon their heads. Their whole appearance was extremely neat and " tidy." They
could not be disciplined to the grave silence observed by the males, but were constantly laughing
and chattering with each other in suppressed voices,
and appeared to take, generally, a livelier interest
in the transactions in which all were equally concerned. The planter approached this line of female
slaves, and inquired of the girl her capabilities as
seamstress, nurse, and ironer. Her price was seven
hundred and fifty dollars. He said he would take
her to his family ; and if the ladies were pleased
with her, he would purchase her. The poor girl
was as much delighted as though already purchased ; and, at the command of the trader, went to
prepare herself to leave the mart. Some other negroes were purchased, several of whom appeared
merely powerful combinations of bone and muscle,

and the only idea suggested to the mind, in gazing upon them, was of remarkable physical energy. In the dull eye and fleshy mouth there was no expression indicative of intellect.

It is the popular opinion, both at the north and south, that the negro is inferior in intellect to the white man. This opinion is not, however, founded upon just experience. The African intellect has never been developed. Individuals, indeed, have been educated, whose acquirements certainly reflect honour upon the race. Uneducated negroes have also exhibited indications of strong intellectual vigour. And because, in both instances, the negro has shown himself still inferior to the white man, he is unhesitatingly pronounced an inferior being, irremediably so, in the estimation of his judges, by the operation of organic laws. That the African intellect, in its present state, is inferior to that of the European, is undeniable : but that, by any peculiarity in his organized system, a necessary inferiority ensues, will not so readily be admitted. Physiologists have agreed, that physical peculiarities may be communicated from generation to generation ; and it is no less certain that mental talents may thus be transmitted also. Dr. King, in speaking of the fatality which attended the house of Stuart, says, " If I were to ascribe their calamities to another cause" (than evil fate), " or endeavour to account for them by any natural means, I should think they were chiefly owing to a certain obstinacy of temper, which appears to have been hereditary, and inherent in all the Stuarts, except Charles the second." The Brahmins are much superior in intellect to all the other castes in Hindostan; and it is mentioned, says Combe, by the missionaries, as an ascertained fact, that the children of the Brahmins are naturally more acute, intelligent, and docile, than those of the inferior castes, age and other circumstances being equal. "Parents," says Dr. Gregory, "frequently live again in their offspring. It is certain that children resemble their parents, not only in countenance and in the form of the body, but in mental dispositions and in their virtues and vices. The haughty "gens Claudia" transmitted the peculiar mental character of its founder through six centuries, and in the tyrannical Nero again lived the imperious Appius Claudius." If this theory be correct, there is something more to be done before African intellect can be fairly developed. If culture will expand the intellect of the untutored negro—take one of the present generation for instance—according to this theory, which experience proves to be true, it is certain that he will transmit to his offspring an intellectual organization, so to speak, superior to that which was transmitted to himself by his parent; the mind of the offspring will be a less rude soil for mental cultivation than was his father's; and when his education is commenced, he will be one step in the scale of intellect in advance of his parents at the same period. When he arrives at maturity, he will, under equal circumstances, be mentally superior to his progenitors at the same period of their lives. His offspring will be superior to himself, and their offspring yet a grade higher in the scale of intelligence, and standing, perhaps, upon the very line drawn between human and angelic intellect. His mind will bear comparison with that of the white man ; and, morally and intellectually, he will stand beside him as his equal.

This is mere theory, but it is theory based upon the operation of laws whose general principles cannot be controverted : and when the negro, by the emancipation of his species, has opportunity for the culture of his own mind—which, if he is disposed to neglect, the philanthopist will not be—a few generations will leave no traces of those mental shackles, which, like chains loaded upon the body, have so long borne him down to a level with the brute. Till time proves this original equi-mental organization of the white man and the negro, which opinion fact has been strengthening for two or three generations in individual instances, it is due, both to philanthropy and justice, to suspend the sentence which condemns him as a being less than man.

Shortly before leaving the slave mart—a handsome carriage drove up, from which alighted an elderly lady, who, leaning on the arm of a youth, entered the court. After looking at and questioning in a kind tone several of the female slaves, she purchased two, a young mother and her child, and in a few minutes afterward, at the solicitation of the youth, purchased the husband of the girl, and all three, with happy faces—happier, that they were not to be separated—flew to get their little parcels, and rode away with their mistress,—the wife and child sitting within the carriage on the front seat—and the man on the coach-box beside the coachman. We soon after mounted our horses, and with George and his wife walking on before us with elastic steps, returned to town.   The slave market, which is the subject of this letter, I have since frequently visited, as well as four or five others in the vicinity of Natchez, where several hundred slaves of all ages, colours, and conditions, of both sexes, were exposed for sale.   I have conversed with a great number of them, from the liveliest to the most sullen, and my impression, which is daily strengthened by a more intimate knowledge of their species, is, that the negro is not dissatisfied with his condition—that it is seldom or never the subject of his thoughts—that he regards it as his destiny, as much as a home about the poles is the Laplander's; nor does he pine after freedom more than the other after the green hills and sunny skies of Italy.   They find themselves first existing in this state, and pass through life without questioning the justice of their allotment, which, if they think at all, they suppose a natural one.   Had the American slave once enjoyed freedom, these circumstances would be changed.   But there is probably not one among them, except some venerable African, who has realized what it is to be free.   So long as he has had any consciousness, he is conscious of having been a slave, and he fulfils his duties as such, without stopping from time to time to put the question to himself, " Is this my original destiny ? Was my first ancestor created a slave ?" With as much propriety might the haughty white man query if more exalted physical beauty and perfection were not once his, and whether man was not originally winged! There are, of course, individual exceptions to this general remark, but in the present darkened state of negro intellect, these exceptions are very few.

During the time they remain in the mart for sale, few men pass their time with more apparent contentment. There are two extensive markets for slaves, opposite to each other, on the road to Washington, three miles from Natchez. These I have passed at least once a week for more than a year, and I have always seen the slaves either dancing to the sound of the violin, played by one of their number, playing at marbles, quoits, practising gymnastics, lounging, sleeping in the sun, or idling about the door, while their masters, the "slave traders," regardless of them, were playing at cards or backgammon, smoking or sitting about the door conversing together, or with a buyer; their presence not producing the least restraint upon the noisy merriment around them. But when a purchaser stops and desires to look at the "lot," the slaves at once leave their several amusements, and draw up into a line, for inspection and purchase; and when the stranger leaves, taking with him one or more of their number, to whom they bid a cheerful good-bye, they return to their former pursuits wholly unimpressed by the event that has just taken place.

Negroes, when brought into market, are always anxious to be sold; and to be sold first is a great desideratum, for in their estimation it is an evidence of their superiority. "None but poor nigger stay for be sol' last." Hence, when a purchaser enters, they strive to appear before him to the best advantage, and by their manner assiduously invite attention to themselves. There are but two things which at all depress the mind of the slave in market; these are, the possibility of obtaining a bad master, and that of being separated from their relations. The first, however, seldom troubles them, and the degree in which they are governed by this apprehension depends wholly upon their former treatment. With individuals who have been blessed with a partial master it may weigh much, but with the generality of slaves it is a light consideration. The latter apprehension is in a great measure lessened by a certainty of being sold together to the same individual, if possible. It is a rule seldom deviated from, to sell families and relations together, if practicable, and if not, at least to masters residing in the neighbourhood of each other. A negro trader, in my presence, refused to sell a negro girl, for whom a planter offered a high price, because he would not also purchase her sister— " for," said the trader, " they are much attached to each other, and when their mother died I promised her I would not part them."

Relatives, except husband and wife, often prefer being sold to different masters in the same neighbourhood. This is to be attributed to the roving propensity of their race, which induces them to prefer a separation of this nature, for a pretence to visit from one plantation to another on Sabbaths and Christmas holydays, at which season the slaves have a temporary freedom for several days. Then the highways, lanes, and streets, in town and country, are filled with gay parties on foot or on plough-horses, caparisoned for the occasion, as happy as the total absence of care, thoughtlessness of to-morrow, plenty of whiskey, and a cessation of all labour, can make them.

XL.

Towns of Mississippi—Naming estates—The influence of towns on the social relations of the planters—Southern refinement—Colleges—Oakland—Clinton—Jefferson—History of the latter—Collegiate system of instruction—Primary departments—Quadrennial classes.

THE towns and villages of Mississippi, as in European states, are located perfectly independent of each other, isolated among its forests, and often many leagues apart, leaving in the intervals large tracts of country covered with plantations, and claiming no minuter subdivision than that of " county." Natchez, for instance, is a corporation one mile square, but from the boundaries of the city to Woodville, the next incorporated town south, there is an interval of thirty-eight miles. It is necessary for the planters who reside between towns so far asunder, to have some more particular address, than the indefinite one arising from their vicinity to one or other of these towns. Hence has originated the pleasing custom of naming estates, as in England; and names so given are always regarded by the planters themselves, and by the community, as an inseparable part of their address. These names are generally selected with taste, such as " Monmouth," "Laurel-hill," "Grange," "Magnolia grove," " The Forest," "Cottage," " Briars," " Father land," and " Anchorage"—the last given by a retired navy officer to his plantation. The name is sometimes adopted with reference to some characteristic of the domain, as " The Oaks," " China grove," " New Forest," &c., but more frequently it is a mere matter of fancy. Towns in this state have usually originated from the location of a county seat, after the formation of a new county. Here the court-house is placed, and forms the centre of an area which is soon filled with edifices and inhabitants. If the county lies on the river, another town may arise, for a shipping port, but here the accumulation of towns usually ceases. A county seat, and a cotton mart, are all that an agricultural country requires. The towns in this state are thus dispersed two or three to each county, nor so long as this is a planting country, will there be any great increase to their number, although in wealth and importance they may rival, particularly the shipping ports, the most populous places in the valley of the west. In these towns are the banks, the merchants, the post offices, and the several places of resort for business or pleasure that draw the planter and his family from his estate. Each town is the centre of

s 2

a circle which extends many miles around it into the country, and daily attracts all within its influence. The ladies come in their carriages " to shop," the gentlemen, on horseback, to do business with their commission merchants, visit the banks, hear the news, dine together at the hotels, and ride back in the evening. The southern town is properly the " Exchange" for the neighbouring planters, and the " Broadway" for their wives and daughters. And as no plantation is without a private carriage, the number of these gay vehicles, filling the streets of the larger towns on pleasant mornings in the winter, is surprising. I have counted between thirty and forty private carriages in the streets of Natchez in one morning. In a small country village, I once numbered seventeen, standing around a Methodist chapel. Showy carriages and saddle horses are the peculiar characteristics of the " moving spectacle" in the streets of south-western towns.

Every village is a nucleus of southern society, to which the least portion is generally contributed by itself. When a public ball is given by the bachelors, in one of these towns—for private parties are scarcely known—the tickets of invitation fly into the retirement of the plantations, within the prescribed circle, often to the distance of thirty miles. Thus families, who reside several leagues apart, on opposite sides of the town, and who might otherwise never associate, unless on " change," or in " shopping," meet together, like the inhabitants of one city. This state of things unites, in a social bond, the intelligent inhabitants of a large extent of country, who are nearly equally wealthy, and creates a state of society in the highest degree favourable to hospitality and social feeling. These social "circles" often revolve within one another, and sometimes enlarge, until they embrace several towns. The Mississippians are remarkable for their "locomotivity;" an organ which they have plainly developed, if we reason, as phrenologists sometimes do, from effect to cause—and whose existence is manifest from their propensity annually to depopulate their state, by taking northern tours during the summer months. During the season of gayety, in the winter months, the public assemblies and private coteries of Natchez are unsurpassed by those of any other city, in the elegance, refinement, or loveliness of the individuals who compose them. If you will bear in mind, that the southern females of wealth are usually educated in the most finished style, at the first female seminaries in the north, and, until recently, not seldom in Europe ; and recollect the personal beauty, sprightliness, and extreme refinement of the southern lady, you will not be surprised that elegant women grace the private circles, and shine in the gay assemblies of southern cities.

But fashion and refinement are not confined to Natchez. In nearly every county reside opulent planters, whose children enjoy precisely the same advantages as are afforded in the city. Drawn from the seclusion of their plantations, their daughters are sent to the north; whence they return, in the course of time, with cultivated minds and elegant manners. Hence every village can draw around it a polished circle of its own; for refinement and wealth do not always diminish here, as in New-England, in the inverse ratio of distance from a metropolis—and elegant women may often be found blooming in the depths of forests far in the interior.

Less attention is paid to the mental or personal cultivation of the male youth of this state, than to that of the females. Many of them are partially educated at home; and, by the time they attain the age at which northern boys enter college, become assistants on the plantation, which they expect one day to inherit; or, at the age of nineteen or twenty, receive from their parents land and negroes, and commence planting for themselves. At the age of twenty-one or two they frequently marry. Many planters are opposed to giving their sons, whom they destine to succeed them as farmers, a classical education. A common practical education they consider sufficient for young gentlemen who are to bury themselves for life in the retirement of a plantation. But Mississippi, in this age and at this juncture, from the peculiar construction of her political and social laws, demands an educated youth. —The majority of the planters are able to educate their children in a superior manner; and if they do this, they will elevate the rising generation high in the scale of society, and give Mississippi an honourable rank among the republics of America. Although education is not indigenous, and is too frequently a secondary consideration in the minds of many, children in the towns are probably as well educated as they would be at the north, under similar circumstances, for no village is without private schools. But the education of young children on plantations is much neglected. Many boys and girls, whose parents reside five or ten miles from any town or academy, and do not employ tutors, grow up to the age of eight or ten, unable either to read or write. Some planters, who have but one or two children, and do not think it worth while to employ a tutor for so small a number, thoughtless of the injury their children may sustain, suffer them to grow up at home, almost ignorant even of the alphabet, till of an age to be sent away to a boarding-school, or an academy, where they first learn to read. In such a state of things, it is not uncommon to meet with very interesting and intelligent children wholly ignorant of those childish studies, and that story-book information, which throw such a charm over their little society, invigorating the intellectual faculties, and laying a foundation for a superstructure of mind. Often several families will unite and employ a tutor; constructing, for the purpose, a school-house, in a central position among their plantations. But those who look forward to a high rank in American and European society for their children, employ private tutors in their own houses, even if they have but one child. Some gentlemen send their children, when quite young, to the north, and visit them every summer. Two-thirds of the planters' children of this state are educated out of it. There is annually a larger sum carried out of the state, for the education of children at the north, and in the expenses of parents in making them yearly visits there, than would be sufficient to endow an institution at intervals of four or five years.

There are three colleges in Mississippi; but Mississippians have so long been in the habit of sending their children away, when it was necesssary, that they still adhere to the custom, when there is no farther occasion for it; and the consequence is, that their own institutions are neglected, and soon fall into decay, while the money which they send for the support of northern colleges, would elevate their own to high literary distinction and usefulness.

Oakland college, twenty-five miles from Natchez, near Rodney, is a flourishing institution under Presbyterian patronage. It is of recent foundation, and has yet no permanent buildings; but handsome college edifices are about to be erected for the accommodation of the students. Its situation is rural and very healthy. Its funds are respectable, and under the presidency of the Rev. J. Chamberlin, a gentleman of learning and piety, it is rapidly rising into eminence. It already has about one hundred students, and its professors are men of talent and industry, one of whom is a son of the late Dr. Payson of Portland. It is thus that young northerners work their way to distinction in the south and west. There is another college at Clinton, of which I have before spoken, and also an academy at Natchez, ranking as high as a south-western college, under the superintendence of J. H. B. Black, Esq. of New-Jersey. Jefferson college, in the village of Washington, six miles from Natchez, is the oldest and best endowed institution in the state. It was founded by private subscription in 1802, and subsequently received a grant of a township of unsaleable land from Congress, exchanged two years since for a more eligible tract, which sold for a very large sum. The income of the college is now about eight thousand dollars, arising from a fund of more than one hundred and fifty thousand. The building is a large, three-story brick edifice, handsomely finished, and capable of containing one hundred students. The location is highly beautiful, in' a grove of majestic oaks, and at the head of a fine green parade, which lies, with a magnificent oak in its centre, between it and the village. A primary department is connected with it; and a pleasant brick building, half surrounded with galleries, on the opposite side of the "green," is appropriated to this branch of the institution. The primary department, which includes a moiety of the students, is under the able superintendence of professor Crane, a native of New-Jersey, and recently from West Point. The history of this institution will confirm what I have stated in my remarks upon education. Since its organization until very recently, it has laboured under pecuniary difficulties, with which it was unable to contend; for a great part of the time it has been without pupils or teachers; and its halls have occasionally been used for private schools. It obtained no celebrity as a college until 1829-30, when Mr. Williston, the author of "Eloquence in the United States," and "Williston's Tacitus," was chosen its president, and the institution was placed under military organization, after the plan adopted by capt. Alden Partridge. The novelty of this mode drew a great number of pupils within its walls. The following year ill health compelled president Williston to resign, and he was succeeded by major Holbrook, formerly principal of the seminary in Georgetown, D. C. During his presidency there were above one hundred and fifty cadets connected with the institution, and it was more flourishing in every respect than any other in the southwest. But the new president, seized with the mania for cotton-planting, which infects all who reside here for any length of time, devoted a portion of his attention to agricultural pursuits, and the patrons of the college, perhaps regarding this additional vocation as incompatible with that of instructing, withdrew their sons, one after another, the novelty of a military education having worn off, and fell into the old mode of keeping them at home on their plantations, or sending them to Kentucky, the great academy for Mississippi youth, to complete their education. During the summer the president died, and the institution again became disorganized. In 1833, capt. Alden Partridge was invited by the board of trustees to assume the presidency, but after remaining a few months, returned to the north, unable to restore it to its former flourishing condition. The college halls became again, and for the sixth time since their foundation, nearly deserted. In the spring of 1834, the board invited two professors to take charge of the college until they could decide upon the choice of a president. The present year, C. B. Dubuisson, Esq. of Philadelphia, one of these professors, was unanimously elected president, and was inaugurated on the 6th of July, 1835. Under the new president, who is a finished scholar and a very amiable and energetic man, the college has become very flourishing, and is rapidly advancing to permanent literary distinction. Professor Symmes, a graduate of the University of Virginia, and an able scholar, is professor of mathematics. Under these two gentlemen, and the professor in the primary department, planters may now have their sons as well educated as at the north. They are beginning to think so. But if they would more generally adopt the opinion, that their sons can be educated at the south by northern professors as well as at the north, the literary institutions of this country would not have to struggle for existence, scarcely able to rise above the rank of an academy. In connexion with the disinclination which southerners have to educating their sons at home, and their disposition to depreciate their native institutions, there exists another cause, with a direct tendency to check their advancement. It is the system of education pursued in their colleges, which, in a great degree, is the result of necessity. Until within a few years, there have been no good preparatory schools in this state, where youth could fit themselves for admission into college. Now, to form the lowest class in a college, it is necessary that those who are to compose it—however large or small their number—should have gone through a prescribed series of preparatory studies. But where there has been no opportunity for pursuing this preparatory course, as here in the south-west, the college must open its doors to unprepared youth, to the great injury of its classes, or, in the absence of other means, provide measures for fitting them for admission. These measures all colleges here are at present taking, by the establishment of primary departments; until the pupils of these departments are qualified for promotion, the college classes remain vacant; and thus, though nominally a college, the institution is, for the time being, an academy, or preparatory school for *itself.* This is the present state of the colleges here, and none of them have advanced so far as to open the junior class. Jefferson College indeed has been, with the exception of its condition under military discipline a few years since, no more than a preparatory department since its organization. It is now rising into the dignity of a college, although the quadrennial course, which in our notions is inseparable from a collegiate education, is not intended by the board to form a part of their system. The method adopted in the University of Virginia, in relation to the routine of studies and succession of classes, will be partially pursued. In the present state of things, this is no doubt the preferable course to follow; but it is to be feared that the college will never be eminent or very permanent, until established on the good old basis of our northern institutions. If this system were adopted, and a professor appointed to fill the chair in each department of science, whether there were students or not—and the freshman

class opened, even by the admission of a single
scholar—the institution, with its immense fund,
would stand upon an immovable foundation. The
classes would increase every year in size, and at the
end of the fifth series, or in twenty years, a class of
seniors would receive their degrees, whom even
aristocratic Harvard would not disdain to acknow-
ledge as her foster children.

XLI.

Indian mounds—Their origin and object—Tumuli near Natchez
—Skulls and other remains—Visit to the fortifications or mounds
at Seltzertown—Appearance and description of the mounds—Their
age—Reflections—History of the Natchez.

THE Indian mounds, those gigantic mausolea of
unhistoried nations, will ever present a subject of
absorbing interest to the reflecting mind. Elevating
their green summits amid the great forests of the
west—mysterious links of the unknown past—they
will stand imperishable through time, encircled by
the cities and palaces of men, silent but impressive
monitors of their grasping ambition. These sepulchres are scattered every where throughout the valley of the Mississippi—itself a mighty cemetery of
mighty tombs. In the pathless forests, and on the
banks of the rivers of the south-west, they are still
more thickly strewed than in the north valley, in-

dicating a denser population. It was recently suggested to me, by a gentleman of antiquarian tastes, that the Indians of the southern valley, by whom these mounds were constructed, and who were a mild and inoffensive people, far advanced in civilization, were, in remote ages, invaded by a horde of northern tribes from the Atlantic shores—as were the effeminate states of southern Europe by the Goths and Vandals—who drove out the original possessors, and took possession of their delightful country; while the fugitive inhabitants crossed the Mississippi, and, moving to the west and south, laid the foundation of the empire of Mexico. This theory is not improbable, and it is supported by many established facts. It is certain that the rude tribes found in this country, by De Soto and his followers, remnants of which still exist, cannot be identified with those by whom these tumuli were erected. Among them there exists not even a tradition of the formation of these mounds.

There have been many curious hypotheses advanced in reference to their object. Some have supposed that they were constructed, after a great battle, of the numerous bodies of the slain; others, that they were the customary burial-places of the Indians, gradually accumulating in a series of years, until, terminating in a cone, they were covered with earth, and deserted for new cemeteries, to be in like manner abandoned in their turn. Others, by a train of analogous reasoning, founded upon the prevailing custom of other aboriginal tribes, have supposed them to be fortifications; and others again believe them temples; or, like the pyramids of Egypt, structures connected with the mysteries of the religion of their builders. But their true origin, like that of their grander prototypes on the plains of Memphis, must for ever be lost in conjecture.

In the vicinity of Natchez, and within three hours' ride of the city, in various directions, are twelve or fifteen of these mounds. Some of them have been partially excavated; and besides many vessels, weapons of war, and ordinary human remains, skeletons of men of a large size have been found in them. On the estate of a gentleman two miles from Natchez, and in the loveliest vale in this region, there are three, situated equidistant from each other, along the bank of the St. Catharine. One of these was recently excavated by Dr. Powell, a distinguished phrenologist of the west; from which he obtained several earthen vessels, neatly made, various fragments, and besides other bones, three perfect skulls—one the most beautiful head I ever beheld, of a young Choctaw girl; another, the skull of a man of the same tribe; and the third, a massive and remarkably formed skull of a Natchez. I have since examined two of these mounds, but was not able to add any thing important to the discoveries of Dr. Powell. The perfect decomposition which has taken place in one of them, would indicate a much greater age than is generally attributed to them. I laid bare a perpendicular face of this mound, ten feet square, and the spade struck but one hard substance, which proved to be the lower jaw, containing seven or eight teeth, of some wild animal, and a few splinters of corroded human bones that crumbled between the fingers. I could easily discern several strata, in this exposed surface, alternately of common earth and a black friable loam, resembling powder to the eye, but soft like paste in the fingers. These black strata were veined with light brown or dingy white streaks, of a firmer consistence. The location of this mound, its height, not exceeding twenty feet, the uniform decomposition, and the regular series of strata, lead to the conclusion, that it was constructed at one time, probably after a battle, of the bodies of men whose deaths took place at the same period, laid in layers, one above another, as the modern slain are buried, by only reversing the process, in deep pits.

The skulls found by Dr. Powell in the mound opened by him, were very perfect specimens. The head of the Choctaw differs not materially from those of Europeans, when considered phrenologically, although its developements of the organs of animal feelings are more prominent than those of the intellectual faculties. The head is generally smaller than that of the European, but the general contour is nearly the same. The skull of the Natchez is remarkable in every respect. It is large, like the German head, very angular, with bold developements. It is shaped artificially in infancy,—a peculiarity only of the skulls of the males—so that the top of the forehead forms the apex of a cone. The compressure necessary to produce this shape has entirely destroyed the organs of veneration, of benevolence, and of the reasoning powers. My examination of this skull was for a moment only, and very superficial, so that I did not ascertain the particular deficiency or developement of any special organ. The heads of the females of this extinct tribe, I am informed by those who have examined them, are very fine, displaying in their graceful, undulating outline, the *beau ideal* of the human cranium.

There is a mound about five miles from Natchez, upon the plantation of a gentleman, whose taste or ambition has influenced him to erect his dwelling upon its summit. A strange dwelling-place for the living, over the sepulchres of the dead! Eleven miles from the city there is another mound, or a collection of mounds, which, in the beauty of its location, the elevation of its summit, and the ingenuity displayed in its construction, either as a fortress or a temple, is entitled to an important rank among these mysterious structures of the western valley. A few days since I left Natchez with a northern gentleman, for the purpose of visiting this mound. Three miles from town we passed the race-course, situated in a delightful intervale. This is the finest "course" in the south, passing round a perfectly level plain in a circle of one mile, whose centre is slightly convex, so that the spectators can obtain a full view of the horses while running. Ladies, on extraordinary occasions, attend the races, although it is not customary. But to south-western gentlemen the race-course is a place of resort of the most alluring character. On the St. Catharine race-course, now alluded to, on great race days, the chivalry of Mississippi will be found assembled in high spirits, and full of the peculiar excitement incident to the occasion. Home is, perhaps, the proper scene for studying the planter's character; but it will never be perfectly understood until he is seen, booted and spurred, with his pocket-book in one hand, and bank bills fluttering in the other, moving about upon the turf.

Three miles from the race-ground, about which is gathered a little village, sometimes called St. Catharinesville, we entered the pretty and rural town of Washington. The whole village was embowered in the foliage of China trees, which thickly lined both sides of the main street. Turning down a street to the left, which led to the college, we alighted there after a short ride over the green, as it was the intention of the president and one or two of the professors to accompany us to the mound. We were shown the college library, comprised in a few shelves filled with volumes of the statutes; and the cabinet, where, besides a few interesting geological specimens, were some bones of a mammoth, or mastodon, found in the neighbourhood.

In the course of an hour we all mounted our horses, and, entering the village, rode down its quiet and shaded streets, and emerged on the brow of the hill or ridge on which the town is built; and shortly after crossed the pebbly bed of the St. Catharines, which, in its serpentine windings, crosses nearly every road in the neighbourhood of Natchez. Beyond this stream, from an eminence over which the road wound, we had a fine view of the village on the opposite hill, with its college, lifting its roof

among the towering oaks; its dwellings, with their
light galleries and balconies, half hidden among the
shade trees; the female academy, with its green
lawn, a high colonnaded private edifice, overtopping
the trees, and its neat unassuming churches.

After a pleasant ride of five miles, through forest
and plantation scenery, over a country pleasantly
undulating, we arrived at the summit of a hill, just
after passing a neat brick cottage, surrounded by a
parterre, and half hidden in the woods; so that it
would not have been observed, but for the wide
gate on the road-side—often the only indication, as
I have before remarked, of the vicinage of a planter's residence.   From this hill we were gratified
with an extensive prospect of a richly wooded and
partially cultivated extent of country, occasionally
rising into precipitous hills, crowned with forest
trees.   About a mile to the north, on our left, in
the centre of a large cotton plantation, surrounded
by an amphitheatre of hills, stood a singular cluster
of eminences, isolated from those encircling them,
whose summits were destitute of verdure or trees.
These were the goal of our excursion—the celebrated tumuli of Mississippi.   Descending the hill,
we passed through a gate, opening into a narrow
lane, bordered on either side with thick clumps of
trees, and the luxuriant wild shrubbery which grows
by the streams and along the roads throughout the
south; and after winding through ravines and crossing bayous, we arrived at the "gin" of the plantation; a large building resembling a northern hay-
press, where some negroes were at work; one of

whom, with a readiness always characteristic of the negro slave, immediately came out to take charge of our horses. Declining his aid, as we had no authority for appropriating his services—a liberty as to which some planters are very punctilious—we hitched our horses to the rail fence. Had the proprietor of the estate been present, we should have solicited the aid of some of his slaves in excavating : but since then I have met with the venerable planter, who, with great politeness, has offered me every facility for making whatever researches or excavations curiosity might suggest.

We ascended the steep sides of the mound with some difficulty, as they were inclined but a few degrees from the perpendicular. On gaining the summit, thirty-five feet from the base, we saw, extended before us, an elliptical area, whose plane was three or four feet lower than the verge of the mound. To the right, at the eastern extremity of the area, rose a super-mound, fifteen feet high ; and on the opposite extremity, to the east, stood another, rising thirty feet from the floor of the area or summit of the great mound we had just ascended, and sixty feet from the level of the surrounding plantation. From the summit of this second mound the eye embraced an irregular amphitheatre, confined by elevated forests, half a league in diameter, whose centre was the mound, from which, on nearly every side, the ground descended, almost imperceptibly, with a few obstructions, to the foot of the surrounding hills.

This peculiarity of its location, so favourable for

a military position, would indicate such to have
been the object of its constructors. The whole
structure, so far as an opinion can be formed from
a careful survey of its general features, was originally a conical hill, now changed to its present shape
by human labour; which nature, in a wayward
mood, placed, like Joseph's sheaf, conspicuous, and
aloof from the hills that surround it on every side.
From its present aspect, the mound, if originally a
natural hill, must have been forty or fifty feet high,
of an oblong form, its greatest diameter being from
east to west, with very precipitous sides.   It consists now of a single conspicuous elevation, oval in
shape, and presenting, on every side, indentations
and projections, not unlike the salient angles of military works, serving to strengthen the opinion that
it was a fortification.   Its summit is perfectly flat,
comprising an area of four acres, surrounded by a
kind of ballustrade, formed by the projection of the
sides of the mound two or three feet higher than
the area. The two super-mounds before mentioned
stand at either extremity of the summit, in a direc-
tion east and west; a position indicating design, and
confirming the views of those who believe the structure to be a temple.   The Indians, by whom the
mound is supposed to have been erected, were, like
the Peruvians, worshippers of the sun and of fire,
and maintained a perpetual sacrifice of the latter
upon their altars.   If this was a temple, the two
super-mounds were its altars; on one of which, toward the east, burned the sacrifice of fire, to wel-
come the rising sun, of which it was a pure and

beautiful emblem ; while the bright flame upon the altar toward the west, mingled with his last expiring beams. Between these two superior mounds are four others of inferior height, two of which border the northern verge of the area, and two the southern, although not exactly opposite to the former. Thus the area upon the summit is surrounded by six tumuli, of various elevations. The largest of them, to the west, before mentioned, is flat on the top, which contains about one-fourth of an acre. Its external sides slope, as do the outside surfaces of the other five, gradually down to the base of the great mound upon which it is constructed.

The whole work is surrounded by the remains of a ditch ; from which, and from the sides of the chief mound, the earth must have been taken to form those upon the summit. The material of which the whole is constructed, is the same alluvial earth as that composing the sides of the ditch and the surrounding plain. Neither stone nor brick forms any portion of the material of the work, nor is the former found any where in the vicinity. In the centre of the elevated area is the mouth of a subterranean passage, leading, with an easy inclination, to a spring without the mound, on the north side of the plain. It is now fallen in, and choked with briers vines, and young trees. There are traces also of another avenue, conducting to the south side, and opening into the country. Against the two eastern angles of the mound, at its base, are two smaller mounds, ten feet high, which might be taken for bastions by one who regarded the work as a fortification. In the

early settlement of this country, the mound was covered with fruit-trees of a large size, whose age indicated uninterrupted possession of their places for
centuries. It is now divested of its trees, and under
cultivation. It is to be regretted that the axe or
plough should ever have desecrated a monument
so sacred to the antiquary.

There is every evidence that formerly this posi
tion was one of great importance. Remains of ex
cavated roads, passing through the adjacent forests,
and converging to this mound as their common
centre, still exist, in which large trees are growing,
whose age—more than two hundred years—gives
an approximation to the date when these roads were
disused, and when, probably, the spot to which they
centred, ceased to be regarded either as a shrine
for the Indian pilgrim—a national temple—or the
centre of their military strength. Human remains
of very large size have been discovered in its vicinity, and also fragments of pottery, weapons,
pipes, and mortar-shaped vessels, covered with ornamental tracery and hieroglyphics, evincing a high
degree of advancement in the arts. If their dwellings and apparel were made with the same skill
which is displayed in the utensils and weapons discovered in these mounds, their fabricators will be
regarded, so far as this criterion extends, as having
possessed a high degree of civilization.

In surveying this mound from the plain, the mind
is impressed with the idea of the vast amount of
human labour expended in thus piling it up—
mound upon mound—like Pelion upon Ossa.

Thousands of human emmets have toiled to rear this hill—their busy hum filled the air, and every spot around us was trodden by their nimble feet. The question is naturally suggested to the mind, while gazing upon the huge pile, " For what was it constructed?"—and imagination, surveying the sad history of the departed nations, who once inhabited this pleasant land, might answer that a prophetic warning of their total annihilation influenced these people to erect a national tomb.   And are they not their tombs ? Are not these the only evidences that they ever have been—and are they not the receptacles of their national remains ? The footstep of the labourer is now stayed for ever ! his voice is hushed in death ! The shout of the hunter—the cry of the warrior—the voice of love, are heard no more.

" The Natchez tribe of Indians," says a beautiful writer, to whom I have before alluded, and who involves in his historical sketch a touching narrative, " who inhabited the luxuriant soil of Mississippi, were a mild, generous, and hospitable people. The offspring of a serene climate, their character was marked by nothing ferocious ; and beyond the necessity of self-defence, or the unavoidable collisions with neighbouring tribes, by nothing martial. Their government, it is true, was most despotic ; and, perhaps, the history of no other nation north of the equator presents a parallel ; and yet no charge of an unnecessary, or unwarrantable exercise of this great power, is made against them, even by their historians, who were also the countrymen of their oppressors.   Their king, or chief, was called " THE

Sun," and the exalted station which he held, was designated by a representation of that luminary worn upon his breast. He united also with his civic function, the priestly power and supremacy— and thus entrenched behind the ramparts of physical force, and wielding the terrors of superstition, he was absolute master of the lives and property of his subjects. His equal, in dignity and power, was his queen, under the title of " The Wife of the Sun." Thus, then, living in undisturbed repose, and in the innocent enjoyment of the bounties of nature, there came in an evil hour to their peaceful shores, a party of French emigrants, who, about the end of the seventeenth or beginning of the eighteenth century, navigated the Mississippi in quest of wealth and territory. They were received with all the cordiality and affection that these guiltless and inoffensive beings could bestow. The choicest gifts of the beneficent Creator had been showered upon them with a lavish hand, and with a spirit, somewhat allied to his who had conferred them, they cheerfully tendered to the houseless wanderers a participation in the blessings they themselves enjoyed. These substantial pledges of amity and good feeling were received with apparent gratitude by the emigrants ; but their immediate wants supplied, they were again thrown back upon their evil passions, that for a moment had been quelled by misfortune, and perpetrated acts of injustice and cruelty which excited the indignation of their benefactors. Driven almost to frenzy, by repeated acts of aggression, they attempted a re-establishment of their rights, but were eventually subdued, and basely massacred. The French, upon their arrival, affected to treat upon terms of reciprocity for the products of the soil; perceiving, however, the unsuspicious temper of these generous Indians, they threw off the mask, and urged novel and extravagant demands; even extending to the fields which supported their wives and children—and not until they were driven in ignominy from them into the depth of the wilderness, were their shameless oppressors satisfied. At this period commenced the league against the French, which embraced all the tribes lying on the east, and to the failure of which, through the unmerited compassion of their queen, they owed their defeat and extermination.

Messengers were despatched to different quarters, and a general massacre of the common enemy was agreed upon. A day was appointed, but being unacquainted with the art of writing, or the use of numbers, the period was designated by a bundle of sticks, every stick representing a day; each of the confederated chiefs prepared a bundle corresponding in number with those of his associates, one of which was to be burned daily; and the committing of the last to the flames, was to be the signal for the attack.

"The wife of the sun," still attached to the French by many recollections, being the strangers whom she had protected and loved—trembling at the torrents of blood which must flow, and forgetting the wrongs which had been heaped upon her country, determined to preserve them, and intimated to their commander the necessity of caution; by some singular incredulity he despised and neglected the counsel thus tendered to him. Frustrated in her purpose of saving those within the limits of her own tribe, she determined, by the anticipation of their fate, to preserve the majority scattered throughout other tribes. Having free access to the temple, she removed several of the sticks there deposited, and the warriors, on repairing thither, finding but one symbol remaining, prepared for the dreadful business on which they had resolved. They then consigned the last stick to the fire, and supposing that the united nations were all engaged in the same bloody work, fell upon the French, and cut them off almost to a man.* Perrein, the commander, with a few more, escaped, and collecting a few of his countrymen, prevailed upon the neighbouring tribes, by threats or promises, to abandon and betray the devoted Natchez; and in one day consigned them to the sword, sparing neither age, sex, nor condition; he burnt their houses, laid waste their fields, and desolation soon marked the spot, once the retreat of an unoffending, peaceful, and happy people. The few who escaped, fled for protection to a neighbouring tribe, then, and now, known as the Chickasaws; a brave, warlike, and independent nation. Their conduct toward these wretched outcasts should be remembered to their immortal honour; they received them with open

* The attack was made on Fort Rosalie, at Natchez, in 1729, the head quarters of the French.

arms, and resisted with unshaken firmness, the earnest and repeated demands of the French for their delivery; and to such an extent did they carry their magnanimity, that they preferred hazarding a doubtful contest, when their own existence was at stake, to a violation of the pledges of hospitality and protection, which they had made to a few persecuted strangers. Three times, with souls bent upon vengeance against the remnant of their ancient foes, and with no less bloody purposes against their defenders, did the French carry war to the Chickasaw boundary, and three times were they driven back with ignominy and loss—nor did they ever obtain their object. The poor Natchez shared the hospitality of their protectors until their necessities and sorrows were alike relieved by death; their bones repose in a land unknown to their fathers; their spirits may be again mingled in the beautiful regions which they believe to be prepared by the Great Spirit for the fearless warrior, the successful hunter, and the faithful and hospitable Indian, beyond the great lakes. Such is the story of the Natchez—such their melancholy end—such the kindness and benevolence extended to the white man in distress—and such the ingratitude, perfidy, and cruelty, with which these favours were repaid. Of the distinguished female, whose humanity and mercy proved so unexpectedly fatal to her race, we hear no more —but it is highly probable, that in the indiscriminate massacre which took place, neither her strong claims to the gratitude of the French, nor her merciful and forbearing disposition, nor her honours, titles, and dignities, nor even her sex, could protect her; but that she fell an undistinguished victim, among her slaughtered people."

XLII.

Slavery in the south-west—Southern feelings—Increase of slaves —Virginia—Mode of buying slaves, and slave-traders—Mode of transportation by sea—Arrival at the mart—Mode of life in the market—Transportation by land—Privileges of slaves—Conduct of planters toward their negroes—Anecdotes—Negro traders—Their origin.

In my desultory sketches of the white and negro population of the south-west, my intention has not been to detail minutely their social relations and domestic economy. To convey a general idea of their condition alone enters into my present plan. Having enlarged upon that of the white population, I will devote a portion of the following pages to a brief sketch of a variety of the human species, which has ever presented an interesting field for the efforts of the philanthropist.

The origin of slavery is lost: but there is no doubt that it prevailed, in the early post-diluvian ages, among all the infant nations of the earth.*

* " Slavery, at a very early period after the flood, prevailed, perhaps in every region of the globe. In Asia it is practised to this day. The savage nations of Africa have at no period been exempted

Sacred history assures us of its existence shortly after the flood ; and divine economy, in regulating the political and domestic state of the Jews, permitted its existence.   But Jewish, and all ancient slavery, was a species of warlike retribution against enemies taken in battle.   Civilization and Christianity had not then established the modern treatment and disposal of prisoners.   Then they were held in bondage by their conquerors during life ; now their detention is but for a limited time ; then, they were individual, now they are national, property. Christianity, in this enlightened age, has taught conquerors to mitigate their severity toward the conquered ; and national policy has found it most expedient to make other disposition of them than holding them in bondage.

But the establishment and preservation of slavery in the south-west, are more immediately the objects

from it.   In Germany, and other countries of Europe, slaves were generally attached to the soil, as in Russia and Poland at the present day.   They were generally employed in tending cattle, and in conducting the business of agriculture."— *Tacitus de moribus Germanorum.*   " Among the ancient Germans, according to the same author, it was not uncommon for an ardent gamester to stake his personal liberty on a throw of the dice.   The latter species of slaves were alone considered as materials of commerce.   In England, now so tenacious of the rights of man, a species of slavery, similar to that among the ancient Germans, subsisted even to the end of the sixteenth century, as appears from a commission issued by Queen Elibeth in 1574.   Colliers and salters were not totally emancipated from every vestige of slavery till about the year 1750.   Before that period the sons of colliers could follow no business but that of their fathers, nor could they seek employment in any other mines than in those to which they were attached by birth. "

Encyclopedia Britan.

of my remarks.   If any people can repudiate with justice the charge of originating it, the Mississippians can do so.   The Spaniards introduced it here ; the first American settlers of this state found slaves attached to its soil, after the Spaniards resigned the country to the government of the United States, and they received them as a portion of the possessions, which fell into their hands by treaty or purchase.   Finding them here they retained them— for the slavery question, like many others in those days of innocence, had not been agitated—or they might have sent them after their Spanish masters.

There was, of course, nothing more natural and easy than the increase of this property.   The process of generation was too slow, however, and men commenced purchasing, not free men from slave ships, but Africans who were already slaves.   Virginia, where the lands were worn out, and slaves were numerous, and almost useless, afforded them facilities for purchasing ; emigrants from that and other slave-holding states also brought great numbers with them, and in a few years this species of property had accumulated to a great extent.   Planters' sons, and all new planters, must be supplied from the same fountain—losses by death and elopement must be made up, till, almost imperceptibly, slavery became firmly established here, and is now a state institution ; and Virginia, with the Carolinas and Georgia, and recently Kentucky, has become the great mart for slave purchasers from the southwest.

The increased demand for slaves led many farmers in Virginia, whose lands were unavailable, to turn their attention to raising slaves, if I may so term it, for the south-western market. Hence a nursery for slaves has been imperceptibly forming in that state, till now, by a sort of necessity, a vast amount of its capital is involved in this trade, the discontinuance of which would be as injurious in a pecuniary point of view, to those who raise them, as the want of the facilities which the trade affords, would be to the planter. Thus Virginia has become the field for the purchaser, and the phrase— " he is gone to Virginia to buy negroes," or " niggers," as is the elegant and equally common phraseology, is as often applied to a temporarily absent planter, as " he is gone to Boston to buy goods," to a New-England country merchant.

Negroes are transported here both by sea and land. Alexandria and Norfolk are the principal depots of slaves, previous to their being shipped. To these cities they are brought from the surrounding country, and sold to the slave-trader, who purchases them for about one-half or one-third less than he expects to obtain for them in the southern market. After the resident slave-dealer has collected a sufficient number, he places them under the care of an agent. They are then shipped for New-Orleans, with as comfortable accommodations as can be expected, where one or two hundred are congregated in a single merchant vessel. I have seen more than one hundred landing from a brig, on the Levée, in New-Orleans, in fine condition, looking as lively and hearty as though a sea voyage agreed well with them. They are transferred, if destined for the Mississippi market, to a steamboat, and landed at Natchez. The debarkation of a hundred slaves, of both sexes and all ages, is a novel spectacle to a northerner. Landing on the Levée, they proceed, each with his bundle, under the charge of their temporary master or conductor, toward the city, in a long straggling line, or sometimes in double files, in well-ordered procession, gazing about them with curiosity and wonder upon the new scenes opening before them, as they advance into the city, and speculating upon the advantages afforded as their home, by the beautiful country to which they find themselves transplanted. Nothing seems to escape their attention, and every few steps offer subjects for remark or laughter; for the risible muscles of the negro are uncommonly excitable.

On arriving on the "Hill," in view of the city, and obtaining a glimpse of the fine country spread out around them, their delight is very great. Full of the impression, which they early imbibe, that the south is emphatically the grave of their race, and daily having it held up before their imaginations at home, *in terrorem*, to keep them in the line of duty, if insubordinate, they leave home, as they proudly and affectionately term Virginia, with something of the feelings of the soldier, allotted to a "forlorn hope." It cannot be denied that many have died shortly after being brought into this country; but this was owing to indiscretion, in transporting them at the wrong season of the year—in the spring, after a winter spent at the north; or in autumn, during the prevalence, in former years, of the epidemics, which once were almost annual visitants of this country. Experience has taught those who introduce slaves, in late years, to bring them quite late in autumn. Hence, the two great causes of mortality being removed, the effects have, in a great measure, ceased; and slaves, when they arrive here, and gaze with surprise upon the athletic figures and gray heads of their fellows, who meet them at every step, as they advance into the city—find that they can live even in the south, and grow old on other plantations than those in " Ol' Wirginny." " I see no dead nigger yet, Jef."—" No—nor no coffin pile up neider in de street,"—said another of a gang of negroes passing through the streets, peering on all sides for these ominous signs of this " fatal" climate, as they trudged along to their quarters in the slave-market. This too common opinion of master and slave must soon be exploded, for it has now no foundation in fact. Passing through the city in procession, sometimes dressed in a new uniform, purchased for them in New-Orleans, but often in the brown rags in which they left Virginia, preceded by a large wagon, carrying the surplus baggage; they are marched beyond the city limits, within which, till recently, they were publicly sold, the marts being on nearly every street. Arriving at their quarters, which are usually old unoccupied buildings, and often tents or booths, pitched upon the common, beside some stream of water, and under the shade of trees, they resort, in the first place, to a general ablution, preparatory to being exposed for sale. The toilet arrangements of one hundred negroes, just from a long voyage, are a formidable affair. Both the rivers, Alpheus and Peneus, would hardly suffice for the process. Two or three days are consumed in it; after which, all appear in new, comfortable, uniform dresses, with shining faces, and refreshed after the fatigue of travel. They are now ready for inspection and sale. To this important period, the day of sale, they cheerfully look forward, manifesting not a little emulation to be "sol' fust." The interim between their arrival and sale—for they are not sold at auction, or all at once, but singly, or in parties, as purchasers may be inclined to buy—is passed in an *otium cum dignitate* of a peculiarly African character, involving eating, drinking, playing, and sleeping. The interval of ease enjoyed in the slave-market is an oasis of luxury in their existence, which they seldom know how to appreciate, if we may judge from the wishful manner in which they gaze upon gentlemen who enter the mart, as though anxious to put a period to this kind of enjoyment, so congenial to their feelings and temperament.

Probably two-thirds of the first slaves came into this state from Virginia; and nearly all now introduced, of whom there are several thousands annually, are brought from that state. Kentucky contributes a small number, which is yearly increasing; and since the late passage of the slave law in Missouri, a new market is there opened for this trade. It is computed that more than two hundred thou-

sand dollars' worth of slaves will be purchased in
Missouri this season, for the Natchez market. A
single individual has recently left Natchez with one
hundred thousand dollars, for the purpose of buying
up negroes in that state to sell in Mississippi.

The usual way of transporting slaves is by land,
although they are frequently brought round by sea;
but the last is the most expensive method, and therefore, to "bring them through," is accounted preferable. This is done by forming them into a caravan
at the place where they are purchased, and conducting them by land through the Indian nations to this
state. The route is for the most part through a continuous forest, and is usually performed by the negroes, on foot, in seven or eight weeks. Their personal appearance, when they arrive at Natchez, is
by no means improved, although they are usually
stouter and in better condition than when they leave
home, for they are generally well fed, and their
health is otherwise carefully attended to, while on
the route. Arrived within two or three miles of
Natchez, they encamp in some romantic spot near
a rivulet, and like their brethren transported by sea,
commence polishing their skins, and arraying themselves in the coarse but neat uniform, which their
master has purchased for them in Natchez.

A few Sabbaths ago, while standing before a village church in the country, my attention was drawn
to a long procession at the extremity of the street,
slowly approaching like a troop of wearied pilgrims.
There were several gentlemen in company, some
of them planters, who gazed upon the singular spec-

tacle with unusual interest. One sooty brown hue
was cast over the whole horde, by the sombre colour of their tattered garments, which, combined
with the slow pace and fatigued air of most of those
who composed it, gave to the whole train a sad and
funereal appearance. First came half a dozen boys
and girls, with fragments of blankets and ragged
pantaloons and frocks, hanging upon, but not covering their glossy limbs. They passed along in high
spirits, glad to be once more in a village, after their
weary way through the wilderness; capering and
practising jokes upon each other, while their even
rows of teeth, and the whites of their eyes—the
most expressive features in the African physiognomy—were displayed in striking contrast to their
ebony skins. These were followed by a tall mulatto, with high cheek-bones, and lean and hungry
looks, making rapid inroads into a huge loaf of bread,
whose twin brother was secured under his left arm.
A woman, very black, very short, and very pursy,
who breathed like a porpoise, and whose capacity
for rapid movement was equal to that of a puncheon,
trudged along behind, evidently endeavouring to
come up with the mulatto, as her eye was fixed very
resolutely on the spare loaf; but its owner strode
forward deliberately and with perfect impunity.
She was followed by another female, bearing an infant in her arms, probably born in the wilderness.
Close behind her came a covered wagon, from which
she had just descended to walk, drawn by two fine
horses, and loaded with young negroes, who were
permitted to ride and walk alternately on the jour-

ney. Behind the wagon, at a long distance, came an old patriarch, at least eighty years of age, bent nearly double with the weight of years and infirmity. By his side moved an old negress, nearly coeval with him, who supported her decrepit form by a staff. They were the venerable progenitors of the children and grandchildren who preceded them. This aged couple, who were at liberty to ride when they chose, in a covered wagon behind them, were followed by a mixed crowd of negroes of all ages, and of both sexes, with and without staff, hatless and barefooted. The office of the negro's hat is a mere sinecure—they love the warm sun upon their heads—but they like to be well shod, and that with boots, for the lower region of their limbs about the ancles is very sensitive. Behind these came a wretched cart, covered with torn, redpainted canvass, and drawn by a mule and a horse; —Sancho Panza's mule and Rosinante—I mean no insult to the worthy knight or his squire—if coupled together, would have made precisely such a pair. This vehicle contained several invalids, two of whom were reclining on a matrass laid along the bottom. Around it were many young slaves of both sexes, talking and marching along in gleeful mood. Two or three old people followed, one of whom, who walked with both hands grasping a long staff, stopped as he passed us, and with an air of affecting humility, and with his venerable forehead bowed to the earth, addressed us, "hab massas got piece 'bacca' for ol' nigger?" An old gentleman standing by, whose locks were whitened with the

snows of sixty winters, having first obtained leave to
do so from the owner of the drove, who, mounted on
a fine blooded horse, rode carelessly along behind
them, gave the old slave all he had about him,
which, fortunately for the petitioner, happened to
be a large quantity, and for which he appeared extremely grateful. Several other negroes, walking
along with vigorous steps, and another white conductor, with a couple of delicately limbed race-
horses, enveloped in broidered mantles, and ridden
by bright-eyed little mulatto boys, and two or three
leashes of hounds, led by a slave, completed the
train. They had been seven weeks on the road,
through the "nation," as the southern wilderness is
here termed—travelling by easy stages, and en-
camping at night. Old people are seldom seen in
these "droves." The young and athletic usually
compose them. But as in this instance, the old
people are sometimes allowed to come with the
younger portion of their families, as a favour; and
if sold at all, they are sold with their children, who
can take care of them in their old age, which they well
do—for negroes have a peculiarly strong affection
for the old people of their own colour. Veneration
for the aged is one of their strongest characteristics.

Nor are planters indifferent to the comfort of
their gray-headed slaves. I have been much affected at beholding many exhibitions of their kindly
feeling toward them. They always address them
in a mild and pleasant manner—as "Uncle," or
"Aunty"—titles as peculiar to the old negro and

x 2

negress, as " boy" and " girl," to all under forty
years of age. Some old Africans are allowed to
spend their last years in their houses, without doing
any kind of labour; these, if not too infirm, cultivate little patches of ground, on which they raise a
few vegetables—for vegetables grow nearly all the
year round in this climate—and make a little money
to purchase a few extra comforts. They are also
always receiving presents from their masters and
mistresses, and the negroes on the estate, the latter
of whom are extremely desirous of seeing the old
people comfortable. A relation of the extra comforts, which some planters allow their slaves, would
hardly obtain credit at the north. But you must
recollect that southern planters are men—and men
of feeling—generous and high minded, and possessing as much of the " milk of human kindness," as
the sons of colder climes—although they may have
been educated to regard that as right, which a different education has led northerners to consider
wrong.

" What can you do with so much tobacco ?" said
a gentleman—who related the circumstance to me
—on hearing a planter, whom he was visiting, give
an order to his teamster to bring two hogsheads of
tobacco out to the estate from the " Landing." " I
purchase it for my negroes; it is a harmless indulgence, which it gives me pleasure to afford them."

" Why are you at the trouble and expense of
having high-post bedsteads for your negroes ?" said
a gentleman from the north, while walking through

the handsome " quarters," or village for the slaves, then in progress on a plantation near Natchez—addressing the proprietor.

" To suspend their " bars" from, that they may not be troubled with musquitoes."

" Master, me would like, if you please, a little bit gallery, front my house." " For what, Peter?" " Cause, master, de sun too hot" (an odd reason for a negro to give,)" " dat side, and when he rain we no able to keep de door open." " Well, well, when the carpenter gets a little leisure you shall have one." A few weeks after I was at the plantation, and riding past the quarters one Sabbath morning, beheld Peter, his wife, and children, with his old father, all sunning themselves in their new gallery.

" Missus, you promise me a Chrismus gif'." " Well, Jane, there is a new calico frock for you." " It werry pretty, missus," said Jane, eyeing it at a distance without touching it, "but me prefer muslin, if you please ; muslin de fashion dis Chrismus." " Very well, Jane, call to-morrow and you shall have a muslin."

These little anecdotes are unimportant in themselves, but they serve to illustrate what I have stated above, of the kindness and indulgence of masters to their slaves. I could add many others, of frequent occurrence ; but these are sufficiently numerous for my purpose.

Probably of the two ways of bringing slaves here, that by land is preferable ; not only because attended with less expense, but by gradually advancing them into the climate, it in a measure pre-

cludes the effect which a sudden transition from one
state to the other might produce. All slaves,
however, are not brought here by negro traders.
Many of the planters prefer going on and purchasing
for themselves, for which purpose it is not unusual
for them to take on from twenty to forty and fifty
thousand dollars, lay the whole out in slaves, and
either accompany them through the wilderness
themselves on horseback, or engage a conductor.
By adopting this method they purchase them at a
much greater advantage, than at second-hand from
the professional trader, as slaves can be bought for
fifty per cent. less there, than after they are once
brought into this market. The number of slaves
introduced into the south-western market is annually increasing. Last year more than four thousand were brought into the state, one-third of whom
were sold in the Natchez market. The prices of
slaves vary with the prices of cotton and sugar. At
this time, when cotton brings a good price, a good
" field hand" cannot be bought for less than eight
hundred dollars, if a male ; if a female, for six hundred. " Body servants" sell much higher, one
thousand dollars being a common price for them.
Good mechanics sometimes sell for two thousand
dollars, and seldom for less than nine hundred.
Coachmen are high, and house servants are worth
at all times, from ten to thirty per cent. more than
field negroes. The usual price for a good seamstress, or nurse, is from seven hundred to qne thousand dollars. Children are valued in proportion to
their ages. An infant adds one hundred dollars to

the price of the mother ; and from infancy the children of the slaves increase in value about one hundred dollars for every three years, until they arrive at mature age.   All domestic slaves, or " house servants," which class includes coachmen, nurses, hostlers, gardeners, footmen, cooks, waiting-maids, &c., &c.—all indispensable to the *menage* of a wealthy planter—are always in great demand, and often sell at the most extravagant prices.   Some of these, born and raised in this climate, (acclimated as they are termed,) often sell for eighteen hundred and two thousand dollars apiece, of either sex. But these are exceptions, where the slave possesses some peculiarly valuable trait as a domestic.

Negro traders soon accumulate great wealth, from the immense profit they make on their merchandise. Certainly such a trade demands no trifling consideration.   If any of the worshippers of Mammon earn their gold, it is the slave-dealer.   One of their number, who is the great southern slave-merchant, and who, for the last fifteen years, has supplied this country with two-thirds of the slaves brought into it, has amassed a fortune of more than a million of dollars by this traffic alone.   He is a bachelor, and a man of gentlemanly address, as are many of these merchants, and not the ferocious, Captain Kidd looking fellows, we Yankees have been apt to imagine them.   Their admission into society, however, is not recognised.   Planters associate with them freely enough, in the way of business, but notice them no farther.   A slave trader is, nevertheless, very much like other men.   He is to-day a plain

farmer, with twenty or thirty slaves, endeavouring
to earn a few dollars from worn-out land, in some
old "homestead" among the Alleghanies; which,
with his slaves, he has inherited from his father.
He is in debt, and hears that he can sell his slaves
in Mississippi for twice their value in his own state.
If there is no harm in selling them to his next neighbour, and coming to Mississippi without them, he
feels that there can be no harm—nay, justice to his
creditors requires that he should place them in the
highest market—in bringing them into this state,
and selling them here. He rises in the morning,
gathers his slaves, prepares his wagons and horses,
takes one or two of his sons, or hires a neighbour,
who may add a few of his own to the stock, to accompany him; and, by and by, the caravan moves
slowly off toward the south and west. Seven or
eight weeks afterward, a drove of negroes, weary
and worn, from a long journey, are seen within two
or three miles of Natchez, turning from the high
road, to pitch their tents upon the green sward, beneath some wide-spreading tree. It is the caravan
from the Alleghanies. The ensuing morning a
bright array of white tents, and busy men moving
among them, excites the attention of the passer-by.
The figure of the old Virginia farmer, mingling
among his slaves, attracts the notice of a stranger. "Who is that old gentleman?" he inquires
of the southerner with whom he is riding in company. "A negro trader," is the reply. This is
the first step of the trader. He finds it profitable;
and if his inclinations prompt him, he will return

home, after selling his slaves, and buy, with ready money, from his neighbours, a few here and a few there, until he has a sufficient number to make another caravan, with which he proceeds a second time to the south-western market. He follows this trade from season to season, and does it conscientiously. He reasons as I have above stated; and if there is no harm in selling the first, there is none in selling the last. This is the metal of which a slave trader is moulded. The humane characteristics of the trade will be, of course, regulated by the tempers and dispositions of the individuals who engage in it.

XXXIX.

Slaves—Classes—Anecdotes—Negro instruction—Police—Natchez fencibles—Habitual awe of the negro for the white man—Illustrations—Religious slaves—Negro preaching—General view of slavery and emancipation—Conclusion.

THERE are properly three distinct classes of slaves in the south. The first, and most intelligent class, is composed of the domestic slaves, or "servants," as they are properly termed, of the planters. Some of these both read and write, and possess a great degree of intelligence: and as the negro, of all the varieties of the human species, is the most imitative, they soon learn the language, and readily adopt the manners, of the family to which they are attached. It is true, they frequently burlesque the latter, and select the high-sounding words of the former for practice—for the negro has an ear for euphony—which they usually misapply, or mis-pronounce.

"Ben, how did you like the sermon to-day ?" I once inquired of one, who, for pompous language and high-sounding epithets, was the Johnson of negroes.—" Mighty obligated wid it, master, de 'clusive 'flections werry distructive to de ignorum."

In the more fashionable families, negroes feel it their duty—to show their aristocratic breeding—to ape manners, and to use language, to which the common herd cannot aspire. An aristocratic negro, full of his master's wealth and importance, which he feels to be reflected upon himself, is the most aristocratic personage in existence. He supports his own dignity, and that of his own master, or "*family*," as he phrases it, which he deems inseparable, by a course of conduct befitting coloured gentlemen. Always about the persons of their masters or mistresses, the domestic slaves obtain a better knowledge of the modes of civilized life than they could do in the field, where negroes can rise but little above their original African state. So identified are they with the families in which they have been " raised," and so accurate, but rough, are the copies which they individually present, of their masters, that were all the domestic slaves of several planters' families transferred to Liberia, or Hayti, they would there constitute a by no means inferior state of African society, whose model would be

found in Mississippi. Each family would be a
faithful copy of that with which it was once connected : and should their former owners visit them
in their new home, they would smile at its resemblance to the original. It is from this class that the
friends of wisely-regulated emancipation are to seek
material for carrying their plans into effect.

The second class is composed of town slaves ;
which not only includes domestic slaves, in the
families of the citizens, but also all negro mechanics, draymen, hostlers, labourers, hucksters, and
washwomen, and the heterogeneous multitude of
every other occupation, who fill the streets of a busy
city—for slaves are trained to every kind of manual
labour. The blacksmith, cabinet-maker, carpenter,
builder, wheelwright,—all have one or more slaves
labouring at their trades. The negro is a third arm
to every working man, who can possibly save money enough to purchase one. He is emphatically
the "right-hand man" of every man. Even free
negroes cannot do without them : some of them
own several, to whom they are the severest masters.

"To whom do you belong ?" I once inquired of
a negro whom I had employed. "There's my
master," he replied ; pointing to a steady old negro,
who had purchased himself, then his wife, and subsequently his three children, by his own manual
exertions and persevering industry. He was now
the owner of a comfortable house, a piece of land,
and two or three slaves, to whom he could add one
every three years. It is worthy of remark, and
serves to illustrate one of the many singularities

characteristic of the race, that the free negro, who "buys his wife's freedom," as they term it, from her master, by paying him her full value, ever afterward considers her in the light of property.

" Thomas, you are a free man," I remarked to one who had purchased himself and wife from his master, by the profits of a poultry yard and vegetable garden, industriously attended to for many years, in his leisure hours and on Sundays. " You are a free man; I suppose you will soon have negroes of your own."

" Hi! Hab one now, master." " Who, Tom ?"— " Ol' Sarah, master." " Old Sarah! she is your wife." " She my nigger too; I pay master five hun'red dollar for her."

Many of the negroes who swarm in the cities are what are called " hired servants." They belong to planters, or others, who, finding them qualified for some occupation in which they cannot afford to employ them, hire them to citizens, as mechanics, cooks, waiters, nurses, &c., and receive the monthly wages for their services. Some steady slaves are permitted to " hire their own time;" that is, to go into town and earn what they can, as porters, labourers, gardeners, or in other ways, and pay a stipulated sum weekly to their owners, which will be regulated according to the supposed value of the slave's labour. Masters, however, who are sufficiently indulgent to allow them to " hire their time," are seldom rigorous in rating their labour very high. But whether the slave earn less or more than the specified sum, he must always pay that, and neither more nor less than that to his master at the close of each week, as the condition of this privilege. Few fail in making up the sum; and generally they earn more, if industrious, which is expended in little luxuries, or laid by in an old rag among the rafters of their houses, till a sufficient sum is thus accumulated to purchase their freedom. This they are seldom refused, and if a small amount is wanting to reach their value, the master makes it up out of his own purse, or rather, takes no notice of the deficiency. I have never known a planter refuse to aid, by peculiar indulgences, any of his steady and well-disposed slaves, who desired to purchase their freedom. On the contrary, they often endeavour to excite emulation in them to the attainment of this end. This custom of allowing slaves to "hire their time," ensuring the master a certain sum weekly, and the slave a small surplus, is mutually advantageous to both.

The majority of town servants are those who are hired to families by planters, or by those living in town who own more than they have employment for, or who can make more by hiring them out than by keeping them at home. Some families, who possess not an acre of land, but own many slaves, hire them out to different individuals; the wages constituting their only income, which is often very large. There are indeed few families, however wealthy, whose incomes are not increased by the wages of hired slaves, and there are many poor people, who own one or two slaves, whose hire enables them to live comfortably. From three to five dollars a week is the hire of a female, and seventy-five cents or a dollar a day for a male. Thus, contrary to the opinion at the north, families may have good servants, and yet not own one, if they are unable to buy, or are conscientious upon that ground, though there is not a shade of difference between hiring a slave, where prejudices are concerned, and owning one. Those who think otherwise, and thus compound with conscience, are only making a distinction without a difference. Northern people, when they come to this country, who dislike either to hire or purchase, often bring free coloured, or white servants (helps) with them. The first soon marry with the free blacks, or become too lofty in their conceptions of things, in contrasting the situation of their fellows around them, with their own, to be retained. The latter, if they are young and pretty, or even old and ugly, assume the fine lady at once, disdaining to be servants among slaves, and Hymen, in the person of some spruce overseer, soon fulfils their expectations. I have seen but one white servant, or domestic, of either sex, in this country, and this was the body servant of an Englishman who remained a few days in Natchez, during which time, John sturdily refused to perform a single duty of his station.

The expense of a domestic establishment at the south, would appear very great in the estimation of a New-Englander. A gardener, coachman, nurse, cook, seamstress, and a house-maid, are indispensable. Some of the more fashionable families add footmen, chamber-maids, hostler, an additional nurse,

if there be many children, and another seamstress.
To each of these officials is generally attached a
young neophyte, while one constantly stumbles
over useless little negroes scattered all about the
house and court-yard.   Necessary as custom has
made so great a number of servants, there seems
to be much less domestic labour performed in a
family of five, such perfect " eye-servants" are they,
than in a northern family, with only one " maid of
all work."   There are some Yankee "kitchen girls"
—I beg their ladyships' pardon for so styling them
—who can do more house-work, and do it better,
than three or four negro servants, unless the eye
of their mistress is upon them.   As nearly all manual labour is performed by slaves, there must be
one to each department, and hence originates a state
of domestic manners and individual character, which
affords an interesting field of contemplation to the
severer northerner.   The city slaves are distinguished as a class, by superior intelligence, acute-
ness, and deeper moral degradation.   A great proportion of them are hired, and, free from restraint
in a great degree, compared with their situations
under their own masters, or in the country, they
soon become corrupted by the vices of the city, and
in associating indiscriminately with each other, and
the refuse of the white population.   Soon the vices
of the city, divested of their refinement, become
their own unmasked.   Although they may once
have ranked under the first class, and possessed
the characteristics which designate the decent, well-
behaved domestic of the planter, they soon lose

their identity. There are of course exceptions to these characteristics, as also in the other classes. Some of these exceptions have come within my knowledge, of a highly meritorious character.

The third and lowest class consists of those slaves, who are termed "field hands."* Many of them rank but little higher than the brutes that perish, in the scale of intellect, and they are in general, as a class, the last and lowest link in the chain of the human species. Secluded in the solitude of an extensive plantation, which is their world, beyond whose horizon they know nothing—their walks limited by the "quarters" and the field—their knowledge and information derived from the rude gossip of their fellows, straggling runaways, or house servants, and without seeing a white person except their master or overseer, as they ride over the estate, with whom they seldom hold any conversation—they present the singular feature of African savages, disciplined to subordination, and placed in the heart of a civilized community. Mere change of place will not change the savage. Moral and intellectual culture alone, will elevate him to an equality with his civilized brethren. The African transplanted from the arid soil of Ebo, Sene-Gambia, or Guinea, to the green fields of America, with-

* "Field hands"—" Force"—"Hands"—"People," and "Niggers," are terms applied to the purchased labourers of a plantation; but "Slaves"—never. "Boys" is the general term for the men, and "women," for females. It is common to address a negro forty years of age as "boy." If much older he is called "daddy," or "uncle;" but "mister," or "man"—never. The females, in old age, become "aunty" "granny," or "old lady."

out mental culture, will remain still the wild African, though he may wield his ox-whip, whistle after his plough, and lift his hat, when addressed, like his more civilized fellows. His children, born on the plantation to which he is attached, and suffered to grow up as ignorant as himself, will not be one degree higher in the scale of civilization, than they would have been had they been born in Africa. The next generation will be no higher advanced; and though they may have thrown away the idols of their country, and been taught some vague notions of God and the Christian religion, they are in almost every sense of the word Africans, as rude, and barbarous, but not so artless, as their untamed brethren beyond the Atlantic. This has been, till within a few years, the general condition of " field hands" in this country, though there have been exceptions on some plantations highly honourable to their proprietors. Within a few years, gentlemen of intelligence, humanity, and wealth, themselves the owners of great numbers of slaves, have exerted themselves and used their influence in mitigating the condition of this class. They commenced a reformation of the old system, whose chief foundation was unyielding rigour, first upon their own plantations. The influence of their example was manifest by the general change which gradually took place on other estates. This reformation is still in progress, and the condition of the plantation slave is now meliorated, so far as policy will admit, while they remain in their present relation. But still they are, and by necessity, always will be, an inferior class to the two former. It is now popular to treat slaves with kindness ; and those planters who are known to be inhumanly rigorous to their slaves, are scarcely countenanced by the more intelligent and humane portion of the community. Such instances, however, are very rare ; but there are unprincipled men everywhere, who will give vent to their ill feelings, and bad passions, not with less good-will upon the back of an indented apprentice, than upon that of a purchased slave. Private chapels are now introduced upon most of the plantations of the more wealthy, which are far from any church ; Sabbath-schools are instituted for the black children, and Bible-classes for the parents, which are superintended by the planter, a chaplain, or some of the female members of the family. But with all these aids they are still, as I have remarked, the most degraded class of slaves ; and they are not only regarded as such by the whites, but by the two other classes, who look upon them as infinitely beneath themselves. It is a difficult matter to impress upon their minds moral or religious truths. They generally get hold of some undefined ideas, but they can go no farther. Their minds seem to want the capacity to receive intellectual impressions, nor are they capable of reasoning from the simplest principles, or of associating ideas. A native planter, who has had the management of between two and three hundred slaves, since he commenced planting, recently informed me, that if he

conveyed an order to any of his " field hands,"
which contained two ideas, he was sure it would not
be followed correctly.

"Dick," said he to one of them, " go to the car-
riage-house, and you will find a side-saddle and a
man's saddle there.   Put one of them on the roan
horse ; but don't put on the ladies' saddle, mind
you."   "Yes, master," said Dick, lifting his cap
very respectfully, and then posted off to the car-
riage-house ; whence he returned in a few minutes
with the roan caparisoned for a lady.

The last idea seems to thrust out the first.   I
have frequently tried experiments to ascertain how
far this was true of them in general, and have convinced myself, that it is very hard for the uneducated, rude field negro to retain more than a single
impression at a time.   A gentleman, who has been
a leading planter for the last twenty years, and who
has nearly one hundred slaves, of all ages, told me,
that, finding the established catechism too hard for
his slaves, he drew one up in manuscript himself,
as simply as he thought it could be done.   But a
few lessons convinced him that he must make another effort, on a plan still more simple : and he ac-
cordingly drew up a series of questions, each containing one idea, and no more ; for every question
involving two had always puzzled them.   Every
question he also made a *leading* one : this he found to
be absolutely necessary.   "Yet," he observed, " after
all my efforts, for many years past, to imbue the
minds—not of the children only, but of the parents,
who were all included in my list of catechumens—

with the plainest rudiments of Christianity, I do not think that I have one on my estate, who comprehends the simplest principle connected with the atonement."

One of these negroes, after a long course of drilling, was asked, "In whose image were you made?" "In de image ob de debil, master," was his prompt reply.

The restrictions upon slaves are very rigorous in law, but not in fact. They are forbidden to leave their estates without a written "pass," or some letter or token, whereby it may appear that they are proceeding by authority. This is a wise regulation, to which I have before alluded; and if its spirit was properly entered into by the community, it would be the best means for public security that could be adopted.

Patrols are organized in the several counties and towns, whose duty it is to preserve order, and apprehend all negroes without passes. This body of men consists of four or five citizens, unarmed, unless with riding whips, headed by one of their number as captain. They are appointed monthly by a justice of the peace, and authorized to visit negro cabins, "quarters," and all places suspected to contain negroes, or unlawful assemblies of slaves; and all whom they may find strolling about, without a "pass," they are empowered to punish upon the spot, with "any number of lashes not exceeding fifteen," or take them to prison. They go out on duty once a week in the towns and villages; but it is considered a bore, and performed reluctantly.

But there is no deficiency of energy and activity in case of any actual alarm.   Soon after the South-Hampton tragedy, during the Christmas holydays, the public mind was excited by a vague rumour that this drama was to be reacted here, as it was known that some of the negroes, supposed to be engaged in it, had been brought out and sold in this state.   During this excitement the patrols were very vigilant.   On the high roads they were increased to one hundred armed and mounted men. But this alarm was groundless, and very soon subsided.

The fencibles—a volunteer military corps in Natchez, composed of the first young gentlemen of the city, and now commanded by the late chancellor of the state—the best disciplined and finest looking body of men west of the Alleghanies, constitute the military police of that city.   They are also the "firemen;" and a more efficient phalanx to battle with a conflagration, cannot be found, even in New-York or Boston.   Patrols go out merely to preserve the peace of the neighbourhood from any disturbance from drunken negroes, rather than to guard against insurrectionary movements.

Though the south has little to apprehend from her coloured population, yet many bold plans, indicating great genius in their originators, have been formed by slaves for effecting their freedom.   But farther than mere plans, or violent acts, of short continuance, they will hardly be able to advance.   The negro is wholly destitute of courage.   He possesses an animal instinct, which impels him, when roused, to the performance of the most savage acts. He is a being of impulse, and cowardice is a principle of his soul, as instinctive as courage in the white man. This may be caused by their condition, and without doubt it is. But whatever may be the cause, the effect exists, and will ever preclude any apprehension of serious evil from any insurrectionary combination of their number. The spirit of insubordination will die as soon as the momentary excitement which produced it has subsided; and negroes never can accomplish any thing of a tragic nature, unless under the influence of extraordinary temporary excitement. The negro has a habitual fear of the white man, which has become a second nature; and this, combined with the fearless contempt of the white man for him, in his belligerent attitude, will operate to prevent any very serious evil resulting from their plans.

A northerner looks upon a band of negroes, as upon so many *men*. But the planter, or southerner, views them in a very different light; and armed only with a hunting whip or walking-cane, he will fearlessly throw himself among a score of them, armed as they may be, and they will instantly flee with terror. There is a peculiar tone of authority, in which an angry master speaks to his slaves, which, while they are subordinate, cowers them, and when they are insubordinate, so strong is the force of habit, it does not lose its effects. The very same cause which enables him to keep in subjection fifty or a hundred negroes on his estate, through the instrumentality of his voice, or mere presence, operates so soon as the momentary intoxication of insurrectionary excitement is over—if it does not check its first exhibition—to bring them into subjection. Nor do I speak unadvisedly or lightly, when I say that a band of insurgent slaves will be more easily intimidated and defeated by half the number of planters, with whips or canes, and their peculiarly authoritative voices, than by an equal number of northern soldiers armed *cap à pie*. Fear, awe, and obedience in relation to his master, are interwoven into the very nature of the slave. They are the main-spring of all his actions; a part and portion of himself, and no extraneous circumstances can enable him to rise superior to their influence.

I could relate many facts illustrative of what I have stated above, respecting the influence of habitual or natural obedience upon the negro. The runaway will sometimes suffer himself to be taken by a white boy not a third of his size. Recently, about midnight, a lady saw, by the light of the moon, a tall negro enter her gallery. She immediately arose, observed him through the window more distinctly as he was peering about with a light step, and satisfied that he was a negro, she threw up the window, and cried "stop, sir! stop!" in the tone of authority peculiar to all who have had any thing to do with negroes. He at first started, and made a motion to run, but on a repetition of the command he submissively obeyed, and suffered himself to be taken by the lady's coachman, whom she called up—

the runaway, as he proved to be, standing till he came and bound him, without moving a limb. This conduct betrayed no uncommon nerve or resolution in the lady, for southern ladies would laugh at the idea of being afraid of a negro. The readiness of the black coachman to arrest his fellow slave, goes far also toward illustrating the views which the slaves themselves entertain of their condition. But this is illustrated still more forcibly by the following incident. I was sitting, not long since, on the portico of a house in the country, engaged in conversation, when an old negro entered the front gate, leading by the arm a negro boy about sixteen years of age. "Ah," said the gentleman with whom I was talking, "there is my runaway!" The old man approached the steps, which led to the portico, and removing his hat, as usual with slaves on addressing a white person, said, "master, I done bring John home. I cotch him skulkin 'bout in Natchy: I wish master sell him where ol' nigger nebber see him more, if he runaway 'gain: he disgrace he family; his ol' mammy cry 'nough 'bout it when she hearn it."

This couple were father and son. A "good negro," in the usual acceptation of the term, feels that there is a kind of disgrace attached to himself and family, if any one of them becomes a runaway.

A negro lad, who had absconded for a few days' play, was apprehended and led by his overseer through the streets on his way home, not long ago, when an old negro wash-woman standing by, exclaimed on seeing him, " La, me ! who 'tink he 'gin so young to act bad !" I will relate an instance of their readiness to arrest each other.

" Missus, dere's a runaway back de garden," said hastily a young negress, as a party were sitting down to the tea table of a lady at whose house I was visiting. " Let me go catch him," " let me go missus," said the waiters, and they could hardly be kept in the hall. Permission was given for one to go, who in a few minutes returned, leading up to the hall-door a stout half-naked negro whom he had caught prowling about the premises. " Here de nigger, missus," said he exultingly, as though he himself belonged to another race and colour.

Negroes are very sensitive. They are easily excited, and upon no subject so much so perhaps, as religion. They are, particularly the females, of a very religious temperament, strongly inclining to superstition. Unable to command their feelings, they give vent to the least emotion in the loudest clamours. They are thereby persuaded that they are converted, and apply for admission into the church in great numbers. Many of them are perhaps truly pious. But the religion of most of them is made up of shouting, which is an incontrovertible argument or proof, with them, of conversion. This shouting is not produced generally by the sermon, for few are able to understand a very plain discourse, of which every sentence will contain words wholly incomprehensible to them. But they always listen with great attention, and so they would do were the sermon delivered in any other tongue. A few of the more intelligent and pious negroes, who can understand most of the sermon, perhaps become affected, and unable, like their better disciplined masters, to controul their feelings, give vent to them in groans and shouts. Those about them catch the infection, and spread it, till the whole negro portion of the audience in the gallery, becomes affected ostensibly by religious feeling, but really by a kind of animal magnetism, inexplicable and uncontrollable.

The majority of the religious slaves are of the Methodist denomination, some of which sect may be found on every plantation in the country, but few of them are practical Christians. They are apt to consider the name as the thing. But I have met with individual exceptions, which reflect honour upon their race, and which I now recall with pleasure. One of the most touching and eloquent prayers I have ever heard, I recently listened to from the lips of an old negro, (who sometimes preached to his fellow slaves,) as he kneeled by the pallet of a dying African, and commended in an appeal,— which for beautiful simplicity and pathos, is seldom equalled—his departing spirit to his God.

I have observed that they are seldom influenced by the principles of religion in their individual conduct. Many, who are regarded by their brother Africans as "shining lights," drink ardent spirits freely and without compunction. "Ben, why do you drink whiskey?" I inquired of an old "member," who was very fond of indulging in this favourite southern potation for all classes—-"It no sin master—don't de Bible say, what enter into de mouth no defile de man?" This was unanswerable.

I asked another, "why he swore?" "Cause, master, nigger no keep de debil down he throat, when oxen so bad."

Negro preaching has obtained here formerly, but the injudicious course taken at the north by those who are friendly to the cause of emancipation, but who do not evince their good feelings in the wisest manner, has led planters to keep a tighter rein upon their slaves. And negro preaching, among the removal of other privileges which they once enjoyed, is now interdicted. It is certainly to be regretted that the steps taken by those who desire to do away slavery, should have militated against their views, through their own unadvised measures, and placed the subject of their philanthropic efforts in a less desirable state than formerly.

The more I see of slavery, the more firmly I am convinced that the interference of our northern friends, in the present state of their information upon the subject, will be more injurious than beneficial to the cause. The physician, like Prince Hohenloe, might as reasonably be expected to heal, with the Atlantic between himself and his patient's pulse, or to use a juster figure, an individual, wholly ignorant of a disease, might as well attempt its cure, as for northerners, however sincere their exertions, or however pure their intentions may be, under existing circumstances, to meliorate the condition of the coloured population of the south.

When the chains of the slave are broken in pieces, it must be by a southern hand—and thousands of southern gentlemen are already extending their arms, ready to strike the blow. And when experience shall tell them the time is at hand, then,

"Thy chains are broken, Africa, be free!" shall be shouted from the south to the north; and

> ————————————winds and waves
> Shall waft the tidings to the land of slaves,
> Proclaim on Guinea's coast, by Gambia's side,
> As far as Niger rolls his eastern tide,
> "Thy chains are broken, Africa, be free!"

I will conclude my remarks upon this interesting subject, with some valuable reflections from another pen. "It avails but little to deprecate now," says the able writer whom I quote, "and even to denounce with holy zeal, the iniquity of those who first established the relations of master and slave in the then colonies of Great Britain, but now United States of America. These relations have been sanctioned by law and long usage, and interwoven with the institutions of the two countries: they cannot be cancelled at once by any law, founded on justice and equity, which should place at once either or both of the parties in a less advantageous position, than the one which they held when connected by the tie of master and slave. However opposed to slavery in the abstract, and alive to its numerous evils in practice; and with whatever zeal we may advocate emancipation, we ought ever, in this, as in all other kinds of reform, political as well as moral, to act with that wise discretion, which should

make the present work a means of future and permanent good.   It should be steadily borne in mind,
therefore, that immediate, unconditional emancipation, while it is detrimental to the master, does no
immediate good to the manumitted slave.   It is not
the boon, so much as a beginning, a hope, and a promise of future good to the African; it is simply one
of the means, a most important and paramount one,
indeed, for acquiring the blessings of rational liberty;
but it is not the blessing itself.   It becomes, therefore, the bounden duty, on every principle of equity
and religion, of those who, either of their own free
will, or by menaces to the master, give emancipation to the slave, to carry out what they have begun,
to realize what they have promised, to fulfil the
hopes which they have raised.   Failing to do this,
and simply content with severing the relations between master and slave, they become, themselves,
the most cruel tyrants, the most unjust men.   They
have hurried on, by their blind zeal, a crisis, which
they are either unable, or unwilling, or know not
how, to turn to the best account, for the cause of
humanity, civilization, and religion.

Previous—and essential preliminaries, to any attempt at emancipation, either by direct advocacy of
the measure in particular quarters, or by legislative
enactments, where such are constitutional and legal
—a full inquiry ought to be instituted under the following heads :—

I. The actual condition of the slaves, which will
include the kind and amount of labour which they

are bound to perform, the treatment which they experience when at work, and the degree of attention paid to their physical wants and moral nature, as to lodging, clothing, food, amusements, and instruction.

II. The immediate effects of unconditional emancipation, on the coloured freeman. Under this head should be investigated his capability, under the circumstances, of providing for himself and family; and of his acting the part of a good neighbour, and a useful, productive citizen.

III. The compatibility of the whites and blacks, the former masters and slaves, and their descendants respectively, living together after emancipation in the same community, with due regard to the feelings, interests, dispositions, and wants of each class.

IV. The measures to be adopted for the interests of each, in case of such incompatibility being evident and impossible to be overcome. The first branch of inquiry results favourably to the cause of humanity, as far as the West Indies are concerned. The state of the slave population in the United States is even still more favourable in the main : and if the comparisons instituted between the slaves in the islands and the operatives in England, have resulted in favour of the superior comforts of the former, I feel very sure that, when made between the latter and the American slaves, they will exhibit these in a still more advantageous position.

All this, however, while it diminishes the fears of the philanthropist, ought not to relax his efforts for a future and gradual melioration. It simply illustrates things as they are, and does not positively show how they should be.

The facts hitherto collected under the second branch of inquiry, are not encouraging. The third head presents a very unsatisfactory aspect to the friends of emancipation, and of the negro race. The problem has not been solved; or if partially so, it goes to show, that there is an incompatibility between the two races, and that both are sufferers by their sojourn in the same land, even though both should be free nominally, and, in the eye of the law, equal. A glance at the condition of the free states of the union, as they are called, in this respect, exhibits the proofs of this condition of things. And so long as these startling anomalies exist—freedom without its enjoyments, equality without its social privileges—we really do not see how the people of the free states can pretend, with any show of propriety or justice, even had they the power by law and constitution, to meddle with the relations between master and slave, in the slave-holding states. They have the right, which all men ought to have, of discussing freely any and every important question in ethics, jurisprudence, and political economy, but not to give their conclusion a direct and offensive application to those portions of their fellow-citizens or fellow-men, to whom they have not yet furnished a clear and satisfactory example, and rule of conduct in the case specially adverted to.

Still more do the difficulties of the subject increase, if the last branch of inquiry has not been satisfactorily carried out—if the necessity of separation of the two races, be denied; or, if admitted, the means of accomplishing it be opposed and reviled, as either impracticable or unjust.   I am myself in favour of emancipation; but this is a conclusion which it seems to us ought to be carried into effect, only after a due consideration of the premises, and with a full knowledge of the remoter consequences, and ability to make these consequences correspond with the claims of justice and peace in the beginning; and the best and permanent interests of the two races, ultimately.   Have those who advocate immediate and unconditional emancipation weighed well these several branches of inquiry on this momentous subject?   It is to be feared, indeed, by their language and conduct, that they have not.   They should beware, while they are denouncing the slave-holder, that they do not themselves incur a still more fearful responsibility, and make themselves answerable for jeoparding, if not actually dissolving, the Union, and encouraging civil, perhaps servile war, with all its horrors and atrocities."

APPENDIX.

NOTE A.—*Title-page—Mississippi.*

Desirous of embodying in the appendix to this work, whatever of an interesting nature relates to the South-west, the author has compiled, principally from the American Almanac for 1835, the following STATISTICAL TABLES of Mississippi, presenting that growing state in a variety of interesting views :—

MISSISSIPPI.

Latitude of Natchez, ... 31° 34´ North.
Longitude in degrees . . . . . . 91 24´ 42´´ West.
" in time, ... 6 5 38.8
Distance from Washington, 1146 miles.

h. m. s.

Relative size of Mississippi, 9.	Extent in square miles, 45,760.

NUMBER OF INHABITANTS TO A SQUARE MILE.

In 1810.	In 1820.	In 1830.
.9	1.6	3

RELATIVE POPULATION.

In 1810.			In 1820.			In 1830.		
Free	Slave	Total	Free	Slave	Total	Free	Slave	Total
20	9	19	24	10	21	24	10	22

RATE OF INCREASE OF FREE AND SLAVE POPULATION.

From 1800 to 1810.			From 1810 to 1820.			From 1820 to 1830.		
Free	Slave	Total	Free	Slave	Total	Free	Slave	Total
334	389.7	356				66.4	100	81

POPULATION IN 1810.

Free	Slaves	No. of free to 1 slave	Total
23,264	17,088	1.35	40,352

IN 1820.

42,634	32,814	1.29	75,488

IN 1830.

70,962	65,659	1.08	136,621

IMPORTS AND EXPORTS IN THE YEAR ENDING

Value of Imports	Value of Exports

Tonnage, 925 Tons.

GOVERNMENT.

	Salary.
HIRAM G. RUNNELS, governor; (term of office expires Nov. 1835.)	$2,500
DAVID DICKSON, secretary of state,	1,200
JAMES PHILLIPS, state treasurer,	1,200
JOHN H. MALLORY, auditor of public accounts,	1,200

GEN. BRISCOE, president of the senate :—ADAMAM L. BIRGAMAN, speaker of the house of representatives. The legislature meets, once in two years, on the 4th Monday in November.

JUDICIARY.

High Court of errors and appeals.

	Salary.
WILLIAM L. SHARKEY, presiding judge,	$2,000
COTESWORTH P. SMITH, judge,	2,000
DAVID W. WRIGHT, do.	2,000
MATTHEW D. PATTON, attorney general,	1,000

This court, which has no jurisdiction, except what properly belongs to a court of errors and appeals, holds two sessions annually, at Jackson, commencing on the first Monday in January and July.

Superior court of chancery.

EDWARD TURNER, chancellor, *Salary* $2,000

This court, which has jurisdiction over all matters, pleas, and complaints whatsoever, belonging to or cognizable in a court of equity, holds two sessions annually, beginning on the first Monday in January and July.

Circuit court.

1st district,	ALEXANDER MONTGOMERY,	judge,
2d do.	JAMES SCOTT,	do.
3d do.	A. M. KEEGAR,	do.
4th do.		do.
5th do.	J. J. H. MORRIS,	do.
6th do.	JAMES F. TROTTER,	do.

The state is divided into six districts or circuits, and one judge and a district attorney are chosen by the electors of each district ; and a circuit court is held in each county twice every year. It has original jurisdiction in civil cases in which the sum in controversy exceeds $50.

BANKS.

Exhibition of their state on the 7th of January, 1834, as laid before Congress, June 24, 1834.

NAME.	Capital stock paid in.	Bills in circulation.	Specie.
Planters' bank, Natchez, Estimated situation of b'ks from which no returns were received.	$2,666,805 45	1,510,426 15	113,220 47
Agricultural bank of Miss. Natchez. State bank of Mississippi, Natchez.	1,000,000 00	590,000 00	43,000 00
Total	$ 3,666,805 45	2,100,426 15	156,220 47

Statement of the banks, as given by a correspondent, under date of August 10, 1834.

NAME.	Place.	Capital.	Branches of Planters' bank.	
Planters' bank,	Natchez,	$4,000,000	Vicksburg,	$500,000
			Port Gibson,	500,000
			Woodville,	500,000
			Manchester,	300,000
			Monticello,	200,000
			Columbus,	200,000
			Jackson,	100,000
			Total of brn's,	$2,300,000
Agricultural bank.	Natchez,	$4,000,000		
	Total	7,000,000		

The capitals of the branches constitute a part of the ($4,000,000) capital of the Planters' bank.

A rail-road is being surveyed this summer from Natchez to

Jackson, for which a charter will be granted at the next meeting of the legislature.

SUMMARY.

The governor of Mississippi is elected by the people. Term begins November, 1833—expires November, 1835. Duration of the term two years. Salary $2,500.

Senators, 11. Term of years, three. Representatives 36. Term of years, one. Total, senators and representatives, 47. Pay per day, $3.

Electors of president and vice-president are chosen by general ticket.

Seat of government, Jackson.

Time of holding elections, in May.

Time of meeting of the legislature, fourth Monday in November, biennially.

Mississippi admitted into the union in 1817.

Note B. *Page* 27.

For the following meteorological table, the author is indebted to the politeness of Henry Tooley Esq. a scientific gentleman who has been a resident of Natchez the third of a century, and who has during the greater part of his life kept a daily register of the weather. The exposure of his thermometer was unexceptionable, and always the same. The tables in the author's possession from various other sources, date back to the year 1799, affording an uninterrupted series of meteorological observations in this climate, down to the present period. An abstract from these tables would be too elaborate for a work of this nature, and would not, indeed, convey any farther important information upon this climate, than is contained in the accompanying abstract from the tables of Dr. Tooley, for the past ten years. The general temperature, though varying much from day to day, is so regular, one year with another, that a meteorological table for any one period of ten years will answer, with slight variations, for almost any other term of the same duration.

The thermometer was examined at 5 A. M. and at 4 P. M. for the extremes.

ANNUAL RESULTS OF METEROLOGICAL OBSERVATIONS MADE AT NATCHEZ IN N. Lat. 31° 34′ Long. 91° 24′ 42″ W.

Year.	Mean. temp.		Warmest.		Coldest.		Number of days.				
			5 A. M.	4 P. M.	5 A. M.	4 P. M.	Clear.	Cloudy.	Rainy.	Snow.	Sleet.
1825	60	$81\frac{1}{6}$	$71\frac{1}{12}$	$81\frac{1}{3}$	$49\frac{1}{2}$	$63\frac{5}{12}$	178	88	99		
1826	$63\frac{1}{4}$	75	$74\frac{1}{3}$	$80\frac{3}{4}$	$48\frac{1}{4}$	$64\frac{9}{12}$	134	120	110	1	
1827	$63\frac{1}{2}$	74	$74\frac{5}{6}$	$73\frac{1}{3}$	$51\frac{1}{3}$	$66\frac{1}{4}$	151	126	88		
1828	64	76	$64\frac{1}{3}$	$77\frac{1}{6}$	$53\frac{1}{2}$	$65\frac{3}{4}$	133	121	112		
1829	54	65	$72\frac{2}{3}$	$76\frac{1}{3}$	$48\frac{1}{12}$	$61\frac{2}{3}$	116	124	134	1	
1830	$62\frac{1}{3}$	74	$72\frac{1}{4}$	$80\frac{3}{4}$	$48\frac{1}{2}$	$66\frac{7}{12}$	161	121	77	2	1
1831	57	$69\frac{1}{2}$	$71\frac{1}{4}$	$77\frac{1}{2}$	$44\frac{1}{2}$	$60\frac{1}{3}$	187	141	34	3	
1832	$61\frac{5}{6}$	$74\frac{1}{2}$	$68\frac{1}{6}$	$84\frac{1}{3}$	47	$64\frac{7}{12}$	185	146	23	2	
1833	$60\frac{1}{2}$	72	$71\frac{1}{12}$	$78\frac{1}{2}$	$48\frac{1}{2}$	65	177	138	50		
1834	$60\frac{1}{2}$	$73\frac{1}{4}$	$73\frac{9}{12}$	$82\frac{1}{3}$	47	65	166	151	46	2	
to June 1835	$21\frac{1}{3}$	$26\frac{1}{4}$	$28\frac{1}{2}$	$30\frac{1}{6}$	15	$22\frac{2}{3}$	62	69	18	2	

1835.

Months.	Mean. temp.		Warm,		Cold,		Cl'r.	Cl'y.	Rain	snow	Sleet
Jan.	46⅔	57	69	64	32	48	12	16	3		
Feb.	36⅓	50	59	61	10	28	13	11	3	1	
Mar.	46	65⅔	68	74	32	50	14	11	5	1	
April,	57⅔	65	71	75	46	64	9	18	3		
May,	69⅔	77⅓	76	88	60	82	14	13	4		
June,											
	21⅓	26¼	28 7/12	30⅙	15	22⅓	62	69	18	2	

Mean temp. obtained by adding mean of months together, and then dividing by the number of months.

1834.

Months.	Mean. temp.		Warm,		Cold,		Cl'r.	Cl'y.	Rain	snow	Sleet
Jan.	29⅔	50	67	74	14	27	5	12	11	2	1
Feb.	52⅔	65	72	73	32	52	13	14	1		
Mar.	47	67	69	78	39	62	9	17	5		
April,	61	76	67	83	49	74	17	11	2		
May,	66	89½	76	93	54	63	14	12	5		
June,	76⅔	87	80	93	71	87	15	15			
July,	77	89⅔	82	83	74	91	21	10			
Aug.	77⅔	90½	83	98	73	89	18	12	1		
Sept.	69⅓	70	77	77	57	77	13	10	7		
Oct.	66½	75½	76	87	41	56	19	9	3		
Nov.	55⅓	63⅔	69	77	31	51	10	15	5		
Dec.	47½	55⅔	67	72	35	52	12	14	5		
	60½	73¼	73 9/12	82⅓	47 1/12	65 1/12	166	151	45	2	1

1833.

Months.	Mean. temp.		Warm,		Cold,		Cl'r.	Cl'y.	Rain	snow	Sleet
Jan.	53½	37½	68	74	31	51	9	17	5		
Feb.	46¾	60	59	72	38	56	11	9	8		
Mar.	51	66	64	71	25	37	13	5	13		
April,	63	76	73	65	55	66	13	16	1		
May,	70	82	76	84	66	73	15	13	3		
June,	75	87	80	92	65	84	18	11	1		
July,	63⅔	89⅔	81	93	69	89	22	9			
Aug.	74	89½	80	93	69	88	19	12			
Sept.	74	86⅓	79	94	62	81	15	12	3		
Oct.	58	69⅔	68	70	37	56	18	8	5		
Nov.	49	63	69	71	30	45	15	11	4		
Dec.	48⅓	58	61	62	36	53	9	15	7		
	60½	72	71 1/12	78 5/12	48 7/12	64 11/12	177	138	50		

The author has been favoured with the following medical report drawn up by a physician of Natchez, who has had long experience in the diseases of this climate.

MEDICAL REPORT.

Return of deaths within the city of Natchez, from 1st June 1822, to first June 1835—including thirteen years :

The population of Natchez is ordinarily between three and four thousand—lessened, probably, in the summer season, from 500 to 1000. With this number of residents, the mortality cannot be regarded as very large. On the contrary, few places of equal magnitude, either north or south, can boast a greater degree of general health than this city. Since the year 1825, it will be perceived, it has been growing gradually healthier—with the exception of the last two or three years,—when, owing in a great measure to the severity of the winter season, a great proportion of the sickness and mortality has occurred in the winter and spring months. Indeed take a period of seven years—from 1825 to 1833, and we challenge any southern or western city, with the same amount of population, to show a less number of deaths—especially in the summer season, than the city of Natchez. The bill of mortality has been considerably augmented of late, by that appalling and sweeping epidemic, which increased in strength, and doubled its roll of victims in proportion as it travelled south—together with small pox and intemperance—for both of which nature has provided specific remedies—but which certain classes continue still to avoid, and will hence continue to suffer and die in spite of Jenner and the temperance societies, as long as incredulity shall exist, and distilleries pour forth their floods of poison in the land. Most of those with the last mentioned diseases, it would seem, have been inmates of the public hospital.

On an average, about $\frac{1}{5}$ to $\frac{1}{4}$ of the deaths annually occur from bilious remittent, congestive and typhus fever. The yellow fever, be it known, has not appeared here as an epidemic for the last five or six years, and may be regarded as quite extinct in the city. Owing to the careless and imperfect manner in which the returns have generally been made—and this we are sorry to say, is too often the case—a large portion of the deaths are from unknown diseases—as to which in regard to the age of the subjects, and the colour, which in this country is somwhat important, we are left generally in the dark. By giving the subject some considerable attention, however, we have been enabled to preserve a degree of accuracy in the proportion, and the general result, we believe, is nearly, if not specifically correct.

The whole number of deaths by fever, during 13 years, is 511 ; cholera 107, consumption 100, intemperance 58, small pox 45, infantile 49, dysentery 30, delirium tremens 23, drowned 10, murder 10, old age 10, suicide 4, unknown 205.

The remainder, which we purposely omit, are by ordinary diseases, which are not peculiar to any clime or season. We have examined a meterological table, kept with a considerable degree of accuracy for the last 10 years : but it presents nothing peculiar—and its details are too minute and comprehensive for our present object. We notice, however, a greater proportion of " cloudy and rainy " days than could be expected in this " sunny clime," while the average degree of heat is by no means greater than in latitudes somewhat farther north. The greatest range of heat is 98, and the greatest cold 10°.—This we are inclined to believe, is not strictly correct, as we have twice, within a few years, seen the thermometer as low as 10° in the neighbourhood of New Orleans.

DEATHS IN EACH MONTH.

Months and years	1822	1823	1824	1825	1826	1827	1828	1829	1830	1831	1832	1833	1834	1835
January		7	4	5	7	5	4	7	5	4	5	4	14	17
February		4	10	7	6	2	7	4	6	5	6	5	16	16
March		8	5	1	3	4	3	7	6	8	3	11	30	18
April		12	6	3	4	4	5	7	2	6	5	8	22	25
May		11	6	5	9	3	6	6	3	11	9	16	19	32
June	9	15	8	6	7	3	9	5	4	6	3	27	44	
July	33	15	19	4	11	4	5	3	7	5	4	9	27	
August	29	102	14	17	9	5	2	6	16	4	3	11	14	
September	28	155	13	33	10	6	12	19	9	4	9	15	17	
October	22	56	8	48	5	26	9	21	10	5	13	30	20	
November	12	8	5	15	4	16	9	16	7	4	10	10	26	
December	6	7	4	4	12	8	3	2	5	12	8	13	20	
Total	139	400	102	148	87	86	74	103	80	74	75	159	269	108—1904
Males	119	315	80	128	62	76	56	80	55	57	55	124	193	79—1479
Females	20	85	22	20	25	10	18	23	25	17	20	35	76	29—425

Note C—*Page* 90.

For the following valuable paper upon the cultivation of cotton, the author is indebted to the kindness of Dr. J. W. Monett, of Mississippi, already well known to the medical world by his treatises published at the north upon the prevailing epidemics of this climate.

THE COTTON CROP.

" Having finished or relinquished the miscellaneous business of winter, such as clearing, building, ditching, and splitting rails, the hands are actively employed in making preparation for another crop. The first thing to be attended to, is the repairing of all the fences, with the light force, such as boys and women ; while the strong hands are employed in chopping, and log-rolling in the new grounds. These operations are commenced generally about the middle of February, and continued two or three weeks, unless the farm is mostly new ; in which case the clearing of the new ground continues four or five weeks until it is time to plant corn, generally from the first to the twentieth of March. During all this time several ploughs, in a well opened place, are kept constantly running (unless prevented by rain), in "listing up" corn and cotton ground. The distance between the ridges for cotton varies according to the strength of the soil, and the consequent size to which the plant grows. In the rich bottoms the distance between the middle or tops of the ridges must be from five to seven feet ; while in the thin upland soil, a space of three or four feet is amply sufficient. In the latter soil, the cotton plant attains the height of three or four feet, and branches laterally about half that distance. But in the rich alluvial lands, the stalk not unfrequently shoots up to six and eight feet, and branches so as to interlock with the other rows six or eight feet apart.

Early in April, and sometimes even in the last days of March, the cotton-planting commences. To open the ridges, a narrow plough is run by one horse along the middle of the ridge, so as to open a narrow shallow furrow, in the mellow ground first ploughed. Immediately behind the opening plough, follows the sower, with his sack of cotton-seed suspended from his neck, walking at the same pace with the plough-man before. At every step or two he throws the seed so as to strew it four or five feet

ahead in the furrow, at each dash of the hand.   The quantity
sown is often unnecessarily large, being frequently twenty times
more numerous than the stalks permitted to remain growing.
This profusion of seed is sown for the purpose of obtaining a
" good stand," after allowing for defective seeds as well as some
which may not be covered, and others that may be covered too
deep, and also for many plants that may sicken and die after they
have vegetated and come above the ground.   This latter circumstance frequently occurs : a stand may be amply sufficient when
first up, but from drought, excessive rain, or chilling winds, one
half in the rows, and sometimes whole acres together, die with
the " rust," " sore skin," or " yellow fever."

After the sower another hand follows closely with a light horse
harrow, drawn over the furrow, for the purpose of covering the
seed.   This throws in the loose earth over the seed, and covers
them so lightly that often one-third of them are still visible, yet
this covering is sufficient, for no seeds require less covering than
cotton-seed.   They will sprout and take root, when left on the
surface of the ground, if a slight shower follows.

On a large plantation where there are, say, fifty effective
hands, there will probably be three or four sets of hands engaged
at the same time in planting ; each set, however, not in any way
interfering with the other ; but all pushing on with a constant
brisk motion.   As a medium task, each set, of three hands, will
very easily plant ten acres, but oftener fifteen in old well broken
land.   During the planting season, or between the first of April
and the middle of May, there are always from one to three wet or
rainy spells, continuing from one to four days each, so that the
planting is necessarily interrupted.   This, however, is an advantage which none complain of, as it facilitates and expedites
the vegetation of the seed already planted ; while it causes the
several portions of the crop to vary eight or ten days in age, and
thereby renders the working more convenient.   Twenty planting
days are sufficient to put in the whole cotton crop, or at least as
much as can be properly tended and secured.   On the rich bottom
lands, when the growth of the cotton is very luxuriant, it is desirable to finish planting always before the first of May ; but in
the hills, especially where the soil is thin, and the cotton plant
attains but a small comparative size, it is preferable to plant be-

tween the fifteenth of April and the twentieth of May. Cotton thus planted in thin soil, will mature and open as soon as that which has been planted three weeks sooner in bottom lands.

When the earth is moist and warm, cotton-seed will sprout, and be up in about five or six days ; but if the soil be dry it takes much longer—or until there is rain sufficient to saturate the loose earth : for the seed, being covered with a thick coat of coarse wool, is not so readily, as some other seeds, acted upon by slight moisture. As the plant first comes out of the ground, it has somewhat the appearance of a young bean, or of the okra plant, being composed at first of two lobate leaflets, which continue, gradually enlarging, until about the end of the first week, when a leaf or two begins to put out between the lobules. The young cotton-plant is extremely tender, and sensible to the most moderate degrees of cold : the slightest frost cuts it off—while it withers and dies from the effects of a few hours of chilling winds.

From the profusion of seed planted, the cotton plant of course comes up very thick and crowded in the row ; in which condition it is allowed to remain a week or ten days, and often of necessity much longer, when it is thinned out, or as it is called, " scraped." During scraping time there is one constant rush, and every hand that can use a hoe is brought into the field. The process of scraping commences by running a light furrow close on each side of the row of young cotton, with the share of the plough next it, so as to throw the dirt from the cotton and trim off the scattering plants : the space left unbroken between these two furrows is about eight or ten inches wide, ready for the hoes. If there are many hoe-hands there are several ploughs " barring off" as it is called. The hoe hands follow close upon the ploughs, each hand upon a separate row, and with hoes sharp, and set particularly for " scraping." Experienced cotton hands run over the rows with great rapidity, and evince great dexterity in striking out all to a single stalk, which is left at the distance, from its next neighbour, of at least the width of the hoe ; and in bottom land, at double that distance. Thus, in thin land, the stalks are desired to be ten or twelve inches apart, and in the rich lands about eighteen or twenty inches, in the row. The cotton plant thus thinned out, continues to grow slowly until the hot weather of June sets in, when it begins to grow rapidly, putting out a blossom at each new joint formed on the branches. This successive florescence continues until frost puts a stop to the growth of the plant, which is generally in October. The pericarp or boll of cotton, from the first bloom, is generally matured in eight or ten weeks, when it begins to crack at the four seams in the bolls, until the four valves spread wide open, remaining attached only at the base or extremity next the *stem*. When the valves are thus open, the cotton with the seed, to which it adheres in a kind of cluster, hangs down from one to four inches. From June until October, the cotton exhibits a successive and continued florescence, while the plant is loading itself with green bolls, from the size of a young peach, having just dropped its blossom, to that of a small hen's egg. About the last of August the matured bolls begin to burst or open their valves and suspend their cotton; and from that time the plant exhibits at the same time, blossoms, and bolls of every size, and every stage of maturity. Toward fall, when the heat of the sun is constant and intense, the bolls will mature and open in six weeks from the blossom.

After the first "scraping out," the cultivation is carried on much in the same manner as in the cultivation of corn, until about the first of August, when it ceases, and the crop is laid by. The same kind of cultivation that would make good corn would make good cotton. In this however there is a difference of opinion : some will hill, or heap the earth up in high ridges with both corn and cotton, while others will keep the soil loose and level about both; the latter is decidedly the proper mode for either.

When the blossom is first unfolded, which generally occurs in the night, in form it resembles the white hollyhock, but is smaller, and is of a faint yellowish white colour, which it retains until about noon; the heat of the sun then being intense, the corolla partially closes, not unlike the four-o'clock-flower, and at the same time its hue is changed to a delicate rose, or lilac. On the following day the flowers become more deeply tinged; toward the close of the second evening they are of a deep crimson, or violet hue. During the succeeding night, and morning, that is, about forty-eight hours after they first open, they always drop off, while of a deep violet colour, leaving the young capsule or boll. The blossoms generally open, as well as fall off, during the night, and early in the morning. Thus a cotton field in July, August, September, and October, exhibits the singular appearance of a continued crop of opening, closing, and falling blossoms, with an almost equal mixture of white, lilac, and purple flowers; while each morning the ground is seen covered with the latter, and the branches replenished with the white.

As the ploughing generally ceases and the crop is "laid by" about the last of July, when the plant is large and brittle, there is but little done in the field during the first three weeks in August, except that a few light hands are kept employed in cutting, or pulling up the "tie-vines" which are sometimes very troublesome: the tie-vine is nothing more or less than the morning-glory, so carefully cultivated in gardens at the north, for the purpose of shading arbours and summer houses.

Toward the last of August, or as soon as there is sufficient open cotton for a hand to pick fifteen or twenty pounds during the day, the light force, consisting of women and children, is put to picking for a week or ten days; when there being sufficient cotton opened, to make a full day's work, all hands are engaged without exception. Then begins another push, which continues until the whole crop is gathered and housed. During "picking time" which continues where full crops are made until the first of December, and in river lands, until the first of January, the hands are regularly roused, by a large bell or horn, about the first dawn of day, or earlier so that they are ready to enter the field as soon as there is sufficient light to distinguish the bolls. As the dews are extremely heavy and cool, each hand is provided with a blanket coat or wrapper, which is kept close around him until the dew is partially evaporated by the sun. Without this protection they would be completely wet from head to feet, in a very short time; and as they would be in the field at least two hours before the sun's rays would be felt, they would be perfectly chilled, if no worse consequence attended. The hands remain in the field until it is too dark to distinguish the cotton, having brought their meals with them. For the purpose of collecting the cotton, each hand is furnished with a large basket, and two coarse cotton bags about the size of a pillow case, with a strong strap to suspend them from the neck or shoulders. The basket is left at the end of a row, and both bags taken along: when one bag is as full as it can well be crammed, it is laid down in the row, and the hand begins to fill the second in the same way. As soon as the second is full, he returns to the basket, taking the other bag as he passes it, and empties both into the basket, treading it down well, to make it contain his whole day's work. The same process is repeated until night; when the basket is taken upon his head and carried to the scaffold-yard, to be weighed. There the overseer meets all hands at the scales, with the lamp, slate, and whip. On the left hand margin of the slate is pasted a strip of paper, with the name of each written in fair large hand. As soon as their baskets are set upon the ground, the weighing commences. Each basket is carefully weighed, and the nett weight of cotton set down upon the slate, opposite the name of the picker. The negroes stand round, to remove and replace the baskets as they are weighed; and occasionally the countenance of an idler may be seen to fall. Then is the time for the overseer to watch close or he may be greatly imposed upon by the cunning and lazy, who are apt, in the crowd, to prevent their baskets from being weighed, by substituting a heavier one which has been passed, or they may fill up their baskets from one already weighed. Sometimes a negro, known to be lazy, will have heavy weight and will probably extort from the overseer expressions of praise and encouragement, unless he examines the basket, when perchance he may find one of his sacks full of moist earth snugly covered up at the bottom; such tricks as these will be continually practised upon an overseer, who is careless or " soft ;" a quality or character, which none can more readily and properly appreciate than the negro. It is not an uncommon occurrence for an overseer, who is even vigilant, amid the crowd of negroes and baskets, with only one lamp, held close to the scales and slate, to weigh some of the heavier baskets several times, their exact weight being changed by taking out, or putting in a few pounds; while the lighter ones pass entirely unnoticed. No inconvenience arises to any one from such incidents, except that the crop is not gathered in as good time as it might otherwise have been, and a portion consequently is wasted.

After the weighing is over, and the baskets are emptied, or turned bottom upward, upon the scaffolds, the overseer takes the slate, and examines the weights attached to each name. Those who are found to have brought in less than their usual quantity, unless for good reasons, are called in the order of their names: the individual advances, and if his reasons are insufficient, he is ordered to lie down upon his face, with his back exposed; when he receives ten, twenty, or fifty stripes with the whip, according to his deserts. In this way the overseer goes over the list, punishing only those who have idled away their time.

No one knows that he is to be punished until his name is called, when he has an opportunity of giving his reasons for his imperfect day's work. As to the quantity which a hand can pick in a day, there is a great difference; some will pick only from 75 to 100 lbs., others from 150 to 200 lbs., while some extraordinary pickers can pick as high as 4 or 500 lbs. in one day. But to pick these last weights requires such brisk and incessant motion, that it could not be done two days in succession without danger of life or health; and is only attempted for a wager, or such like reason. The average weight picked by all the hands on a place, will seldom exceed 150 or 160 lbs., in good picking. Children from ten to fifteen years of age generally pick nearly as much as grown hands. The scaffolds for drying cotton are mostly temporary, being made anew every summer, of common boards or plank. Upon these the cotton is suffered to lie spread out to the sun, at least one day to dry; while some old or decrepid hand stays at the scaffold, to turn and spread it, as well as to pick out leaves and trash.

It may not be improper to make a remark or two relative to whipping. This is generally performed with as much care and humanity as the nature of the case will admit. A person standing at the distance of two hundred yards, being unacquainted with the mode, and hearing the loud sharp crack of the whip upon the naked skin, would almost tremble for the life of the poor sufferer. But what would be his surprise, after hearing fifty or one hundred stripes thus laid on, to go up and examine the poor fellow, and find the skin not broken, and not a drop of blood drawn from him! Yet this is the way in which the whip is generally used here upon slaves: very few planters would permit them to be whipped on the bare back with a raw-hide, or cow-skin, as it is called. Though, as in every thing else, there is a great difference in the degree of severity exercised by different masters: yet we must take the general rule, as applicable to the great class of planters. The common overseer's whip consists of a stout flexible stalk, large at the handle, tapering rapidly to the distance of about eighteen inches, and thence continued with cord or leather; the whole is covered with a leather plat, which continues tapering into, and forms the lash—the whole together being about three feet and a half long. To the end of the lash is attached a soft, dry, buckskin cracker, about three eighths of an inch wide and ten or twelve inches long, which is the only part allowed to strike, in whipping on the bare skin. So soft is the cracker, that a person who has not the sleight of using the whip, could scarcely hurt a child with it. When it is used by an experienced hand it makes a very loud report, and stings, or "burns" the skin smartly, but does not bruise it. One hundred lashes well laid on with it, would not injure the skin as much as ten moderate stripes with a cow-skin.

But to return from this digression:—Every day, when the weather will admit, beholds a repetition of the ceremony of picking, weighing, and drying, as before detailed. Those who have gins, as all planters should have, generally keep the stand running during the picking season, so as to gin out the cotton as fast as it is picked. If there are forty or fifty good pickers, it requires one stand to be kept running constantly to keep up with them. In such cases, during wet weather, when the hands cannot pick cotton, the ablest of them are kept baling the cotton which has been ginned since the last rain, or within the last eight or ten days. When there are not more than twenty, or twenty-five, the gin will be able to keep up, by ginning the last three days in the week, in addition to all rainy weather; and the able-bodied hands will be able to do all the pressing and baling during the wet days.

Gin, in the common acceptation, signifies the house and all the machinery required to separate the *lint* from the seed, and to press it into large bales, weighing generally from 400 to 500 pounds. The house is a large enclosed roof, resting upon blocks or posts, which support it at about eight or nine feet from the ground. The common area covered is about forty by sixty feet, the rafters resting upon plates, and the plates upon flooring beams, or joists, upon which the floor is laid. About the distance of one-third the length of the house, two gearing beams are laid across, for supporting the machinery. These rest upon the top of the blocks, or on posts framed into them. On the ground floor is the horse-path for drawing the main wheel and counter wheel; the last of which carries a broad band, which passes over and turns the cylinder and brush of the gin-stand alone. The large plantations are adopting steam engines, and erect for the purpose very large and expensive buildings, in which are placed two, three, or four stands. A gin-stand is a frame, in which runs a wooden cylinder with an iron shaft running through it; this cylinder is encircled at every inch by a very thin circular saw, with sharp hooked teeth, upon which the seed cotton is thrown, running through parallel grates. The teeth of the saws catch and carry through the lint from the seed. Just behind the cylinder is a fly-wheel brush— that is, a fan, with a brush on its extreme circumference; this brush, running considerably faster than the cylinder, takes off the cotton from the teeth, and blows it back. The space or room above is divided into two apartments; one for the stand and seed cotton, and the other for ginned cotton; the latter of which will contain cotton for twenty or thirty bales. A good gin-stand, with sixty or sixty-five saws, running constantly from daybreak in the morning until eight or nine o'clock at night, will gin out as much as will make three or four bales.

At the other end of the house, and immediately under the room containing ginned cotton, is the press. It consists of two large wooden screws, twelve or sixteen inches in diameter, with reversed threads cut on each end to within eighteen inches or two feet of the middle, through which there is a mortice for the lever. These screws stand perpendicularly, and about ten feet apart, and work into a large heavy beam above, and into another firmly secured below. The upper moves up or down (when the screws are turned), between four strong upright posts, framed together, two on each side, so as to come down strait and steady when pressing.

The lower sides of the press are composed of very strong batten doors; when the beam is brought sufficiently low, a spring is struck, and they fly open; when they are removed, leaving the naked bale standing on its edge under the press. A piece of bagging, cut to the proper size and shape, was put in the bottom of the press-box, before filling in the cotton, and another on top, immediately under the follower. These two pieces are brought together in such manner as to cover the cotton neatly, and there sewed with twine. The rope passed under and over it, through the grooves left in the bed-sill and in the follower, by means of a windlass, is drawn extremely tight and tied with double loop knots.　When all is finished, the screws are turned backward, the beam rises, and the bale is rolled out.　Notwithstanding there are seven bands of strong rope around it, the bale will swell and stretch the rope, until its breadth is at least two or three inches more than when in the press.　To press and bale expeditiously requires at least four or five hands and one horse.　When the box has been sufficiently filled, generally eight or nine feet deep, the men bring down the beam by turning the screws with hand levers as long as they can turn them ; then a large lever is placed in the screw, with a strong horse attached to one end, and a few turns of the screws by the horse bring the beam down to the proper point, within thirty or thirty-four inches of the sill.

The requisite number of hands will put up and bale with a common press about ten or twelve bales a day, by pushing.　After the bales are properly put up, the next thing is to mark and number them on one end.　For this purpose a plate of copper, with the initials, or such mark as is fancied, cut in it, is applied to the end of the bale and the letters and figures painted through it with black marking ink.

The next trouble is to haul them to market, or the nearest landing for boats ; sometimes this is a very troublesome and difficult task, especially in wet weather, when the roads, from the immense quantity of heavy hauling, in getting the crops to market, are much cut up, and often almost impassable.　The planter who is careful to take all proper advantages of season and weather, will have his cotton hauled early in the fall, as fast as it is ginned, when the roads are almost certainly good.

The quantity of cotton produced to the acre, varies with the quality of the soil and the season.　The best kind of river and alluvial lands, when in a complete state of cultivation, and with a good season, will produce on an average from 1500 to 2000 lbs. of cotton in the seed per acre ; while new land of the same quality will not yield more than 1200 or 1400 lbs. per acre.　The highlands, where the soil is fertile, will yield under the most favourable circumstances about 1400 lbs., while those lands which have been many years in cultivation, where the soil is thin, will not yield more than from 800 to 1000 lbs. per acre ; and some not more than 600 lbs. As a general rule 1300 or 1400 lbs. of seed cotton, will, when ginned out, make a bale of 400 lbs. or more. This is according to the correct weight of the daily picking in the cotton book; although after being weighed, it must lose some weight by drying.

The quantity of cotton raised and secured by good management most commonly averages about five or six bales to the hand: and the quantity, among the mass of planters, more frequently falls below, than rises above this estimate. Some, with a few choice hands, may sometimes average nine or ten bales to the hand by picking until January.

When the crop is all secured, which, as we observed before, varies from the first of December until some time in January, according to the season, hands, and extent of the crop, the hands are employed during the winter in clearing, chopping logs in the field, splitting rails, or ditching, if necessary. About the middle of February they resume preparations for " another crop."

NOTE D.—*Page* 258.

A recent writer, in speculating upon the possible result of an insurrectionary movement in the south, says, in the course of his remarks,—

" Here, where the whites so far outnumber the blacks, as to render such a struggle hopeless on their part, there is little or nothing to apprehend ; but in the south, where the case is reversed, the consequences will probably be what they were in St. Domingo—the extermination or expatriation of the whites, the loss of tens of hundreds of thousands of lives, and hundreds or perhaps of millions of property."

In reply, and in confutation of this opinion, Gen. Houston of Natchez, addressed a very sensible and well-written paper to the editor of the New-York Courier and Enquirer, in which he says—

" There are but two states in the Union where the slaves are equal in numbers to the whites, and in these they have a bare majority ; in other states they have but a third and in others a fourth or fifth. Now is there any man who supposes that an equal number of negroes, unacquainted with arms, undisciplined, without combination, without officers, without a rifle or a musket, or a single cartridge, can in any way be formidable to an equal number of whites, well armed and equipped, well supplied with all the necessaries of war, well organized, and well officered? The notion is absurd. I will go farther; take a body of negroes, furnish them with arms, equipments, and every thing necessary for war; let them have twelve months to combine, to train, and to acquire a knowledge of the use of arms, and my life on it, they would be nothing more at the end of the time than an ignorant disorderly rabble, who could not form a line of battle, a thousand of them would not stand the charge of a single volunteer corps, they would disperse at the first volley of musketry, and a body of white men would feel debased to compete with such foes.

"There is no southern state that apprehends any injury from its slaves—that seeks protection from any power on earth—not one of them values the Union one particle as the means of guarding them on that score.

"There are no people on earth better supplied with arms, more accustomed to their daily use, and I may say more ready to use them, than the people of the south. Go into any house in Mississippi, Alabama, South Carolina, Kentucky, Virginia, Tennessee, or any other southern state, and you will generally see a good rifle and fowling-piece; and every neighbourhood has its men who can throw a deer running at full speed at the distance of one hundred yards. Do such men seek protection or apprehend danger from an inferior number of unarmed, ignorant and enslaved negroes? Most assuredly not.

"Experience has shown that the militia of the United States are frequently able to combat successfully with the regular troops of Europe. And many a well-fought field has shown that the militia of the southern states are equal to any in the Union, I will not be invidious and say superior. If such is the case, what lessons do the wars and experience of Europe teach us? There it is a received maxim that ten thousand disciplined troops are superior to an army of forty thousand undisciplined peasantry, even when they are equally supplied with arms. And to this maxim history shows but few exceptions, as in Switzerland and the Tyrolese mountains, where the peasantry are much favoured by the mountains and defiles, are inured to hardships, trained in the chase and in the use of arms.

" Have not the peasantry ef Europe more acquaintance with arms, more means of acquiring them and other necessaries for war, more military information, more means of combination, and more intelligence, than the negroes of the south ? Most assuredly they have, and yet they are generally held in subjection by a comparatively small body of men. I merely glance at this, but could, if time and space permitted, give many striking illustrations.

" If the south are so safe, it may be asked why are they so sensitive on this subject ? I will answer :—they are sensitive from motives of interest and humanity.

" He who makes my negroes dissatisfied with their situation, makes them less useful to me, and puts me under the necessity of dealing more rigorously with them.

" Throughout the whole south it is considered disgraceful not to clothe and feed negroes well, or to treat them cruelly, and there are very few who have the hardihood to brave public sentiment. And on many plantations, when they are orderly and obedient, they have many indulgences and privileges, such as to raise and sell poultry, &c.: to cultivate a small piece of ground and sell the products ; and time is allowed them for such purposes. But if negroes become disorderly, discontented, and disobedient, the necessity requires that they should either be set at large at once, or their privileges curtailed, and discipline made more rigorous till they are brought into complete subjection ; there is no middle course. Again—if negroes become dissatisfied, disobedient and rebellious, there is a possibility that they may do damage in a single neighbourhood, and destroy the lives of a few women and children—the consequenee of which would be that then whites would be under the necessity of putting great numbers of the misguided wretches to death. Such was the case at Southampton. This we would avoid, both from motives of interest and humanity, not that we apprehend any more serious injury, and you may rest assured that if the negroes were to rebel and do any considerable injury, the havoc and destruction made amongst them would be dreadful ; and it would be difficult to prevent its extending to those who were innocent.

" Those, therefore, who are instrumental in making the negro dissatisfied with his condition, make it much worse, for they constrain his owner to be more rigorous in his treatment, and they tempt him to rebellion, which must lead to death and extermination."

THE END.

Date Due